PREPARE AND DEFEND

PREPARE AND DEFEND

Keeping Yourself and Others Safe from Mass Murder Attacks

Robert L. Snow

ROWMAN & LITTLEFIELD
Lanham • Boulder • New York • London

Published by Rowman & Littlefield
An imprint of The Rowman & Littlefield Publishing Group, Inc.
4501 Forbes Boulevard, Suite 200, Lanham, Maryland 20706
rowman.com

6 Tinworth Street, London SE11 5AL, United Kingdom

British Library Cataloguing in Publication Information Available

Library of Congress Control Number: 2019047109

ISBN 9781538129203 (cloth : alk. paper) | ISBN 9781538129210 (epub)

∞ ™ The paper used in this publication meets the minimum requirements of American National Standard for Information Sciences Permanence of Paper for Printed Library Materials, ANSI/NISO Z39.48-1992.

For Melanie, proofreader and soul mate.

CONTENTS

1

MASS MURDERS IN THE UNITED STATES

On May 18 at 8:45 a.m., Andrew Kehoe became the worst mass murderer of schoolchildren in US history. At that moment, an alarm clock he had wired to 500 pounds of dynamite mixed with a military incendiary went off in a three-story Bath, Michigan, schoolhouse. Kehoe had spent the previous weeks smuggling in the explosives a bit at a time and hiding them in the basement ceiling. Thirty-eight children would die in the blast, or shortly thereafter, along with six adults. Fifty-eight others would suffer minor to serious injuries. And although many readers may believe that the mass murder of schoolchildren is a recent trend, what became known as the Bath School Massacre occurred in 1927, more than ninety years ago.

Kehoe, a fifty-five-year-old farmer who lived close to Bath, Michigan, a small town about ten miles northeast of Lansing, the state capital, had lived a seemingly normal life. In his youth he studied electrical engineering at nearby Michigan State College in East Lansing, and for a time he had worked as an electrician in St. Louis. In 1912, he married Nellie Price and they eventually bought a 185-acre farm near Bath. Neighbors would later give differing versions of what kind of person Kehoe was. Some described him as dependable and friendly, often willing to help out his neighbors. Others described him as combative and mean-spirited, telling of how he killed a neighbor's dog that had irritated him, and how he shot one of his own horses when it didn't perform to his standards.

In 1922, the town of Bath and the surrounding township established the Bath Consolidated School. This brought all the children of Bath and the surrounding area to one large three-story school building. Before this, most of the children had gone to one-room schoolhouses scattered around the area. This consolidation, thought to be in the best interests of the children, wasn't cheap, and, to pay for it, the school taxes in the area increased more than 60 percent. This infuriated Kehoe, who at the time was struggling with his personal finances.

Kehoe won an election to the local school board in 1924, and the board members named him as the school board treasurer. Always a very frugal man (he reportedly left the Catholic faith after being assessed $400 for the building of a new church), Kehoe argued endlessly for lower taxes and for cutting the expenses of running the school. He consequently fought constantly with other school board members over expenditures and reportedly had nothing but disdain for School Superintendent Emory Huyck, who he often publicly accused of wasting money.

A *New York Times* article on May 20, 1927, quoted a school board member as saying, "He fought the expenditure of money for the most necessary equipment."[1]

In 1925, because of the death of the Bath Township Clerk, Kehoe found himself appointed to the position. However, he soon found himself out of the job when he lost an election for the position in the spring of 1926. Many people later thought that much of the bitterness that led to the school bombing started with this defeat.

As mentioned above, for several years before the bombing Kehoe had suffered from serious financial difficulties. He couldn't keep up the mortgage payments on his farm and had stopped making mortgage payments months before the explosion, apparently expecting that he would soon lose ownership of the farm. He had also seemingly given up on farming, deciding not to harvest his crops in the fall of 1926. Kehoe's wife, Nellie, thought to be suffering from tuberculosis, also began running up extensive medical bills. She had been in and out of hospitals and sanitariums for several years and had just been discharged from the hospital on May 16, 1927.

Several months before the school bombing, Kehoe had volunteered to perform some electrical work at the school, and naturally the school board felt grateful to have a trained and experienced electrician doing the work for them. However, what this actually did was allow Kehoe to have free access to the school when no one was there. Authorities who later investigated the bombing believed that this was when he brought in and wired the hidden explosives that would eventually bring part of the school crashing down.

In preparation for the explosion, Kehoe traveled to Lansing, where he purchased several cases of dynamite and pyrotol. Pyrotol, an explosive processed from World War I military surplus, caused an incendiary blast when mixed with dynamite. Because farmers in those days regularly used dynamite and pyrotol to remove stumps, these purchases didn't raise any suspicion. Kehoe also purchased a bolt-action rifle, which would figure prominently in his plan.

Sometime in the two days before the explosion, Kehoe murdered his wife by a blow to the head, destroyed all of the fences on his property, sliced through the bark of many of his trees in order to kill them, and cut all his grapevines and then repositioned them so the damage wouldn't be apparent. On the morning of May 18, 1927, Kehoe used dynamite and pyrotol to blow up most of the buildings on his property. This would happen just before the bomb at the school exploded. A number of neighbors, hearing the explosion, hurried to Kehoe's farm to see if they could help. Kehoe reportedly told them that they needed to get out of there and head for the school, which had just exploded. According to testimony at the coroner's inquest, Kehoe told them, "Boys, you are my friends. You better get out of here. You better go down to the school."[2]

Kehoe waited at his property for a while, apparently wanting to be certain that everything was destroyed. Then he got into his Ford truck, which he had laden with explosives and metal shrapnel, and headed for the school. He would arrive there about a half hour after the explosion at his farm.

At 8:45 a.m. on May 18, 1927, the last day of classes before summer vacation, along with the blast at Kehoe's farm, another huge explosion rattled the town of Bath. The north wing of the three-story brick school building collapsed from the force of the explosives Kehoe had hidden there. A first-grade teacher, Bernice Sterling, told the Associated Press on May 19, 1927, "It seemed as though the floor went up several feet. After the first shock I thought for a moment I was blind. When it came the air seemed to be full of children and flying desks and books. Children were tossed high in the air; some were catapulted out of the building."[3]

According to the book *The Bath School Disaster*, Monty Ellsworth, a witness who arrived at the school shortly after the explosion, said, "There was a pile of children of about five or six under the roof and some of them had arms sticking out, some had legs, and some just their heads sticking out. They were unrecognizable because they were covered with dust, plaster, and blood."[4]

When Kehoe finally drove up to the site of the school explosion, the scene was naturally one of mass confusion as dozens of parents hurried to the school and began looking for their children. Many immediately raced into the explosion site and began pushing the rubble aside, searching for survivors. Kehoe got out of his truck and saw School Superintendent Huyck standing nearby. He reportedly motioned for the superintendent to come over to the truck. When he did, Kehoe fired the bolt-action rifle he had purchased into the truck, causing the explosives hidden there to detonate. The resulting blast killed Kehoe, Huyck, and two other adults. Sadly, Cleo Clayton, an eight-year-old who had survived the blast at the school, died from shrapnel the bomb in the truck hurled outward.

During the hours following the blast at the school, hundreds of individuals searched through the rubble looking for any survivors. In one of the classrooms searchers found the body of a teacher holding the bodies of two dead children. The would-be rescuers found a surprise, however, in the undamaged south wing: 500 pounds of explosives wired to an alarm clock. Kehoe had intended to take down the entire school building. Experts who recovered the explosives believed that the blast in the north wing had blown a wire loose, which prevented the second bomb from exploding. The alarm clock had been set for 8:45 a.m. Reportedly, searchers also found a container of gasoline wired to explode, apparently as a backup to the bombs.

The Michigan State Police, who investigated the blast at the school, also searched through the rubble of Kehoe's farm. At first, they believed that Kehoe's wife, Nellie, still resided in a sanitarium somewhere in Michigan, so they put out the word to search for her. It wasn't until the day after the explosion that investigators found her charred body crammed into a wheelbarrow in the burned-out rubble of the farm.

They also found that Kehoe had wired the legs of his horses together so they couldn't escape the explosion and resulting fire.

Kehoe's sister would later claim his body and bury it in an unmarked grave. Naturally, the Bath School Massacre, as it was called, occupied the national news for several days, but was soon pushed aside as Charles Lindbergh's flight across the Atlantic captured the nation's attention. Regardless, reportedly more than 100,000 automobiles filled with sightseers passed through the Bath area in the days following the bombing.

In all, forty-four people, including thirty-eight children, died in the Bath School explosion, and fifty-eight others were wounded. It remains the worst school mass murder in US history.

* * *

As can be seen by the above incident, school mass murders, while seeming to be a development of the last few decades, have actually been around for some time. For example, on September 15, 1959, Paul Harold Orgeron bombed an elementary school in Houston, Texas, killing or wounding twenty-four people. On August 1, 1966, Charles Whitman climbed to the top of the clock tower at the University of Texas in Austin and killed or wounded forty-eight people. On December 30, 1974, Anthony Barbaro killed or wounded fourteen people at Olean High School in Olean, New York. On September 23, 1988, Clemmie Henderson killed or wounded six people at a Chicago school. On January 17, 1989, Patrick Purdy killed or wounded thirty-seven people at a school in Stockton, California. The list goes on and on.

For the purposes of this book, a mass murder, such as those in the examples above, is defined as an event in which a person kills three or more people (not including himself or herself) in a single incident. This follows the definition of mass murder given in the federal Investigative Assistance for Violent Crimes Act of 2012. This definition is different from that of a serial killing, in which the murderer kills his or her victims during separate incidents over an extended period, occasionally traveling long distances looking for new victims. And, despite all the examples above, mass murders don't occur just in schools. As shown below, they can occur anywhere.

* * *

To his neighbors, twenty-eight-year-old Howard Unruh seemed harmless enough. Viewed by many as a "mama's boy," he didn't have a job and lived quietly with his mother in an apartment on River Road in Camden, New Jersey. Unruh, a veteran of World War II, had attended pharmacy classes at Temple University for three months, but then dropped out, seeming content to live off his mother's income as a soap packer at the Evanson Soap Company. Unruh had served admirably during the war as a tank gunner, taking part in a number of battles in Italy, Belgium, and Germany. His superiors had given him good reviews while he was in the army.

However, another Howard Unruh existed that no one knew about. Unruh was a homosexual during a time when such behavior was criminal, the laws against homosexual intimacy remaining on the books in New Jersey until 1978. But along with worrying about hiding his sexual orientation, Unruh also seethed with anger at his neighbors, particularly the Cohens, who owned a drugstore and lived next door to him and his mother. He had had constant run-ins with them about his use of their gate and yard to gain access to his apartment. The Cohens, however, weren't his only "enemies." Unruh also felt certain that many of the other people in his neighborhood talked badly about him behind his back. Consequently, he kept an extensive written record of his complaints against his neighbors, often with the code "retal" next to their names, which meant retaliation for their misdeeds against him.

Unruh's mother, trying to stop his run-ins with the Cohens, had a new gate installed that would allow him access to their apartment without having to go through the Cohens' yard. She hoped this would calm her son down.

On September 5, 1949, Unruh traveled to Philadelphia, where he visited the Family Theater on Market Street and watched a double feature of *I Cheated the Law* and *The Lady Gambles* several times. He left the theater at a little after 2:00 a.m. and returned home at 3:00 a.m., only to find that someone had removed the gate that his mother had had installed the previous day. Many people would later believe that this was the trigger that pushed Unruh into committing the crime he had been planning and dreaming of for some time.

At around 9:00 a.m. on September 6, 1949, Unruh's mother woke him up as he had asked and made him breakfast. After finishing the meal, he reportedly threatened his mother with a wrench. She fled the house and raced to a neighbor's.

Once she had left, Unruh went to his room and put on a brown suit, white shirt, and striped bow tie. He then grabbed a German Luger he owned, two magazines filled with bullets, sixteen loose bullets, a knife, and a teargas pen. Leaving his apartment, Unruh first fired a shot at a bread delivery man but missed. Unruh, unperturbed, then walked down River Road to the store of a shoe cobbler, and without saying anything he fired a round at twenty-seven-year-old John Pilarchik, the owner of the store. Shot in the chest, John fell to the floor. Unruh calmly walked over and shot him in the head, killing him. He ignored a young boy who had hidden behind the counter, leaving and walking to the barbershop next door.

The barbershop featured a white wooden horse that children would sit on while getting their hair cut. At that moment, six-year-old Orris Martin Smith sat on the horse getting his hair cut by thirty-three-year-old Clark Hoover. Unruh shot the boy in the head, killing him, and then went for the barber. Clark dashed away in terror and tried to dodge the bullets while using a barber chair as a shield. It didn't work; Unruh shot and killed him. The six-year-old's mother, Catherine, raced over and grabbed her fallen child, screaming frantically while Unruh strolled unperturbed out of the barbershop.

Next, while walking down the sidewalk, Unruh fired a shot at a seven-year-old boy looking out of a window but missed. He then approached a tavern, but the owner, Frank Engel, had heard the shots and locked the door. Unruh fired several shots through the door but didn't hit anyone. Frank ran for his own handgun, firing at Unruh from an upstairs window. The bullet hit Unruh in the thigh, but he didn't seem to notice. He was headed for the main target of his rampage: the Cohens.

A local insurance salesman, James Hutton, had just come out of the Cohen drugstore as Unruh approached. Unruh said, "Excuse me, sir" to James, and then shot and killed him when he didn't move out of the way fast enough. The gunshot alerted the Cohens, and Unruh saw them fleeing up the stairs to their apartment. Thirty-eight-year-old Rose Cohen quickly hid her young son in a closet, and then hid herself in another closet. However, Unruh saw her and fired several shots through the closet door, killing her. Forty-year-old Maurice Cohen had climbed out of a window and onto a porch roof, but Unruh also shot and killed him, sending him tumbling to the sidewalk below. Following this, Unruh entered a nearby bedroom and shot and killed sixty-three-year-old Minnie Cohen, Maurice's mother, who was on the telephone trying to call the police. He then left without harming the young boy in the closet.

Exiting the drugstore, Unruh next encountered twenty-four-year-old Alvin Day, who just happened to be driving down River Road. Unruh leaned into the car as Alvin stopped to look at the body of James Hutton, and shot and killed him. Next, Unruh fired into another car that had stopped for a red light, killing two women in the front seat and wounding a nine-year-old boy who sat in the back. The boy would later die at the hospital. Unruh then shot and wounded eighteen-year-old Charlie Peterson when he and two friends stopped their car to look at the body of James Hutton. Following this bit of random shooting, Unruh continued toward the next on his list of specific targets. He entered Tom Zegrino's tailor shop but found him gone, the store being watched over by Helga, Tom's bride of only a month. Although she begged for her life, Unruh shot and killed her.

After leaving the tailor shop, Unruh shot and killed two-year-old Thomas Hamilton, who happened to be looking out of a window. He then tried to gain access to a small grocery store but found the door locked. Unruh fired several shots through the door but didn't hit anyone. Hearing sirens approaching, Unruh dashed into a nearby alleyway and broke into a home behind his apartment, where he shot and wounded a mother and son who lived there.

Now out of bullets and knowing the police were nearby, Unruh retreated to his apartment, which soon became surrounded by more than fifty police officers. A brief standoff ensued, during which the police fired dozens of machine-gun, shotgun, and revolver rounds into the apartment, none of them hitting Unruh. During the standoff, an editor for the *Camden Evening Courier* called Unruh on the telephone. When the editor asked how many people he had shot, Unruh replied, "I don't know yet, I haven't counted them. But it looks like a pretty good score."[5]

Finally, the police lobbed two teargas canisters (the first one proved to be a dud) into the apartment and Unruh surrendered. In less than twenty minutes, Unruh had killed thirteen people and wounded three.

According to a *New York Times* article on September 8, 1949, during questioning Unruh would say, "I shot them in the chest first, and then I aimed for the head."[6] The police questioned Unruh for several hours before someone noticed a puddle of blood gathering under Unruh's chair. It was only then that they discovered he had been hit by the bullet fired by tavern owner Frank Engel.

Unruh would later be determined to be mentally ill and committed to the New Jersey Hospital for the Insane. He would remain locked up until his death in October 2009. During the remainder of his life he never showed any remorse for the killing spree. According to the *History of World Crime*, Unruh told a psychologist toward the latter part of his life, "I'd have killed a thousand if I had enough bullets."[7]

* * *

As the above narrative shows, and as I will discuss in a later chapter on secondary victims, even if a mass murderer has specific victims in mind, and is making every effort to kill them, that doesn't mean that total strangers won't also become victims of the rampage. Quite often, just being in the vicinity of a mass murder can put a person's life in danger.

Readers will no doubt notice that both narratives in this chapter took place many years ago. I have included them in the first chapter to show readers that, although mass murders may seem to be a recent phenomenon, they have been around for some time.

However, even though there may have been a number of mass murder incidents in the past, many people believe—correctly—that these events have become much more prevalent in the last few decades. Several studies have shown that mass murders have become much more common, particularly in the twenty-first century.

A study published in 2018 by the Office of Research & Public Affairs stated, "Studies of mass killings strongly suggest they began to increase in incidence in the 1980s, and that the incidence is increasing."[8]

A study by the FBI in 2013 concerned mass murders involving firearms. They found that the average number of mass murder events involving firearms averaged 6.4 events per year from 2000 to 2006. However, for the years 2007 to 2013, the average had grown to 16.4 events per year.[9] A study reported by the *New York Times* in 2000 of one hundred "rampage killings" found that twenty-seven such events occurred between 1949 and 1989, but that seventy-three events occurred from 1990 to 1999.[10]

Following this further, another FBI study on mass murders showed a steady increase starting in the year 2000. In that year only seven victims died in mass murders; the number grew to 51 in 2003, to 126 in 2007, to 208 in 2012, and to 729 in 2017.[11] As further proof of the increase of mass murders, the lead author of a study published in the *Journal of Child and Family Studies* stated, "In less than 18 years, we have already seen more deaths related to school shootings than in the whole 20th century." Both interesting and disturbing, this study also found that while 60 percent of the mass shootings at schools in the United States during the 20th century had been committed by juveniles aged eleven to eighteen, that percentage had risen to 77 percent in the twenty-first century.[12]

Mass murders, as discussed earlier, can occur anywhere. The comic strip *Pearls before Swine* had a strip on November 27, 2018, that showed one of its characters with a list of "Places I can go and still feel safe in America." All the places on the list were crossed out except for a synagogue. Then, reflecting on the mass murder at a synagogue in Pittsburgh the previous month, the next panel showed the word synagogue crossed out.[13] The FBI recently released a report that unfortunately verified this. A study that investigated 160 mass murder incidents in the United States found that the largest number of them, 45.6 percent, occurred in commercial areas, both open and closed to the public. The next largest percentage, 24.4 percent, occurred at schools, followed by 10.0 percent on government properties, 9.4 percent in open spaces, 4.4 percent at residences, 3.4 percent in houses of worship, and 2.5 percent at healthcare facilities. (The percentages above don't total exactly 100 percent because of rounding.)[14] As a report on the mass killing in Las Vegas in 2017 stated, "This week's massacre at a country music festival in downtown Las Vegas, which left at least 59 people dead and more than 500 injured, reminds us that the locations and circumstances of mass shootings in America are unpredictable."[15]

Basically, what all the above statistics show is that mass murders are definitely increasing in number and can occur anywhere. Consequently, they can involve anyone and everyone. But the public is not helpless to this growing problem. There are numerous ways to spot a potential mass murderer, and also numerous ways to avoid becoming the victim of a mass murder. For example, there are definite signs that these events are likely to occur. In its *A Study of the Pre-Attack Behaviors of Active Shooters in the United States between 2000 and 2013*, the FBI stated that "in the weeks and months before an attack, many active shooters engage in behaviors that may signal impending violence." The above study also showed that many mass murderers will spend from weeks to months planning and preparing for their upcoming murder spree. During this time, many of them will give clues as to what they are planning and preparing for. The study reported that on average a mass murderer displayed four to five "concerning behaviors" before actually carrying out the attack.[16] In 2000, the *New York Times* published the results of a study by their staff of one hundred "rampage killings." In the cases they researched, they found "63 involved people who made threats of violence before the event, including 54 who threatened specific violence to specific people." James Calvin Brady, for example, reportedly told psychiatrists he wanted to kill people. Days later he went on a shooting rampage in an Atlanta, Georgia, shopping mall.[17]

Along with watching for these signs of an impending attack, individuals can take actions that will greatly lessen their chances of becoming a victim if they find themselves caught up in a mass murder event. I will show readers these actions and how to use them, to save not only themselves but also others nearby.

2

WHO ARE THE MASS MURDERERS?

On Friday, April 3, 2009, at around 10:30 a.m., forty-one-year-old Jiverly Antares Wong, a naturalized citizen from Vietnam, entered the American Civic Association in Binghamton, New York. Binghamton is a city of about 50,000 people in central New York State, just north of the Pennsylvania state line. The American Civic Association assists refugees and immigrants with their assimilation into American life. Wong had taken English classes there from January to March 2009. A minute or so before coming through the front door of the center, he had used his father's car to block the rear door, the only other exit from the building.

Wearing a bulletproof vest over a bright green jacket, Wong, carrying two handguns, a 9mm Beretta semiautomatic pistol, and a .45 caliber Beretta semiautomatic pistol, entered the building without speaking. He walked over to the two female receptionists and shot one in the head, killing her instantly; he then shot the other in the stomach. Sixty-one-year-old Shirley DeLucia fell to the floor and pretended to be dead. When Wong moved away from the reception area, she hid under a nearby desk and called 911. The police said the call came in at 10:38 a.m. Shirley stayed on the line with the police for nearly forty minutes during the ordeal, keeping them updated on what she could see from her hiding spot. Along with the guns, the police said Wong also carried a hunting knife in his waistband and a bag of ammunition around his neck.

After shooting the receptionists, Wong moved on to a nearby classroom, where an English class was in session. Once more without speaking, Wong began shooting the students. Other people in the American Civic Association building, hearing the gunfire and the screams of the victims, escaped to the basement and hid in a closet.

The police responded to the scene within minutes. On their way there, the officers requested the help of a local high school teacher, who was fluent in Vietnamese, to assist them in negotiating with the gunman. However, what the police didn't know, but later learned from witnesses, was that Wong, upon hearing the police sirens approaching, had put one of the guns to his head and killed himself. In a matter of just three minutes, Wong had fired almost one hundred rounds, killing thirteen people and injuring four others.

Immediately after setting up a perimeter around the building, the police attempted to contact Wong. Of course they were unsuccessful because, unbeknownst to them, he had already committed suicide. Eventually the police, finding themselves unable to engage in negotiations, entered the building and cleared it. After discovering Wong's body and determining that he was the only shooter, the police evacuated twenty people who had escaped the shooting.

Who was Jiverly Antares Wong and what would make him want to commit such an act?

Wong, of Chinese descent, was born in South Vietnam in 1967. His father had been a captain in the South Vietnamese army. Wong immigrated with his family to the United States in 1990. He lived at first with his family in Binghamton, New York, but didn't get out much. Members of the Vietnamese community said that he very seldom interacted with them. Around 1992, Wong moved to Inglewood, California, where he lived for fifteen years. His family knew very little about his time there, other than that he had become a US citizen in 1995 and had changed his name from his given name of Linh Phat Voong. No one knows why. His family also later found out that he had gotten married and divorced while living in California. Family members said that Wong barely kept in contact with them during the fifteen years he lived in California, calling them only a few times and never writing.

In 2007, Wong finally called his father and asked if he could come home. He had lost his job, and because of his poor English skills couldn't find another one. Wong's father would later say that the son who returned home wasn't the same one he knew. Wong had become withdrawn and quiet, rarely interacting even with his family. He had no friends. And while Wong appeared to be having psychological problems in 2007 when he returned home, he had begun showing signs of serious mental problems soon after arriving in America. His father reported possible delusions when at twenty-two years old, sitting on the porch with his father, Wong had said that there were individuals who were trying to harm him. "They're in front of me and trying to capture me," he told his father.[1] Wong pointed to a spot in front of him as if someone were there. His father, naturally concerned, convinced him to go to a local hospital. Wong agreed, apparently wanting to get away from the people who were trying to capture him. A few hours later, the doctors released Wong, saying there was nothing wrong with him. However, despite the doctors' opinion, Wong's delusions of persecution continued and got worse.

Several days after the shooting at the American Civic Association, *News 10 Now* television in Syracuse, New York, received a package from Wong postmarked the day of the shooting. Inside the package they found Wong's driver's license, gun permit, and a letter. In the letter, printed in all capital letters and two pages long, Wong first apologized for his poor English and then complained about being persecuted by an undercover police officer. The officer, he said, constantly followed him and tried to get him involved in car crashes. The officer would also monitor him twenty-four hours a day using high-tech hidden cameras, and would burn chemicals in his house that made the air unbreathable and cause him to vomit. Along with this, he claimed the officer would change the channels on his television, adjust his fan, and make music play in his ears. Additionally, he said that the undercover police officer spread false rumors about him and caused him to get fired from his job. Interestingly, when Wong moved from Inglewood, California, to Binghamton, New York, the harassment by the undercover police officer, he said, continued unabated. When in New York, the undercover officer, Wong wrote in the letter, would sneak into his room while he slept, once stole $20.00 from his wallet, and had even shot him with a Taser.

At the close of the letter, Wong said that the undercover police officer, not he, was responsible for the shooting. He ended the letter with "And you have a nice day."[2]

As for possible signs of the impending attack, they were extremely subtle. Wong's father said that for two weeks before the attack, Wong had locked himself away in his room, not coming out to eat, watch television, or even converse with his family.

"He avoided being in the house at the same time with me," Wong's father said. "At first, I thought maybe he was mad about something and was planning to ask him. This tragedy occurred before I even had a chance to ask him."[3]

* * *

Many readers, when hearing about mass murders in which the murderers slaughter the victims for no apparent reason, likely think that the killers must be psychotic and delusional, such as Jiverly Wong in the incident above. Many believe that to just walk into a building and begin shooting people whom the murderers often don't know, at random and with no mercy, is obviously the work of individuals suffering from severe psychosis—people who, like Wong, have lost their grip on reality and are responding to whatever dark fantasy is playing out in their heads. Unfortunately, the mass murderers who fit this description have received a lot of media time that exaggerates their number—people like Adam Lanza, who killed twenty-six people, including twenty first graders, at the Sandy Hook Elementary School, and James Holmes, who killed twelve people at a movie theater in Aurora, Colorado.

However, research on mass murderers doesn't support this idea. After-action investigations of mass murders show that only about 20 to 30 percent of mass murderers suffer from severe mental illness like Wong. The FBI's *A Study of the Pre-Attack Behavior of Active Shooters in the United States between 2000 and 2013* says that of the sixty-three cases they studied, "the FBI could only verify that twenty-five percent of active shooters in the study had ever been diagnosed with a mental illness. Of those diagnosed, only three had been diagnosed with a psychotic disorder."[4] Of course, in many mass murder cases, mental evaluation is difficult because the perpetrators killed themselves or the police killed them. If these individuals didn't have a formal mental evaluation beforehand, their mental state is then only a guess. But still, investigators for the study above always spoke afterward with the family and loved ones of the mass murderers, and found that, unlike Wong, most of the individuals studied showed no apparent psychotic behavior. In fact, far too many mass murderers instead follow the personality profile in the following narrative.

* * *

On May 18, 2018, the expected high temperature in Santa Fe, Texas, a small town of about 13,400 residents thirty miles southeast of Houston, sat at ninety-four degrees. Regardless, and as he had done for some time, seventeen-year-old Dimitrios Pagourtzis wore a long black trench coat and military boots to high school. On the trench coat he had attached a number of pins and buttons, including a hammer and sickle and an Iron Cross. While all of this might seem strange, the teachers and other students at Santa Fe High School saw no reason for concern; he had been dressing like this for a long time. But what the teachers and students didn't know was that hidden under the trench coat that day Pagourtzis carried a Remington 870 pump shotgun and a .38 caliber revolver. These weapons belonged to his father, who had purchased and owned them legally. Also, before entering the school, Pagourtzis had stashed outside the building several homemade explosive devices, including a pressure cooker containing nails and wired to a clock, two CO_2 canisters duct taped together, and a Molotov cocktail.

Interestingly, along with the fact that no one was alarmed by Pagourtzis's attire, neither was anyone suspicious of him because of his personality, lifestyle, or previous actions. Pagourtzis had been a member of Santa Fe High School's junior varsity football team, an honor roll student, and a singer at his church; he had also competed in a national history contest for the school. He had told everyone that he intended to join the Marines in 2019. Pagourtzis simply didn't appear to be dangerous. He didn't seem to be seething with anger, wasn't rebellious of rules and teachers, and didn't appear to be a danger in any way. Pagourtzis had never come to the attention of the local police or school security; he was simply a quiet kid who didn't appear to have any major life problems.

"He was quiet, but he wasn't quiet in a creepy way," said Valerie Martin, one of Pagourtzis's teachers.[5]

However, at 7:50 a.m. on May 18, 2018, Pagourtzis walked into the high school's art complex, made up of four rooms connected by interior hallways. Once he got into one of the rooms, he reportedly shouted "Surprise!" and pulled out the shotgun. Pagourtzis then began shooting the students in the room. Apparently spotting a student he didn't like, Pagourtzis allegedly told him, "I'm going to kill you," and then shot the student.[6] Naturally, panic broke out in the classroom and students attempted to dive for cover or flee the room as Pagourtzis continued shooting student after student.

"We heard the first shot and heard probably almost 20 shots," said Zack Lawford, who sat in a nearby classroom.[7]

Several students attempted to barricade themselves in a storage closet, but Pagourtzis shot through the door and hit several of the students hiding there. From the initial classroom, Pagourtzis next moved to the ceramics room and began shooting more students. The students in the room he had just left tried to barricade the door, but Pagourtzis returned and pushed through the barricade, shooting another student in the chest.

A nearby teacher, hearing the gunfire and knowing what it was, pulled the school's fire alarm in order to get the other students out of the building and harm's way. Most of the students thought it was just an ordinary fire drill and left the school with no fear—that is, until several of the teachers began shouting that this wasn't a drill, that they had an active shooter, and for the students to run. The students then began racing away from the school, most hiding behind nearby buildings.

A school safety officer, who happened to be a retired Houston police officer, along with another officer, arrived within just a few minutes of Pagourtzis entering the art classroom and called to Pagourtzis from the hallway. They demanded that he lay down his weapons and surrender. Pagourtzis, however, argued loudly with the officers and fired several shots, wounding one of the officers. In situations like this, police officers find themselves facing many obstacles. They must try to stop the suspect, protect themselves, and do everything possible to avoid any more loss of life. Since Pagourtzis had stationed himself inside a room full of students, the officers had to be extremely cautious about firing back at him for fear of hitting innocent bystanders. Therefore they continued to try to reason with him. The standoff would last another twenty-five minutes before Pagourtzis finally surrendered to the police. He would later tell investigators that his original plan had been to kill himself rather than be arrested, but that he simply lacked the courage to go through with it.

After the police had Pagourtzis in custody, they began immediately looking for victims. A call for multiple ambulances went out as officers found that Pagourtzis had killed two teachers and eight students, including an exchange student from Pakistan, and had wounded more than a dozen others. Searching the grounds of the high school, police officers found the explosive devices Pagourtzis had brought with him. A later analysis determined that the pressure cooker and CO_2 canisters were not operational. Still, a warning went out to Santa Fe residents to be extremely cautious if they came upon any strange items lying around, and to call the police immediately.

The police would eventually charge Pagourtzis with ten counts of capital murder and numerous counts of aggravated assault. The Department of Justice said that they would be looking into federal charges against Pagourtzis, including the use of weapons of mass destruction. Naturally, a search also began for a motive. What would make a seemingly normal seventeen-year-old high school student with no criminal record and no obvious psychological problems go on a killing rampage like this?

"He was kind of a quiet kid," said fellow student Aidan Gomez. "Every time you'd try to start a conversation with him he'd just kind of like laugh, wouldn't really continue on with the conversation." When asked about Pagourtzis being the shooter, Gomez said, "I didn't think he was that kind of kid."[8]

Some people put forth the theory that the shooting stemmed from Pagourtzis being bullied, telling about incidents of teachers lecturing him about his personal hygiene. But others said that they had never seen any bullying and that he had never complained of it.

"People on the news said he was being bullied a lot," said fellow student Rey Montemayor III. "I never seen him being bullied. I never bullied him. He was cool to me."[9]

The mother of one of the female students who was killed said that Pagourtzis had been pestering her daughter to go out with him and had lately become more and more aggressive. Her daughter, the mother said, finally stood up to him and plainly and bluntly told him that she wasn't interested. The mother's belief was that this was possibly what had caused the deadly rampage, especially since Pagourtzis had selected the young girl as one of those who would die.

During his interrogation by the police, Pagourtzis admitted to the shooting, although he claimed he didn't remember much about the incident. The attorneys hired to represent Pagourtzis also said that he claimed he couldn't remember much about that day. This claim, however, is common among individuals who have committed extraordinarily heinous acts. It allows the individuals to accept responsibility without accepting the blame. However, Pagourtzis also told the police that he didn't shoot anyone he liked. He wanted them to still be around to tell his story, which contradicts the claim that he couldn't remember anything about what he did. The police, following their investigation, couldn't officially confirm any motive for the killings.

Pagourtzis's parents, like everyone else, appeared stunned by the incident. Pagourtzis's family insisted that they had seen no signs of whatever problems had led Pagourtzis to carry out these murders. They said they were praying for the families of the victims. "While we remain mostly in the dark about the specifics of yesterday's tragedy, what we have learned from media reports seems incompatible with the boy we love," the family said in a statement.[10]

A search of Pagourtzis's cell phone and computer showed that he had been planning the shooting for some time. People also pointed to several of his social media postings as possible signs of what he had intended to do. One of these postings showed a photograph of a T-shirt with the words "Born to Kill" printed on it—the shirt he had worn the day of the shootings. Pagourtzis had also posted a photograph of a gun and a knife and a photograph of the black trench coat he wore with an explanation of what the pins on it meant. The Iron Cross, he said, represented bravery, the hammer and sickle meant rebellion, the rising sun meant kamikaze tactics, and so forth. But while many people pointed to these social media posts afterward, they hadn't raised any alarms ahead of the attack; they had appeared to be normal postings for a seventeen-year-old boy.

The police sent Pagourtzis to the Galveston County Jail, where he was put in solitary confinement and on suicide watch. A judge ordered him to be held without bond. While ordinarily anyone convicted of ten counts of capital murder would face the possibility of the death penalty, Pagourtzis, because he was only seventeen, could not. The US Supreme Court in *Roper v. Simmons* ruled in 2005 that juveniles could not be put to death. He could not even face life imprisonment without the possibility of parole. The Supreme Court ruled in the 2012 case of *Miller v. Alabama* that juveniles could not be given this penalty. Pagourtzis would instead face up to forty years in prison.

Because of this tragedy in Santa Fe, Texas, Netflix canceled the premiere of the second season of *13 Reasons Why*. The plot reportedly included a storyline about a school shooting that had been prevented.

Eventually, the parents of several of the students killed at the high school filed lawsuits against the parents of Pagourtzis. In the lawsuits the parents claimed that Pagourtzis's parents had not properly secured their weapons, thus making them available for Pagourtzis to use, and that they had also ignored signs of their son's possible violence. The lawsuits, in addition, complained that Pagourtzis's parents had neglected to get mental health counseling for Pagourtzis, and had failed to properly warn the community that he could be a danger.

The entire incident that occurred at Santa Fe High School, which lasted about thirty minutes, was actually a very long time for this type of incident. They usually wrap up in a much shorter time. A study by the US Secret Service of twenty-eight mass murders that occurred in the United States in 2017 found that more than half of the events ended within five minutes of the first shot fired or the first person harmed.[11]

Interestingly, Santa Fe High School had had a detailed plan for dealing with an active shooter and had conducted several drills. However, drills can never completely mimic real life. Although plans and drills are extremely important, a certain amount of chaos always surrounds large-scale incidents like this; chaos that can interfere with the best-laid plans.

As boxer Mike Tyson once said, "Everyone has a plan until they get hit in the face."

＊ ＊ ＊

The above narrative should be disturbing to most readers because many mass murderers fit this profile. The most common response from people who knew mass murderers is shock. Most say that they never thought the murderers were violent or that they would ever do such a thing. And while some of these seemingly normal individuals who became mass murderers have had minor run-ins with the police, and perhaps with school authorities, most, like Pagourtzis above, have never raised any alarms that would make people believe they are a danger or could be capable of committing a mass murder.

"Often offenders are so pathologically secretive about their abnormal behavior that they arouse no suspicion or 'the not quite right' feeling in an observer," Joel Shults, a former police chief in Colorado and now CEO of Shults Professional Services, told me.[12]

And yet, while this large percentage of mass murderers may not be suffering from a severe psychosis that would be identifiable to those who came in contact with them, this is not to say that they don't suffer from mental health issues. They do, but usually not to the level that would raise alarm and intervention by the authorities. Most mass murderers, experts claim, suffer from some type of personality disorder. However, these personality disorders, when enhanced and magnified by stressors such as relationship conflicts, employment reverses, financial problems, and rejection by peers, can push the individuals toward violent behavior.

Many mass murderers, for example, suffer from pathological narcissism. "They believe themselves to be special, to have the right to do and say, but also to act out as they wish, feeling omnipotent in their beliefs and assured that only they have the wisdom, vision, and understanding of the problem and of course the solution," says Joe Navarro, a retired FBI agent and now CEO of JN Forensics.[13] Because of this narcissism, these individuals often have very little empathy for anyone else; therefore, when they do strike out, they can kill both those whom they have targeted and those whom they haven't.

Pathologically narcissistic individuals believe that they are elite beings and therefore have entitlements that the common person doesn't. However, when life doesn't give them these entitlements the individuals begin building up rage at the unfairness of it. This rage continues to grow and fester after each slight until these individuals finally feel that they must punish those who are receiving the entitlements to which they believe they are entitled. "He is tormented by beliefs that privileged others are enjoying life's all-you-can-eat buffet, while he must peer through the window, an outside loner always looking in," says Dr. Allen J. Frances in an article in *Psychology Today* magazine.[14]

Like pathological narcissism, many future mass murderers suffer from grandiosity, a feeling that they are many steps above all others in the world. And yet, even though they feel this way, these individuals find themselves struggling to understand why they can't succeed in school, in their careers, or in their personal life. Because they are so much smarter and wiser than anyone else in the world, they finally decide it has to be sabotage by lesser individuals. This paranoia about sabotage can grow and fester until it leads to violence; these individuals eventually see this as the only way to correct the situation. Also, individuals suffering from grandiosity can sometimes become involved in a mass murder because they feel that through the mass murder they can become godlike, that they will be the one who decides which individuals will live and which individuals will die. One of the gunmen in the Columbine High School mass murder said, "I would love to be the ultimate judge and say if a person lives or dies—be godlike."[15]

Along with these personality disorders, some future male mass murderers can feel a significant loss of their masculine identity by various events in life. They lose a job and can no longer support their family; they suffer reverses or rejection in their romantic lives; other people obtain awards and accolades that they feel they deserve. These events can sometimes be so demeaning and humiliating that these individuals eventually feel that they must strike back at the people who are stealing their masculine identity.

Quite often, adults involved in mass murders will also have a history of domestic violence. If the relationship they're in breaks down and the victims of the domestic violence leave, these individuals can feel a severe loss of masculine identity and will want to strike out at others to regain their feeling of masculinity. According to *Fox News*, a study showed that 54 percent of mass shootings between 2009 and 2016 involved domestic or family violence.[16] The FBI's study of sixty-three mass murderers, referenced earlier, found that 62 percent of the individuals studied had a history of acting in an abusive, harassing, or oppressive manner, which included domestic violence and stalker-related conduct.[17]

This group worried about the loss of their masculine identity also includes many of the young school shooters. Research has shown that many of these individuals feel that they don't live up to what other teenagers perceive as being masculine, which is almost exclusively determined by their peers. These future mass murderers are often viewed by classmates as being sissies, possible homosexuals, or just weird. This then leads these individuals to being shunned by classmates, and consequently fuels their anger at their classmates who seem to be getting all the rewards that they themselves should be getting. Not being accepted by the "cool group," being turned down by girls they like, and generally being denied an opportunity to take part in social activities because of their lack of masculinity can eventually drive some of these individuals into committing the ultimate masculine act: shooting up the school. What could be more manly than that?

Often members of this group, because of the lack of acceptance by their peers at school, suffer from social isolation and become known as loners. Consequently, their anger and rage grow. Without a group that will allow for venting and compassion, this resentment increases unabated. In a study that appeared in the *Journal of the American Academy of Child and Adolescent Psychiatry*, the author stated that in a study of 115 potential school shooters over a nine-year period researchers found that higher levels of threat were present in the most socially lonely or teased kids, who were harboring secret retaliatory thoughts.[18] An article in *Psychology Today* listed a number of traits for school shooters. Almost all, the article said, were male, most had been bullied, felt mistreated by teachers, tended to be socially awkward, would often retreat into fantasy, and many times had a sense of hopelessness.[19]

Along with all the above problems, many future mass murderers also suffer from paranoia. These individuals begin to see threats everywhere. For them there are no innocent actions, but rather slights and plots against them. This paranoia can build until the individuals feel certain that an attack against them is imminent. While these fears can seem irrational or nonsensical to most people, they are not to the individuals suffering from paranoia. They are concrete threats.

These paranoid individuals can also often be "wound or injustice collectors." They remember every slight they have ever received, every insult, every injustice they believe they have suffered. And they don't just remember them; they dwell on them constantly, daily reviewing and reliving them, which only further fuels their anger and paranoia. An article in an academic journal said "the more people think about them the angrier they get, and the angrier they get, the harder it is to think about anything else."[20]

"People who collect wounds, who intentionally go out of their way to see social slights as personal attacks, then nourish these psychological wounds by constantly reminding themselves of them," said retired FBI agent Joe Navarro in an interview. "These grievances or psychological wounds, when repeatedly reinforced and nourished, leave the person in a constant state of agitation or hypersensitivity. At some point, a life stressor triggers these pent up grievances and the person will act out with violence."[21] When these individuals finally do strike out at others in a mass murder, they feel that their actions are totally justified because of how badly they have been treated by their enemies, who were bound to strike out at them soon anyway.

Naturally, because of the consequences of the personality disorders discussed above, many mass murderers also suffer from depression. This is a natural outgrowth of feeling slighted and cheated by life, of feeling rejected by their peers, or of feeling that they don't match up to society's image of masculinity. Often this depression can lead to thoughts of suicide, but some individuals commit suicide only after they have taken out the ones who have wronged them.

Readers may have noticed that so far all the narratives in this book have involved male perpetrators. This is because more than 90 percent of all mass murderers are male. A study by researchers Alexia Cooper and Erica L. Smith of mass murders between 1980 and 2008 found that women committed 6.4 percent of them.[22] Other researchers agree, many also finding that women commit between 6 and 7 percent of all mass murders. "[Female mass murderers are] so rare that it just hasn't been studied," says James Garbarino, a psychologist at Loyola University Chicago.[23] But as the following short narratives show, women do commit them. Consequently, readers should never have a false sense of security just because the person acting strangely is a woman.

✽ ✽ ✽

Forty-four-year-old Cherie Lash Rhoades lived in the Native American enclave of Cedarville Rancheria in Cedarville, California, a town of about 500 residents in the northeast corner of California. She worked at a filling station and convenience store owned by her tribe, and for several years had been chair of the thirty-five-member group of Native Americans. In early 2014, however, she had been ousted as the chair. Some time before this, a federal investigation had been launched into $50,000 in federal grant money meant for the tribe that had gone missing from a fund she oversaw. As punishment for the missing money, the new leadership of the tribe began proceedings to have Rhoades evicted from Cedarville Rancheria, the harshest punishment the tribe could impose.

People in the area told the news media that they always worried about violence erupting during an eviction hearing. "Anytime you evict someone from their home, you're going to worry about this," said Linda Stubblefield, whose daughter worked for the tribe. "And you're taking their Indian rights from them."[24]

On February 20, 2014, Rhoades's brother, fifty-year-old Rurik Davis, the new chair of the tribe, and several other board members held a meeting at their headquarters building in Alturas, California, to discuss the eviction of Rhoades. However, during the meeting, Rhoades burst into the room and began shooting at them with a semiautomatic pistol. She killed her brother, Rurik; her nineteen-year-old niece, Angel Penn; her thirty-year-old nephew, Glenn Calonicco; and forty-seven-year-old Shelia Lynn Russo. Apparently running out of bullets, Rhoades then brandished a knife, stabbed one woman, and chased another one of her nieces out of the building.

The authorities, alerted when a blood-covered woman ran to the Alturas City Hall building close by, sent officers to the scene. They saw Rhoades slashing the knife at her niece as she chased her. A tribal member helped the police tackle and disarm Rhoades. The police later charged Rhoades with four counts of murder, several counts of attempted murder, child endangerment (there had been several children in the tribe's headquarters building that day), and brandishing a weapon. This, however, wasn't Rhoades's first outburst of violence. She was known around the area as being easily angered and violent.

"She bullied her way through life," said Sandra Parriott, a longtime resident of Cedarville. "But I would never think she would start blowing people away in a meeting."[25]

In December 2016, a jury found Rhoades guilty of four counts of first-degree murder and two counts of attempted murder. A judge eventually sentenced her to death for the murders and 150 years' imprisonment for the attempted murders.

✿ ✿ ✿

Twenty-six-year-old Snochia Moseley had been hired in September 2018 as a temporary employee at the Rite Aid Drugstore warehouse near Aberdeen, Maryland. This large facility employed about one thousand people, and Moseley had worked there for only two weeks as a security guard. The warehouse was gearing up for the 2018 holiday season.

On September 20, 2018, Moseley came to work at her usual time of 6:30 a.m. and got into an argument with someone lined up to go into the building. Less than an hour later, Moseley left the facility and went home to retrieve her 9mm Glock semiautomatic handgun. She arrived back at the warehouse parking lot at 8:53 a.m. That was when, outside the building, she pulled out the Glock and killed forty-five-year-old Sunday Aguda, who was standing nearby. Moseley then fired shots at several other people, but missed. At 9:05 a.m., she went inside the warehouse and fired thirteen rounds, hitting five people. Two of these people, forty-one-year-old Brindra Giri and forty-one-year-old Hayleen Reyes, died. Moseley then turned the gun on herself and fired two shots. The first shot only grazed her, but the second shot found its mark. She died later at the hospital.

The police received their first call about the shootings at 9:09 a.m. and arrived at the scene within minutes. But by then the shooting was over. Along with the handgun, the police would also find handcuffs and pepper spray on Moseley's body. These would have been part of her security guard equipment.

Moseley had no criminal record and had only come in contact with the police over traffic violations. No one she knew could imagine a motive for the mass murder. Her family, however, did say that she had become increasingly agitated during the previous few weeks and that it had concerned them. They also said that she had been diagnosed with an unknown mental illness several years before.

The local sheriff's department served a search warrant at Moseley's residence. "While no evidence directly related to the shooting was recovered," said Harford County Sheriff Jeffrey Gahler, "evidence that the shooter was suffering with a mental illness was identified."[26] However, the sheriff didn't release any information about the type or severity of Moseley's mental problems. Whatever her problem was, however, it apparently wasn't serious enough to stop Moseley from purchasing a firearm.

* * *

Forty-four-year-old Jennifer San Marco had worked for the US Postal Service for six years, retiring in 2003 on a medical disability due to psychological problems. She had been known to behave very bizarrely while employed at a mail processing center, once having to be forcibly removed from the facility by the police after they had pulled her from a hiding place under a postal sorting machine. However, the Postal Service wasn't alone in noticing San Marco's strange behavior. Her neighbors had reported her several times for shouting loudly to herself, and she had been known to order food at a restaurant and then race out of the establishment before touching it. In addition, she would often stop her car to kneel and pray at the edge of the road, would occasionally strip naked in public parking lots, and had once undressed at a filling station.

Several people had tried without success to get help for San Marco. Darlene Hayes, who worked at a mental health clinic, had found San Marco kneeling and praying in a post office parking lot. San Marco talked loudly about people being there with her, but she was alone. Darlene called the police to get her help. "It seemed like she was acting delusional," said Darlene Hayes. "I wanted the police to make contact with her and hold her for 24 hours so they could determine whether she needed a physician."[27]

Sadly, San Marco didn't get any help, and on January 30, 2006, after shooting and killing fifty-four-year-old Beverly Graham, a former neighbor who had complained about her loud singing, San Marco drove to the mail processing center where she had worked in Goleta, California. In the car with her, she carried a 9mm Smith and Wesson semi-automatic pistol that she owned. She had purchased it at a pawn shop and had cleared the background investigation because she had never been formally diagnosed as mentally ill or been committed to a mental health facility for a mental illness.

Walking around the parking lot, San Marco first shot thirty-seven-year-old Ze Fairchild in the head, then shot twenty-eight-year-old Maleka Higgans and forty-two-year-old Nicola Grant. Some of the employees inside, hearing the gunfire, raced to the windows to see what was happening. They said San Marco smiled at them.

San Marco then entered the building using another employee's key-card. Once inside, she shot forty-four-year-old supervisor Charlotte Colton and fifty-three-year-old Lupe Swartz and fifty-seven-year-old Dexter Shannon, who were employees. She then turned the gun on herself and committed suicide. The seven people she shot that day would die at the scene or later at the hospital.

The police later searched San Marco's home. They found some of her writing, which indicated she believed there was a conspiracy at the mail processing center and that she was their target. San Marco, who was white, had also been known to harbor a dislike for minorities and had once applied for a license to publish a newsletter called *The Racist Press*. All of San Marco's victims had been minorities.

* * *

As the above three narratives show, no one should be counted out as a possible mass murderer. Actually, it is difficult to mark any group as more likely than another to be mass murderers. The age makeup of mass murderers, for example, is certainly spread out. In the FBI's study of sixty-three mass murders, referenced earlier, the ages of the individuals in the study ranged from twelve to eighty-eight. The two peak age groups were eighteen to twenty-nine and forty to forty-nine. Interestingly, 65 percent of the mass murderers studied by the FBI had no prior criminal convictions, and just 5 percent had a felony violent crime conviction. The educational level of the mass murderers was also widely spread, ranging from no high school up to a doctorate.[28] As for the racial makeup of mass murderers, statistics gathered by *Mother Jones* magazine showed that the makeup of mass murderers pretty closely mirrored the racial makeup of the United States.[29] Whites committed 64 percent of the mass murders, blacks committed 16 percent, Asians committed 9 percent, and the rest were committed by Hispanics, Native Americans, and unknown. "If you look at the whole list, it turns out that whites and blacks are pretty proportionate to their population, very close," says David Cullen, author of *Columbine*.[30] Finally, research has shown that drug and alcohol use is minimal in mass murderers. There is a good reason for this. Most mass murderers have decided to carry out their plans because in doing so they hope to right the wrongs they believe they have suffered. Mass murderers don't want drugs and alcohol to cloud or muddle the experience; rather, they want to enjoy their moment of retribution to the fullest.

Everything I've talked about in this chapter shows that there is no single description that fits all mass murderers. Readers simply cannot rely on the belief that only certain types of people can commit such heinous acts. The truth is, almost anyone could become a mass murderer. The FBI in its study of mass murderers reported that these sixty-three active shooters did not appear to be uniform in any way such that they could be readily identified prior to attacking *based on demographics alone*.[31]

"Profiling is fascinating to the public and law enforcement alike, but has been found of dubious reliability," said former chief of police Joel Shults in an interview. "The problem with all personality profiles is that most characteristics are found in the general, non-murdering populace."[32]

While almost all the mass murderers I've described so far, with the exception of the first narrative in this book, committed the mass murder using firearms, that is not the only weapon they have used. As we will see in the next chapter, a variety of weapons are available to those contemplating a mass murder.

3

WEAPONS OF MASS MURDERERS

Sixty-four-year-old retiree Stephen Paddock of Mesquite, Nevada, a town of about 19,000 people eighty miles northeast of Las Vegas, checked into the Mandalay Bay Hotel and Casino in Las Vegas on September 25, 2017. He asked for an upper-level suite that would be facing the outdoor Route 91 Harvest Festival to be held across the street from the hotel on October 1. The hotel knew Paddock to be a high roller and wanted to accommodate him, but the requested suite wasn't immediately available. However, several days later they did move him into a thirty-second-floor suite, room 32-135, which had the requirements he requested. Paddock then went to work.

Making a number of trips, Paddock brought two dozen guns to the room, including fourteen AR-15s equipped with bump stocks that made the semiautomatic assault rifles fire like fully automatic assault rifles, eight .308 caliber AR-10s, one .308 caliber Ruger American Bolt Action rifle, and one .38 caliber Smith and Wesson revolver. He also brought in thousands of rounds of ammunition for these weapons, including 100-round magazines. The police would also later find unused explosive material in his car. In addition to all of this, Paddock set up hidden cameras to keep track of what was going on in the hallway outside his room. He wanted to be prepared for the eventual police assault.

The hotel staff had been in Paddock's room a number of times but didn't notice anything suspicious. They could see that he had more than a dozen suitcases, but that really wasn't any of their business. "It wasn't evident that he had weapons in his room," said Clark County Sheriff Joseph Lombardo.[1]

At 9:40 p.m. on October 1, 2017, the Route 91 Harvest Festival had gotten under way and country singer Jason Aldean stood on the stage. At 10:05 p.m., the crowd of 22,000 people, enjoying the balmy weather and great music, didn't seem to have anything to worry about. That changed quickly. Suddenly, gunfire erupted from the windows on the upper floors of the Mandalay Bay Hotel. Paddock had broken the windows out a few moments before with a hammer. Most of the concertgoers at first thought that the sound was just fireworks; then they saw people in the audience begin spouting blood and falling to the ground. The crowd, although stunned for a few seconds, naturally panicked because no one knew what was going on, and the thousands of people suddenly began dashing for their lives in all directions. During the frenzied escape no one was certain at whom the next volley would be aimed, but they prayed that it wouldn't be at them as they raced for safety.

Up on the thirty-second floor, Paddock used a number of his weapons to fire at the crowd below. From his position he likely couldn't see any individual targets, but with many thousands of people packed so closely together he couldn't miss hitting someone just by firing into the crowd. But along with firing at the people, Paddock also fired at some nearby fuel tanks, apparently hoping to add to the panic. Although he hit them several times, the fuel tanks didn't ignite. Before he stopped, Paddock would reportedly fire hundreds of rounds at the terrified concertgoers.

A minute or so before the shooting started, Jesus Campos, a security guard for Mandalay Bay Hotel, had been sent to investigate an open door on the thirty-second floor. While coming up the stairs he found that someone had barricaded the door to the thirty-second floor. "There was a metal bracket holding the door in place," said Campos.[2] Paddock had seemingly done this to slow down the police when they responded to the shooting. Campos informed the hotel of this and then took the elevator to the thirty-second floor. He said he heard what sounded like drilling coming from Paddock's room and went to check on it. Apparently Paddock saw the security guard approaching his room on the hidden cameras he had installed and shot at Campos through the door, hitting him in the right upper thigh. Campos went for cover and alerted hotel security. He remained on the thirty-second floor and advised them of the situation until the police arrived.

The police set up a staging area on the thirty-first floor at 10:12 p.m. By then Paddock had fired at least a dozen volleys with various weapons at the crowd below. At 10:17 p.m., two officers arrived on the thirty-second floor. Campos, the wounded security guard, directed them to the room where the shooting had come from. By that time, for an unknown reason, Paddock had stopped firing at the crowd.

Within minutes, eight additional police officers arrived on the thirty-second floor. Since the shooting had stopped, rather than assaulting the room, the officers began evacuating guests from the floor in case more shooting erupted when they did attempt to take the shooter or shooters into custody. By 10:24 p.m., the officers had positioned themselves outside of Paddock's room and called for the SWAT team. An active shooter alert from the Las Vegas Police Department also went out, letting taxi drivers and others know to avoid the area around the Mandalay Bay Hotel. The police department also put out a Twitter alert about the shooting.

The officers outside of Paddock's room radioed in and asked for permission to force entry into the room, but they were told to wait for the SWAT team. Although many people might not agree, this was a very sound tactical decision that had to be made. The police command staff knew that there was obviously a heavily armed and very dangerous shooter or shooters in the room, armed with automatic weapons. SWAT team officers are specially trained and equipped for the best and safest methods for making room entry in just such a situation. And since the shooting had ceased, and the person or persons in the room had been contained by the officers outside, there was minimal risk and danger in waiting for SWAT.

At 11:20 p.m., the police SWAT team had arrived and used an explosive charge to blow open the door to Paddock's room. Doing this not only allows for immediate entry into a room, but it is hoped that the explosion will also momentarily stun anyone inside the room, giving SWAT a few seconds of advantage. The advantage wasn't needed in this case; Paddock lay dead on the floor, having shot himself in the head. The police, however, also blew open a closed door inside the suite, in case Paddock had accomplices hiding there, but they didn't find anyone. Paddock had been the only shooter. However, it was still a little over an hour before the police officially confirmed that Paddock had been the only shooter. This is simply a precaution the police must take to be absolutely certain he was the only shooter. They don't want the public to believe that they are safe and stop being cautious, in case it turns out there actually were more shooters.

The final toll of the shooting would be fifty-eight concertgoers killed and more than 800 wounded. But of course, in any panicked crowd like this, many of the injuries didn't come from the shooting itself, but from being knocked down and trampled by others trying to flee. Even so, this was just the physical toll. No one knows what the future emotional and psychological problems will be for the thousands of concertgoers who fled for their lives as the shots rang out from above, for the concertgoers who saw others nearby shot and killed, and for the concertgoers who had to jump over dead bodies as they escaped.

"People were getting shot at while we were running, and people were on the ground bleeding, crying and screaming," said Dinora Merino, who was at the concert with a friend. "We just had to keep going."[3]

Naturally, hospitals in the area began filling up with patients. "I can only describe the hospital ED as a war scene . . . something you would see in the movies," said Dorothy Grillo, a nurse at Sunrise Hospital. "There were patients everywhere and people just kept coming through the doors. Ambulances, cars, and trucks were lined up and unloading wounded people, some fatally injured."[4]

Naturally, a case of this magnitude would involve many detectives trying to figure out what happened and why. The police investigated the case for almost a year but could never come up with a definite motive.

"This individual purposely hid his actions leading up to this event," said Sheriff Lombardo. "And it is difficult for us to find the answers to those actions."[5]

Who was Stephen Paddock, the man who killed fifty-eight people he didn't know?

Paddock had no criminal record and no known ties to any terrorist groups. He had worked for the post office and as a tax auditor, but neither of these jobs paid as well as he had hoped. Paddock eventually went into the business of flipping houses and made a lot of money. From all reports he seemed to be very well-off financially. He owned several houses, a couple of airplanes, several apartment buildings, and was known around Las Vegas as a high roller. But few people really knew Paddock well. He appeared to be an extremely private person who didn't socialize much. Paddock's girlfriend, Marilou Danley, later told investigators that he appeared to be having problems, both mentally and physically, in the months before the shooting.

Paddock's family also commented on him and the mass murder. "I wish I could tell you he was a miserable bastard, that I hate him, that if I could have killed him myself I would have," said Eric Paddock, Stephen's younger brother. "But I can't say that. It's not who he was. We need to find out what happened to him."[6]

Whatever it was that was happening to Paddock before the shooting seemed to relentlessly drive him toward mass violence. He began making plans for a mass slaughter some time before the Las Vegas shooting. Paddock had reportedly scouted hotels around Fenway Park in Boston and had berated the front desk personnel at a hotel in Chicago in order to get a room that overlooked the Lollapalooza festival. He claimed that he had met his wife at the festival. The hotel finally did reserve a room for him in September 2017, but for some reason he didn't use it. Paddock also reportedly stayed at the Ogden Hotel in downtown Las Vegas. The hotel overlooked the Life Is Beautiful festival.

It is likely that no one will ever know what caused Paddock to go into his deadly shooting spree. Was it declining physical health? Declining mental health? Personal life issues? We can only guess.

❊ ❊ ❊

The reason I selected this narrative to begin the chapter is that Stephen Paddock used the most common weapon of mass murder, and he used a lot of them: firearms. There are several good reasons why firearms are the weapon of choice in most mass murders in the United States. Firearms are relatively easy to obtain, they are usually deadly, and they are much more impersonal than other weapons. When using a firearm there is no contact with the victims. A mass murderer can stand back from the victims while they are killed.

The type of firearms used in mass murders can vary. A study of more than one hundred mass shootings from January 1982 to November 2018 found that well over three-quarters of the shootings involved the use of handguns, both revolvers and semiautomatic pistols.[7] The semiautomatic pistol was often the choice for these mass murderers because of the availability of fourteen- or fifteen-round magazines and the ease of reloading the weapon. With a revolver, the cylinder usually only holds five or six rounds and reloading takes a bit longer. There are, however, speed loaders available for revolvers. This is a bullet holder in the shape of a revolver cylinder. Rather than having to reload a revolver one bullet at a time, all of the chambers can be reloaded at one time. This makes reloading a revolver much faster.

Along with the popularity of handguns, a little less than 50 percent of the mass shootings examined involved the use of some type of rifle, ranging from hunting rifles to military assault weapons. The AR-15 assault rifle has been a very popular choice for mass murderers because it can be equipped with hundred-round magazines and its power is deadly. It was used in the Las Vegas shooting, the Pittsburgh synagogue mass murder, at Marjory Stoneman Douglas High School, Sandy Hook Elementary, a church in Sutherland Springs, Texas, and other mass murders. While a pistol bullet travels, on average, about 700 to 800 miles per hour, an AR-15 bullet travels several times faster, giving it much more force and allowing it to do extreme damage to human tissue. On *60 Minutes*, during an episode on the AR-15 and why it's so popular with mass murderers, Scott Pelley talked with Cynthia Bir, who operates a ballistics lab at the University of Southern California. She demonstrated how a bullet from a 9mm semiautomatic pistol, when fired at a gelatin block that represented human tissue, passed straight through the gelatin block with one continuous hole the size of the bullet. However, when the AR-15 was used it tore a large cavity in the gelatin.

"Organs aren't just going to tear or have bruises on them," she said. "They're going to be, parts of them are going to be destroyed."[8]

And while the AR-15s sold to civilians are semiautomatic, meaning that they can fire only one bullet with each pull of the trigger, they can be made to fire faster. Stephen Paddock used a bump stock that made the AR-15s he used fire much faster. Also, with the right tools and expertise, a semiautomatic AR-15 can be converted into a fully automatic one. Several years ago, while writing a book about the American Militia Movement, I attended a militia conference in Atlanta, Georgia, that had a lot of assault weapons for sale. When I inquired about the possibility of buying a fully automatic weapon, one of the vendors offered to throw in a booklet on how to convert one to fully automatic. Information about how to do this can also be found on the internet.

Last, about 25 percent of the mass shootings in the United States from January 1982 to November 2018 involved the use of a shotgun. These weapons can come in various forms, from one shot to double barrel to a pump shotgun that can hold six or more rounds depending on the model. While not very useful at long distances, shotguns can do devastating damage at close range, and by using a pump shotgun the operator can fire as quickly as he or she can pump a new shell into the chamber. (The percentages for the study add up to more than 100 percent because in many instances more than one type of weapon was used.)[9]

Interestingly, a news article from 2016 made the following observation: in countries with strict gun laws, mass murderers must resort to other weapons, often knives. According to the article, on July 26, 2016, twenty-six-year-old Satoshi Uematsu broke into a center for the disabled in Japan. Once inside, he stabbed more than fifty people, killing nineteen of them. His motive? He told the police that he wanted to purge disabled people from society.[10] In addition to this, according to the BBC website, in 2018 Great Britain saw the highest number of fatal stabbings since record keeping began in 1946.[11] As the following narrative shows, the same situation can happen in America. Occasionally, for various reasons, mass murderers cannot obtain a firearm or enough ammunition, so instead they grab a knife.

✳ ✳ ✳

When thirty-four-year-old Noe Martinez Jr. didn't show up for work for two days, a fellow employee called the police and asked them to check on him. The police went to the Martinez home in the 5700 block of South California Avenue in the Gage Park neighborhood of Chicago and discovered a gruesome scene. When no one answered the door and the police could find no forced entry, the officers looked in a window and could see a body covered with blood lying on the floor. Forcing their way in, the police found, along with the one body seen from outside, the bodies of five other members of the Martinez family. Although at first suspecting this might have been a murder-suicide, the police later determined it to be a mass murder. One of the victims, thirty-two-year-old Maria Martinez, had been shot to death, the other five bludgeoned and stabbed to death. For a time the police wondered if the killer or killers had mistaken the Martinez household for another.

However, after deciding that the killer or killers had the right household after all, the police didn't believe that it had been just a random attack; they suspected that the Martinez family had been targeted for some reason. "Everything from a domestic incident, possible robbery, or even possibly something nefarious that could have targeted the family is being explored," said Chicago Police Department spokesperson Anthony Guglielmi. [12]

As the investigation continued, suspicion fell on twenty-two-year-old Diego Uribe, a frequent visitor to the home who was related to Maria's ex-husband. After talking to several witnesses, the detectives found that it was well known there was bad blood between Uribe and Maria; Uribe felt that Maria had treated her ex-husband badly. During their investigation, the police had asked Uribe and other family members to submit DNA samples; they all agreed. The DNA in blood the police had collected from under Maria's fingernails matched Uribe. Detectives arrested him and nineteen-year-old Jafeth Ramos, Uribe's girlfriend and the mother of his child.

Upon questioning, both Uribe and Ramos admitted to the crime. People who knew the family appeared stunned by the news because Uribe had been a regular visitor to the house and, except for Maria, all of the family members seemed to be on good terms with him.

"[He] played with those kids all the time," a neighbor of the Martinez family said. "That family loved him." [13]

In his confession, Uribe told the police that he and Ramos arrived at the Martinez house late in the afternoon of February 2, 2016, and that he had planned at that time to rob and kill the family. He and Ramos, Uribe claimed, needed baby supplies and enough money to buy a car. Some time after arriving at the house, Uribe and Maria argued in an upstairs bedroom, and he subsequently shot her four times in the head, killing her. Noe Martinez Jr., hearing the gunfire, raced up the steps to see what had happened, but was struck in the head with Uribe's gun, which had apparently run out of bullets.

Uribe then ran downstairs and grabbed several knives from the kitchen and stabbed both Noe Martinez Jr. and fifty-eight-year-old Rosaura Martinez to death. He then threatened two young boys in the house with the knives and forced them to bring him all the cash in the home, about $500.00. Uribe also took an Xbox gaming console and some jewelry, both of which he later pawned for $150.00. After he had collected all the valuables in the house, Uribe stabbed and killed Maria's sons, ten-year-old Alexis Cruz and thirteen-year-old Leonardo Cruz. The thirteen-year-old boy reportedly begged for his life, pleading with Uribe, "Please no! Please don't! I just want to live!"[14]

Once the five family members had been killed, Uribe and Ramos waited until sixty-two-year-old Noe Martinez Sr., who had gone to get some food for the family, returned home. Uribe also stabbed him to death.

The police charged Uribe, who had no criminal record, with multiple counts of murder. They also charged Ramos with the murders. She had only come in contact with the police once before on a shoplifting charge. Even though she didn't do any of the actual killings, Ramos was a willing participant in the crime and had spent some of the proceeds.

"After 30 years as a prosecutor, I thought I had seen and heard just about anything and everything when it comes to violent crime, but a case like this is something I have never seen before," said Cook County State's Attorney Anita Alvarez. "This was not an armed robbery, this was a methodical slaughter."[15]

* * *

Although the incident above was certainly tragic, there was a much, much larger mass murder that involved the use of knives. The 9/11 terrorists took control of four airplanes with the use of box cutters, resulting in almost 3,000 deaths. But it's not just terrorists and family friends who commit mass murder with knives. Sometimes it can be individuals no one would suspect.

On October 23, 2018, the police in Bartow, Florida, arrested two middle school students, eleven- and twelve-year-old girls. They had come to school with the intention of killing at least fifteen younger students and drinking their blood. The police said the girls had four knives on them that they had smuggled into school. The girls told the police that they planned to kill themselves afterward and be forever with Satan.

"They wanted to kill at least 15 people, and were waiting in the bathroom for the opportunity to find smaller kids that they could overpower to be their victims," said Bartow Chief of Police Joe Hall.[16]

The plot started with a weekend of watching scary movies. Afterward, the girls went online to find the most efficient way to kill someone with a knife. Fortunately, another middle school student heard about the plot and alerted the police before anyone was hurt.

Some mass murderers don't want contact this close with their victims. Also, any time a mass murderer tries to kill someone with a knife there is always the possibility of being overpowered. Therefore, a number of mass murderers have used motor vehicles as their weapon of choice. For example, on October 24, 2015, Adacia Chambers, a twenty-five-year-old woman who claimed to be feeling suicidal, drove her 2014 Hyundai Elantra around a barrier the police had set up to block traffic for Oklahoma State University's homecoming parade in Stillwater, Oklahoma. Once past the barrier, Chambers sped up and plowed her car into a crowd of people watching the parade. Before she stopped, she had killed four people and injured forty-six others. One of the dead was a two-year-old boy.

"The evidence indicates Chambers consciously drove through a red light, around a police barricade, over a police motorcycle and farther into a large crowd of highly visible, innocent people enjoying the OSU homecoming day festivities," said Payne County District Attorney Laura Austin Thomas.[17]

The police arrested Chambers and had her blood tested for alcohol and narcotics, on the belief that this was why she had driven into the crowd. She tested only .01 for alcohol (far below the legal limit necessary to arrest for drunken driving) and had no narcotics in her system. The police then charged her with four counts of second-degree murder and forty-six counts of assault. Before her trial could begin, however, Chambers accepted a plea deal under which she would serve fifty-five years in prison before her first possible release.

"If only I could change the past," Chambers said at her sentencing. "I was suffering from psychosis that day."[18]

More recently, on October 31, 2017, twenty-nine-year-old Sayfullo Saipov, a Russian immigrant and permanent resident of the United States, steered a rented Home Depot pickup truck onto the Hudson River Greenway, a bicycle path along the Hudson River on the west side of Manhattan. For nearly a mile he rammed the truck into bicyclists and pedestrians, killing eight of them and injuring eleven more. He eventually crashed into a school bus and jumped out of the truck, brandishing what looked like two handguns, but which would later be found to be a paintball gun and a pellet gun. A responding police officer, seeing the guns, shot Saipov in the chest—a wound he would survive.

Friends would later say that Saipov had a bad temper and would often get into disagreements that cost him jobs. Saipov told the police that he had scouted the greenway a week earlier and had purposely chosen Halloween for his attack because he thought there would be more people out.

Saipov's attorney would eventually offer the prosecution a deal under which his client would plead guilty to all charges and accept a life sentence if the death penalty were taken off the table. However, in September of 2018, prosecutors said that they would seek the death penalty if Saipov was convicted.

For many mass murderers, though, knives, blunt force, and even motor vehicles are too close, personal, and messy. They prefer something more detached, like a bomb. When talking about a mass murder by bombing, many readers will likely think of Timothy McVeigh and the bombing of the Alfred P. Murrah Federal Building in Oklahoma City in 1995. But actually there have been many other mass murders in the United States perpetrated by a bomb. Along with the Bath Consolidated School bombing discussed in chapter 1, a bomb set off at a labor rally in Chicago's Haymarket Square in 1886 ended with four attendees and seven police officers being killed. The state of Illinois hanged four people for this act. In October of 1910, during another labor dispute, two union leaders, who later pled guilty, dynamited the *Los Angeles Times* building, resulting in twenty-one deaths. Ten years later, in September of 1920, a bomb exploded in the financial district of New York City, killing thirty-eight people and injuring hundreds of others. Although the police had suspects, no arrests were ever made.

More recently, in January of 1975, a bomb at the Fraunces Tavern in New York City exploded, killing six people and injuring dozens. In December of the same year, someone placed a bomb in a locker in the baggage claim area of the TWA terminal at LaGuardia Airport in New York City. Eleven people died and seventy-four suffered injuries. No arrests were made. Almost twenty years later, in February 1993, a van loaded with a bomb went off in the underground garage of the World Trade Center in New York City. Six people died and hundreds suffered injuries. The police convicted six people for this crime. Additionally, on April 15, 2013, two pressure cooker bombs set up at the finish line of the Boston Marathon exploded. Three people died and hundreds suffered injuries. One of the bombers died in a shootout with the police and the other received a death sentence.

Along with bombing, though, fire is also an efficient way to commit a mass murder. The following narrative illustrates just how efficient a fire can be.

✿ ✿ ✿

Julio Gonzalez was born in Holguin, Cuba, in 1954. In his early twenties, he deserted from the Cuban Army. The Cuban authorities eventually caught up with him and sent him to prison for three years. In 1980, Gonzalez faked a criminal record as a drug dealer so that he could join the Mariel boatlift to the United States. After arriving in Florida, he traveled to Arkansas and Wisconsin before finally settling in New York City. There Gonzalez met Lydia Feliciano and they began a six-year on-again, off-again relationship.

By March 25, 1990, Gonzalez, then thirty-six, had lost his job at a lamp factory several weeks before, and he wanted his girlfriend back. They had broken up six weeks earlier. Gonzalez also wanted Feliciano to quit her job in the coat check room at the Happy Land Social Club. The club, which operated illegally, occupied a condemned building in the East Tremont neighborhood of the Bronx. The building had been condemned because it lacked sufficient exits, fire alarms, and a fire escape. Gonzalez went there at about 3:00 a.m. on March 25 and argued with Feliciano about quitting her job. She didn't want to quit her job and told him that their relationship was over and that she didn't want anything to do with him. A bouncer for the club then threw Gonzalez out. Gonzalez swore at them and yelled that he would shut the club down.

Gonzalez ran to a nearby Amoco gas station and purchased one dollar's worth of gasoline, which he pumped into a plastic container. Returning to the club at around 3:30 a.m., Gonzalez splashed the gasoline around the entrance to the enclosed front stairway, the club's only exit, and set it on fire. He then went home and fell asleep.

The fire spread quickly through the old, rickety building, and the patrons naturally panicked when they found that a raging fire blocked the only exit. The crowd of people cried and screamed in terror as they trampled each other trying to escape the flames that had raced up the stairs and into the social club. Some of the patrons attempted to break through a wall to escape, but in the end eighty-seven people perished in the blaze, most from trampling and smoke inhalation; only six people escaped with just injuries.

"There was no way out; they never had a chance," said Thomas Doyle, executive director of the New York City Emergency Medical Service.[19]

After putting out the fire, the authorities stacked body after body in a makeshift morgue in the building next door, waiting for identification by relatives, who were gathered at a nearby school. The police would take Polaroid photographs of the victims for the relatives to identify.

Feliciano, one of the six survivors, told the detectives about her argument that morning with Gonzalez. The police arrested Gonzalez the next day and he admitted to setting the fire. "I got angry, the devil got to me, and I set the fire," he told the detectives. Gonzalez would die in prison in 2016 at the age of sixty-one. He had been serving eighty-seven sentences of twenty-five years to life in Dannemora Prison.[20]

✿ ✿ ✿

There have been a number of horror stories about the use of poison gas in warfare during the last part of the twentieth century and even into the twenty-first. On March 16, 1988, for example, during the Iraq-Iran War, the Iraqi city of Halabja had fallen to Iranian forces. Iraq then attacked the city with both mustard and nerve gas. Reportedly, as many as 5,000 people died in this attack.

More recently, the civil war in Syria has seen a number of attacks by poison gas. In 2013, the city of Aleppo suffered an attack by nerve gas. In August of 2016, the United Nations blamed the Syrian military for the use of chlorine bombs on the towns of Talmenes and Sarmen. Other attacks with poisonous gas have also occurred during this conflict.

While the use of poisonous gas, as seen above, has occurred mostly during wartime, civilian mass murderers have also been known to use this weapon. As the following narrative shows, this can lead to deadly results.

✿ ✿ ✿

At around 8:00 a.m. on March 20, 1995, during the peak of the morning rush hour, several individuals set down five containers of the deadly nerve gas sarin at different locations in the Tokyo subway system. The sarin had been frozen to make transporting it safe, and the individuals planting the sarin used sharp-pointed umbrellas to puncture the containers. At that time of the morning, of course, hundreds of thousands of people going to work crowded the subways. Suddenly, as the sarin began melting, the containers started spewing the deadly gas, and commuters, overcome by the fumes, fell to the floor dead or thrashing in agony. This naturally started a panic as the crowds of people attempted to escape the deadly toxin, screaming in terror and shoving against the people in front of them as everyone tried to flee the subway system at once. Even though the threat quickly became known to the authorities, it took some time to completely evacuate the subway system and to safely neutralize the gas. Twelve people would die in the attack and more than 5,500 would need medical attention; seventy-five of them were in critical condition.

It didn't take the authorities long to discover who had been behind the attack. The police raided the headquarters of the Aum Shinrikyo (Supreme Truth) cult, located in a small village about seventy miles southwest of Tokyo. There, the authorities found a maze of hidden rooms and secret passages. They also found the laboratory where the sarin had been manufactured. Along with this, the police uncovered $7.9 million in cash and twenty-two pounds of gold (the cult was later found to have more than a billion dollars in assets). In the various hidden rooms and tunnels the authorities found numerous high-ranking members of the cult hiding, including the scientist who had produced the sarin and the cult's leader, Shoko Asahara, who claimed to be the reincarnation of Jesus Christ.

Why would Aum Shinrikyo want to do this? Why would they target innocent citizens? What would they gain from this act?

The leader of the cult, who claimed he could levitate, fly, and walk through walls, would show potential recruits to the cult doctored videos of him performing these wonders. He assured the recruits that if they became faithful members of his group they would also be able to perform these amazing feats. Interestingly, not just misfits and disaffected youth joined the cult. It also began to attract highly educated individuals, including doctors, lawyers, military leaders, and scientists from various professions, including the chemist who manufactured the sarin.

Although advertised as a religion of peace and love, the group was anything but that. Any opposition to the cult met with swift retribution. An attorney who represented a group of parents who had children in the cult, called Parents of Aum Children, was found murdered, as were his wife and small child, by members of the cult. The cult also had a special "action squad," run by a former underworld criminal who had joined the cult. This group would go out and snatch back any members of the cult who had tried to leave.

After being soundly rejected by voters when some of its members ran for public office, Aum Shinrikyo quickly became a doomsday cult. Shoko Asahara began preaching that the end of the world was quickly approaching. Only members of Aum Shinrikyo would survive the apocalypse to rebuild the world. The subway sarin attack, the cult's leader believed, would hasten his prophesied end of the world.

"The attack was launched so that the guru's prophecy could come true," said Dr. Ikuo Hayashi, a cardiac specialist who had planted one of the containers of poison gas in the subway system.[21]

After lengthy trials, more than one hundred cult members received various prison sentences for their part in cult crimes, and more than a dozen members received the death sentence. In July 2018, Japan executed thirteen members of Aum Shinrikyo, including its leader.

Of course, many readers will think that this is just a weird cult in a country halfway around the world. They were no threat to the United States. This is far from the truth. Aum Shinrikyo had plans to commit similar crimes with sarin gas in the United States.

"The guru has ordered us to release sarin in several places in America," said Dr. Hayashi.[22]

Along with this, the Aum Shinrikyo cult used trucks to spray deadly botulinum and anthrax germs on areas near US military bases. The germs, fortunately, proved too weak to cause illness, sparing the United States a catastrophe that might have killed hundreds of innocent Americans.

* * *

The United States, incidentally, has had its own cult-motivated public poisoning. In 1981, Bhagwan Shree Rajneesh, a spiritual guru from

India, purchased a 65,000-acre ranch in Antelope, Oregon. Rajneesh intended this to be the headquarters for his cult called Osho. This group, at its height, had more than 200,000 members and dozens of learning centers around the world. As hundreds of people flocked to the cult, the population of the cult headquarters quickly became so large that its inhabitants were able to vote themselves into all of the public offices in Antelope. However, Rajneesh had higher aspirations and wanted to control the entirety of Wasco County.

This idea, however, ran into problems. While the cult had enough votes to control the town of Antelope, they didn't have nearly enough votes to take over the county. To overcome this disadvantage, the group purchased a small sample of salmonella germs and then began growing their own stock in a laboratory at the ranch. The plan was to put the salmonella into the county's water supply and thereby incapacitate enough voters on Election Day to win the county offices they wanted. As a test run, they contaminated the salad bars and coffee creamers in ten restaurants. The plan worked and the germs sickened 751 people, but the result turned out badly for the cult.

"They apparently didn't expect it to be such a huge success," says Leslie L. Zaitz, a reporter for *The Oregonian*. "The attention attracted by the salad bar escapade brought hordes of health officials and investigators into The Dalles (Wasco County Seat). It dashed the cult's plans to do worse on Election Day."[23]

Finally, there is a weapon of mass murder that can and has been used, but which few readers would think of as a weapon: persuasiveness. How could this be used to commit a mass murder?

∗ ∗ ∗

In 1971, during a stay at a mental hospital in an attempt to cure his homosexuality, Marshall Herff Applewhite met registered nurse Bonnie Lu Nettles, who dabbled in astrology and spirit channeling. They had an immediate, though reportedly nonsexual, attraction, and quickly began a relationship that would last until Nettles's death in 1985. The couple began developing a belief system that centered on the two of them being more than just humans. At first, they claimed that they were the two witnesses described in chapter 11 of Revelation. They preached their philosophy anywhere they could reach listeners and soon began to attract followers into a cult that would eventually be called Heaven's

Gate. At first, they told followers that the two of them would be killed by nonbelievers but then brought back to life in a cloud of light three and a half days later.

As ridiculous as this might sound, especially since the group slept in parks and had to beg for food, the cult soon began attracting followers few would expect, including a former military officer, an accountant, college students, a film editor, and even a wealthy real estate developer. Interestingly, as the cult continued to gain members, Applewhite's and Nettles's belief system began to change. It went through a number of alterations until finally they told the cult members that they were actually alien entities who came to Earth in a spaceship and took over Applewhite's and Nettles's bodies. But more importantly, another spaceship was en route to pick them up along with the members of the cult.

Like most cults, life inside the group became increasingly strict and regulated. Everyone had to obey the leaders without question and one of the biggest sins was "thinking for yourself." No one was ever allowed to be alone, but always had to have a partner nearby to prevent backsliding. Applewhite and Nettles wrote up an inches-thick manual that told the cult members how to perform every task imaginable, even things as mundane as shaving and eating. The cult members would eventually look to their leaders for every decision, no matter how small, and learned never to question them.

The belief system about the leaders being alien entities, however, often ran into failures. Several times Applewhite and Nettles took the cult somewhere, telling the members that they had received a telepathic message that a spaceship would pick them up there, only to be disappointed.

In July 1995, astronomers announced the discovery of comet Hale-Bopp, which would soon become visible in the night sky. A photographer claimed that he had photographed an object tailing the comet, and a number of so-called psychics confirmed that it was a spaceship full of aliens trailing the comet. This misinformation seemed to catch on, and it was repeated, published, and discussed in dozens of places, including on a national radio program.

Applewhite became convinced that this was finally the ship they were waiting for, even though scientists proved that there was nothing following the comet. The cult purchased an expensive telescope to view the spaceship. When they couldn't find anything behind the comet, they returned the telescope, telling the store that it didn't work. The cult members, by this time, had been so programmed and indoctrinated that the only proof they needed was Applewhite's word that there was a spaceship there. They had been conditioned to never question anything he said.

In preparation for the spaceship's arrival, Applewhite preached to his group that the only way to board the spaceship was by ridding themselves of their human bodies. So, on March 23, 1997, the day of comet Hale-Bopp's closest approach to Earth, thirty-nine members of the Heaven's Gate cult took lethal amounts of phenobarbital, washed down with vodka. They then tied plastic bags over their heads and, covered with purple shrouds, lay down on their beds. They were discovered three days later by a cult member who had been away from the group. In the days following the mass death, several more members of the group, who hadn't been with them, killed themselves in the belief that they would also be transported to the spaceship.

Even though the coroner eventually ruled all the deaths to be suicide, a number of people disagreed. "I don't consider it suicide," said cult expert Janja Lalich. "I consider it murder. [Marshall Applewhite] controlled it, he called the shots. These people were pawns in his personal fantasy."[24]

❈ ❈ ❈

As we have seen in this chapter, there is no weapon that mass murderers won't use to accomplish their crimes. In the next chapter, we will see how mass murderers plan and carry out their crimes. This will be extremely important because, as we will see in later chapters, this planning can often give a warning to potential victims.

4

TACTICS OF MASS MURDERERS

Twenty-year-old Arcan Cetin purchased a ticket to the first evening showing of the movie *Snowden* at the Cascade Mall in Burlington, Washington, a town of about 8,000 people sixty-five miles north of Seattle. September 23, 2016, was a Friday night and the mall was crowded. Once inside the theater, Cetin used his cell phone to prop open an exit door and then left the theater. He planned to later access the theater, carrying a weapon, through that door. This idea bore close resemblance to the movie theater mass murder in Aurora, Colorado, in 2012, in which James Eagan Holmes propped open an exit door of a theater with a piece of plastic. However, before Cetin could come back through that door, a moviegoer discovered his cell phone and turned it in to theater personnel.

With his mass murder plan at the movie theater foiled, Cetin walked out of the mall and into the parking lot, where he got into his blue sedan and moved it close to the entrance of Macy's department store. He then retrieved a Ruger 10/22 rifle from the trunk of the car and walked into Macy's. Apparently not having any specific target in mind, Cetin began shooting at the customers randomly. He first shot and killed a teenage girl looking at clothing, then shot and killed three women and a man at a cosmetics counter. Two of the victims at the cosmetics counter were husband and wife. They tried to flee when the shooting started, but the wife fell. Cetin shot them both as the husband was trying to help his wife get up. The entire incident inside Macy's, according to security video, took about a minute.

After killing these five people, Cetin threw the rifle onto the cosmetics counter and raced for the door. He ran out into the parking lot, jumped into his vehicle, and then sped away. Because this crime could have possibly been terror related, the FBI and ATF joined with the local police to help solve it. As it turned out, Macy's security video system captured relatively good pictures of the shooter, and the next day the police arrested Cetin as he walked down a street in Oak Harbor, Washington, where he lived. Oak Harbor is about thirty miles southwest of Burlington. The officers described Cetin as "zombie-like" and docile.[1]

Cetin eventually confessed to the killings. Actually, there was little choice for him about confessing since he had left the weapon with his fingerprints on it at the crime scene and the police had a clear video of him committing the mass shooting. The state charged him with five counts of murder, charges that could carry the death penalty. Unlike many of the mass murderers we've discussed so far, Cetin was no stranger to the criminal justice system. He had been arrested and charged more than a half dozen times before, including a charge of assault for which he had to undergo mental health counseling.

As for a motive for Cetin's acts, the police drew a blank. Although he confessed to the crime, Cetin never gave the police a motive. "I don't know what his motivations were to do this," said Lieutenant Chris Cammock of the Mount Vernon Police Department. Mount Vernon is just south of Burlington. "I don't know what his motivations were to continue [shooting]. I don't know what his motivations were to stop."[2]

Cetin had been born in Turkey but came to the United States as a youngster when his mother married a US citizen. He became a naturalized citizen and eventually graduated from Oak Harbor High School. Some of the people who knew him in high school liked him, while others couldn't stand him. He appeared to have held aggressive feelings toward females and was reported to have made vulgar comments and attempted to grope a number of them in high school.

"He would touch them inappropriately when they didn't want it," said Miranda Schnecker, a classmate of Cetin's.[3]

After high school, Cetin attended college and worked as a bagger at the Base Commissary at the Naval Air Station on Whidbey Island, just north of his home in Oak Harbor. He also reportedly worked as a dishwasher. Although arrested and charged, Cetin never stood trial for his crimes. On April 16, 2017, sheriff's deputies found Cetin dead in his cell. He had hanged himself.

The victims of this mass murder included a sixty-one-year-old Boeing maintenance worker, a sixty-four-year-old probation officer, her ninety-five-year-old mother, and a fifty-two-year-old makeup artist for Macy's. Also included on this list of victims was sixteen-year-old Sarai Lara, a sophomore at Mount Vernon High School. Sadly, Sarai had been a cancer survivor whom her mother described as the perfect child. Sarai's friends loved and respected her.

"She was a strong girl, she told me a lot about her life and I trusted her with everything," a friend told the news media. "She gave me advice and helped me through a lot. She told me about (losing) her hair and everything."[4]

* * *

As is obvious from this narrative, Cetin did little planning and preparation for his mass murder. At first, he was just going to mimic James Eagan Holmes's crime in Aurora, Colorado, in 2012. When that didn't work out, he simply walked into the Macy's department store and began shooting randomly, apparently without a plan or specific targets. Another fact that showed how uncoordinated and unplanned his attack was is that he dropped the murder weapon at the crime scene with his fingerprints all over it. Escaping the scene in his vehicle was futile because he had been arrested a number of times, and it didn't take the police long to trace the fingerprints on the weapon back to him and then track him down.

While a number of mass murders in the United States over the last few decades have been unplanned and simply spontaneous acts of violence like this one, this has not always been the case. As the following narrative will show, some mass murderers can do weeks, months, and even years of research and planning before carrying out their mass slaughter.

* * *

Before beginning his mass murder spree on December 14, 2012, Adam Lanza first killed his mother. Following Lanza's rampage, the police went to his house and found fifty-two-year-old Nancy Lanza still in her pajamas in bed, shot in the head four times. Lanza, just twenty years old, would be described by those who knew him as weird and a recluse. He reportedly suffered from Asperger's syndrome, depression, and obsessive-compulsive disorder. Because of these problems, he apparently couldn't maintain personal relationships, even with those who shared similar interests, such as computer gaming. Following the murder of his mother, Lanza took an XM15-E2S assault rifle his mother owned and 300 rounds of ammunition in ten clips to Sandy Hook Elementary School in Newtown, Connecticut, a town of about 28,000 people, located about seventy-five miles northeast of New York City.

For protection against active shooters, the elementary school had security procedures in place that required all the doors to the school to be locked at 9:30 every morning. This security procedure, however, didn't stop Lanza. He simply shot out the glass panel next to the door to make entry. Once inside the school, wearing a green vest over black clothing, Lanza first encountered the school principal, the school psychologist, and a teacher. The three had left a meeting after hearing the shots that broke out the glass. Upon seeing Lanza with his gun, they reportedly shouted, "Shooter! Stay put!"[5] This likely saved the lives of the other people in the meeting, who hunkered down in the conference room. Lanza shot and killed the principal, forty-seven-year-old Dawn Hochsprung, and the psychologist, fifty-six-year-old Mary Sherlach. The teacher with them, forty-year-old Natalie Hammond, also suffered gunshot wounds but managed to crawl into a room and block the door.

Janitor Rich Thorne next encountered Lanza but managed to escape him and run down the hallways to alert the classes that they had an active shooter. It was also reportedly announced over the school's public address system. Even with this warning, however, Lanza still managed to force his way into a first-grade classroom, where thirty-year-old substitute teacher Lauren Rousseau was trying to hide the first graders in a bathroom. Another woman in the room, twenty-nine-year-old Rachel D'Avino, a behavior therapist for a special needs child, also tried to hide the children. Lanza shot and killed both Lauren and Rachel, along with fifteen first graders. Fourteen of the children would die at the scene and one later at the hospital. One child in the room survived the assault. Crammed into the bathroom with fifteen other children, she played dead and apparently fooled Lanza. She later told her mother, "Mommy, I'm okay, but all my friends are dead."[6]

When it appeared that everyone was dead, Lanza went to another first-grade classroom nearby. The teacher, twenty-seven-year-old Victoria Leigh Soto, had hidden the children in a closet, a bathroom, and under desks. Lanza saw the children under the desks and began shooting them. Jesse Lewis, one of the first graders, shouted for his classmates to run. Many did and would survive; however, Lanza shot and killed Jesse. Soto tried to shield the children with her body and Lanza killed her. He also killed fifty-two-year-old Anne Marie Murphy, a teacher's assistant, whose body would be found shielding a six-year-old student. Lanza's gun then jammed and he had to stop shooting in order to clear it, allowing more students to flee. Eleven students from the classroom would survive.

The mass shooting by Lanza would cease at 9:40 a.m., only five minutes after the rampage began. Police officers, who had arrived just a minute before, would hear just one more shot. This would be Lanza shooting himself in the head with a 10mm Glock semiautomatic handgun. The authorities later found the assault rifle, the Glock, and a 9mm Sig Sauer semiautomatic pistol near Lanza's body.

The final death tally at Sandy Hook Elementary School would be twenty first graders, eight boys and twelve girls, all ages six and seven, and six adults, all women. All but two of the victims, the coroner would find, had been shot multiple times. The later investigation of the mass murder showed that Lanza had fired a total of 156 shots in the five-minute murder spree.

Investigators would later determine that the first 911 call about the shooting came in to the police at 9:35 a.m. The first police officer arrived at the school at 9:39 a.m. However, the entire incident was over in only five minutes, too quickly for the police to do anything to stop it. This is why the final chapters of this book are so important. Schools and other targets of mass murder must have plans to take action against the mass murderers themselves. The police often simply can't be there quickly enough to stop them.

Searching Lanza's body and his home, the police didn't find a suicide note or any explanation for why he would want to do this. The investigation into the mass murder became even more difficult when the police discovered that Lanza had destroyed the hard drive from his computer. Although some early reports about the mass murder suggested that Lanza's love of violent video games had fueled his desire for mass murder, later investigation showed that the games he most often played were *Mario Kart* and an interactive dance game named *Dance Dance Revolution*.

The police were able to discover, however, that Lanza had researched mass murders extensively and had downloaded videos about the Columbine mass murder and two videos about how to commit suicide with a firearm. He had also reportedly drawn up a seven-by-four-foot spreadsheet containing information on nearly 500 mass murders. Lanza became so obsessed by mass murderers that he even named several of his Tumblr accounts after them. All this research by Lanza, the authorities believed, could have taken several years. A GPS device that Lanza owned showed that on the day before the mass murder he had scouted Sandy Hook Elementary School.

In Lanza's home, along with the above items, the police also discovered several samurai swords, newspaper clippings about another mass murder, and a gun safe with three additional weapons owned by Lanza's mother, who was apparently a gun enthusiast. The police found that she had taken Lanza to shooting ranges with her many times and had let him shoot most of the guns she owned. Lanza had even passed a gun safety course offered by the National Rifle Association.

Afterward, many people wondered why Lanza had picked Sandy Hook Elementary School as his target. One likely reason was that he had attended the school for four and a half years, but probably more important, many mass murderers look for soft targets for their crimes, locations where the victims likely will not fight back. An elementary school certainly fits this description.

As for a definite motive for the mass murder, the police simply couldn't uncover any evidence that pointed toward one. A report on the mass murder concluded, "The obvious question that remains is: 'Why did the shooter murder 26 people, including 20 children?' Unfortunately, that question may never be answered conclusively, despite the collection of extensive background information on the shooter through a multitude of interviews and other sources."[7]

Still, all the research Lanza had done on mass murders played a very important part in this crime because this research helped make Lanza's plans successful. From all his research he knew the best target to pick, and he knew that he had to accomplish his task in a short time before the police responded and stopped him. The State Attorney's report on the Sandy Hook incident says, "The evidence clearly shows that the shooter planned his actions, including the taking of his own life, but there is no clear indication why he did so, or why he targeted Sandy Hook Elementary School."[8]

The FBI's final report on the Sandy Hook Elementary mass murder says, "The shooter was fascinated with past shootings and researched them thoroughly."[9]

* * *

In terms of tactics and planning, the two narratives above are polar opposites, one carefully planned and carried out, and the other simply a spur-of-the-moment crime. And of course, in addition to these two types there are many mass murders that fit somewhere in between. For example, the mass murder of the Martinez family, described in chapter 3, had been partly planned in that Uribe had a specific location identified and went to the Martinez house with the intention of robbing and killing specific targets. However, he only brought along a handgun with limited ammunition, and had to grab weapons at the scene to complete the crime. In the incident involving Jiverly Wong in chapter 2, the attack appeared a little better planned. Wong had a specific target in mind, wore a bulletproof vest, brought weapons with sufficient ammunition, and had blocked the rear door in order to keep his victims from escaping. The Stephen Paddock incident in Las Vegas, discussed in chapter 3, showed even more planning and better tactics. Not only did Paddock bring enough weapons and ammunition; he also found the perfect vantage point for the killings that provided him cover so that he couldn't be stopped easily. In addition, he installed hidden cameras to monitor activity outside of his room, and also traveled across the country scouting out possible sites for his mass murder.

In terms of planning, tactics, and execution, there exists a very dangerous mass murderer that Dr. James L. Knoll describes in an article in the *Journal of the American Academy of Psychiatry and the Law* as a "pseudocommando." Dr. Knoll describes this individual as "a type of mass murderer who kills in public during the daytime, plans his offense well in advance, and comes prepared with a powerful arsenal of weapons. He has no escape planned and expects to be killed during the incident."[10] As might be imagined, because of the planning and decision to die at the scene, this type of mass murderer can be extremely dangerous to both the public and the police.

While Arcan Cetin, in the narrative at the beginning of this chapter, did very little planning, the FBI, in *A Study of the Pre-Attack Behavior of Active Shooters in the United States between 2000 and 2013,* says that 77 percent of the mass murderers studied spent at least a week or longer planning their attacks, and that 26 percent spent a month or more.[11] But while all this research about the planning of mass murders is frightening enough, Andre Simons, agent in charge of the FBI's Behavioral Analysis Unit, said, "I'm aware of offenders who do so even more meticulously."[12] What all of this information is saying is that the planning and tactics of mass murderers can run the gamut, but no matter what type of planners and tacticians they are, all mass murderers are dangerous.

When thinking about the planning and tactics of mass murderers, it is a widely held belief that completely psychotic individuals, people operating in their own realm of reality, cannot put together a methodical and detailed assault plan for a mass murder. While this may sound like common sense, it is far from the truth. Many psychotic mass murderers, although totally breaking from reality, still have enough presence of mind to purchase weapons, conduct surveillance, and also realize that they are threatened when the police arrive. In addition, psychotic mass murderers can be extremely dangerous because they often select complete strangers as their victims, and no one knows what or who the deluded mass murderers think the strangers are.

Many mass murderers, like Adam Lanza above, not only scout their targets, but also research previous mass murders extensively and can see through this research what went wrong in incidents where the potential mass murder was stopped before it got started. But they can also see what made some mass murders successful and try to emulate that. Lanza, for example, made sure to scout his crime location beforehand to find the best way to quickly access the building and get immediately into battle mode. He obviously knew from his research of other mass murders that to be successful he had to finish the act before the police arrived, because they would kill him if he tried to continue his rampage. Hence, he had apparently planned to stop and kill himself when he knew the police were near, as did Jiverly Wong in chapter 2. Historically, once the police arrive, the mass murderer is killed, commits suicide, or is taken into custody. Mass murderers, even those who plan exten-sively, seldom escape from the police for long.

Regardless of whether a mass murder is planned, semi-planned, or spontaneous, they are all dangerous. Readers, if they should ever find themselves in such a situation, will need to use the tips I give in later chapters on how to survive a mass murder incident.

Of course, the most common question that people ask about a mass murder is why. What motivates a person to want to go on a mass mur-der spree? In the next chapter we will see that there are numerous reasons and motivations for a mass murder.

5

THE MOTIVATION BEHIND MASS MURDER

The two young men wanted to surpass the death toll of Timothy McVeigh's bombing of the Alfred P. Murrah Federal Building in Oklahoma City in 1995. They wanted to be more famous than any other mass murderer in history. One of them even bragged in a video he made that their mass murder would be the biggest in US memory. To carry out these goals, the two young men planned to attack the staff and students at Columbine High School, hoping to kill hundreds. They meticulously planned the attack for a year, planned it to be more vicious and more deadly than anyone could ever imagine.

But yet, no matter how carefully they planned it, not everything would work out the way they had hoped it would. Still, the attack at Columbine High School by Eric Harris and Dylan Klebold would create a months-long media storm. It would have reporters questioning over and over why these two young men would want to do this. And although not rising to the level Harris and Klebold had hoped for, the attack would still give birth to many thousands of young admirers, and also to numerous copycat mass murders.

In late 1998 and early 1999, in preparation for their attack at Columbine High School, which sits in the southwest Denver metropolitan area, Harris and Klebold had several adult friends purchase them two 9mm semiautomatic pistols, a Hi-Point carbine (basically an assault rifle) with thirteen ten-round magazines, two shotguns that they shortened the barrels on, and a TEC-9 semiautomatic handgun. The TEC-9 came with a fifty-two-round magazine, a thirty-two-round magazine, and a twenty-eight-round magazine. Harris and Klebold weren't old enough to purchase these weapons themselves. The adult friends who purchased the firearms would later be sentenced to prison for providing the guns to Harris and Klebold.

Harris and Klebold, using instructions found online and in the book *The Anarchist's Cookbook*, also built dozens of homemade bombs. These included pipe bombs, propane tanks made into bombs, Molotov cocktails, and others. They planned to use the bombs to kill school staff and students, and to stop the police from entering Columbine High School. The two young men planned to place some of the bombs where they would explode when first responders arrived at the school, killing them and any bystanders. A huge part of their plan, the part that would kill the most people, would be setting off several massive bombs during lunch hour in the school cafeteria, with the goal of killing hundreds of students and then using their guns to pick off the survivors. In addition, they had timed several bombs left in their cars to go off after the police, other emergency responders, and the crowds of people, including worried parents, had shown up at the school. They knew that the news media would also be there by that time, and with such a huge body count, which they had figured would have to be at least in the mid-hundreds, their story would be broadcast worldwide. They would be famous. Everyone would know their names and faces. One of them bragged in a journal that movie directors and producers would fight for the rights to their story.

On Tuesday morning, April 20, 1999, Harris and Klebold planted two duffel bags containing propane tank bombs among the hundreds of backpacks sitting on the floor of the cafeteria. They had set the bombs to explode at 11:17 a.m., when the cafeteria would be filled with students. Although the duffel bags were visible on security video, no one monitoring the cameras saw them as dangerous. The two young men also placed bombs in the kitchen. Harris and Klebold then left school and dropped off backpacks filled with explosives in two locations several miles from the school. They meant these to be a diversionary tactic that would draw emergency responders away from Columbine High School before the attack began. They needed this free time to carry out their slaughter. However, only a few of the bombs in the backpacks detonated, causing only a small fire that the fire department quickly extinguished.

The two young would-be mass murderers arrived back at Columbine High School at 11:10 a.m. in separate cars that they had rigged with explosives; they parked in separate parking lots. Harris encountered a friend in the parking lot and warned him not to go to school that day. "Get out of here. Go home," he told the friend.[1] The friend took the warning seriously and left the school grounds.

There was a group of students at Columbine High School called the "Trench Coat Mafia" who all wore long trench coats to school. Although not a part of this group, Harris and Klebold wore long trench coats that day, hiding their weapons beneath. The two would-be mass murderers, after parking their cars, climbed to the top of a hill that would give them a good view of the exit doors to the school's cafeteria. Their plan was to watch the explosion in the cafeteria and then shoot any survivors who tried to escape afterward.

Students Rachel Scott and Richard Castaldo sat on the grass nearby having lunch. The bombs in the cafeteria failed to explode, fortunately for the 488 students eating there, and Klebold, in frustration, threw a pipe bomb in the direction of a parking lot. It only partially exploded; everyone thought it was simply a senior prank.

Upon finding that their grand plan to bomb the cafeteria had failed, Harris and Klebold, infuriated, both pulled out weapons from under their trench coats and began firing at Rachel and Richard. Rachel died after being shot with the carbine Harris carried. Richard would be shot eight times, but he survived, though he was paralyzed. The two shooters then began firing at three students standing at the bottom of the hill. One of them would die. Harris and Klebold next began firing at five other students nearby, wounding two of them. The other students escaped unharmed.

Descending the hill and approaching the cafeteria, Klebold shot one of the already dead students with a shotgun, and then shot one of the wounded students in the face with the shotgun. Klebold carefully opened the door to the cafeteria, likely to check on what had happened to the bombs in the duffel bags, but didn't shoot anyone. Harris, meanwhile, had remained on top of the hill shooting at other students. Klebold rejoined Harris and they both continued shooting, this time at students on a nearby soccer field, but missed hitting anyone. A witness heard them shouting, "This is what we always wanted to do! This is awesome!"[2]

The two gunmen then headed for the cafeteria, where they injured a teacher and a student inside when they shot out the glass in the door. The teacher had just been opening the door to see what was happening outside. Even though injured, she ran down to the library and called 911. Harris and Klebold stepped into the cafeteria.

A custodian at the school, seeing what was going on, radioed sheriff's deputy Neil Gardner, the school's resource officer, and told him that they needed help. Another radio caller warned, "Neil, there's a shooter in the school!"[3] Harris opened and stood at the door to the cafeteria and fired ten shots from his carbine at Gardner when he arrived. Gardner fired back with his service pistol and Harris ducked back inside. Neither one hit the mark. Harris would pop out of the cafeteria a few moments later and fire additional shots at Gardner; again he missed.

Two more police officers joined Gardner at the shooting scene; they exchanged shots with Harris, but once more no one was hurt. Harris and Klebold then left the cafeteria and headed for the school's north hallway, tossing pipe bombs and shooting at anyone they spotted.

Walking the hallways of the school, Harris and Klebold shot another teacher. They then headed for the library, where more than fifty students, two teachers, and two librarians had retreated. The two shooters exploded a bomb in the hallway outside the library, and then entered the library, ordering everyone to get up.

Klebold first shot and killed disabled student Kyle Velasquez, and then both mass murderers reloaded their weapons. They next tried to identify the jocks in the room by the white hats worn by students who participated in sports, but most of the students had already discarded them. Interestingly, however, even though both Harris and Klebold had complained before the attack of being bullied, later investigation would show that neither had suffered any significant long-term bullying or harassment at Columbine, and that in their selection of victims they didn't pick out any specific people, as would have been expected had they been bullied. Investigators afterward believed that their statements were simply meant to mask their real motive: to become famous.

At that moment, the two shooters noticed that the police had shown up in force. They fired out the windows at the police, and the police returned fire, but once more no one suffered any injuries. Klebold then shouted for everyone with a white hat to stand up. No one did, and Klebold fired a shotgun at the students nearby, injuring three of them. Harris also began firing, killing one student and injuring another. He then walked over and knelt beside a female student hiding under a desk. He reportedly said, "Peek-a-boo," and then shot the student in the head with a shotgun, killing her.[4] Witnesses would later say that the two gunmen laughed and joked as they killed people.

In his killing of the girl hiding under the desk, however, Harris had been holding the shotgun with one hand, and the recoil sent the shotgun barrel smashing into his face, breaking his nose. Bleeding heavily and seeming a bit disoriented, Harris taunted another student by asking her if she wanted to die. She said no, and for some reason he spared her.

Klebold next shot at a student trying to administer first aid to a wounded student, injuring the would-be rescuer. He then noticed a black student hiding under a desk. Making a number of racially derogatory remarks, he shot and killed the student and then another.

The two shooters then walked around the library indiscriminately shooting students, killing several more and injuring others. After they had shot and killed ten people and wounded twelve others in the library, Harris and Klebold seemed to tire of the massacre. They left the library and returned to the cafeteria, firing shots and throwing handmade bombs along the way. In the cafeteria, one of them fired a shot at the duffel bags containing the propane tank bombs they had planted there, but it had no effect. Klebold then threw a Molotov cocktail at them and started a fire. The cafeteria sprinkler system, however, quickly extinguished the flames.

Following this, the two young mass murderers wandered the hallways and fired their weapons randomly. They would stop and taunt students they could see trying to hide, but they didn't fire at them. They eventually returned to the library, now empty of survivors except for two students too injured to be moved, with the intention of watching the cars they had rigged with explosives blow up and kill those outside. These bombs also failed to go off, and the two frustrated gunmen exchanged more gunfire with the police. Once again, no one suffered any injury.

With the car bombs not exploding and the police massing outside, Harris and Klebold decided that their massacre was over. They sat down in the library, and Harris stuck a shotgun in his mouth, while Klebold placed the TEC-9 up against his head. They both then fired their weapons, killing themselves.

The event at Columbine High School had lasted almost an hour. The two gunmen fired a total of 188 rounds. Fifteen individuals at the school (including Harris and Klebold) would die at the shooters' hands, and twenty-four suffered injuries. Interestingly, throughout the massacre at Columbine, the police didn't enter the school, even though Harris and Klebold were killing people inside. As was the standard police procedure then, they simply set up a perimeter around the school to contain the incident and waited for the SWAT team to arrive. This would lead to some brutal criticism and a change in how the police nationally handled such incidents, which I will discuss in a later chapter.

The police handling of the Columbine mass murder also resulted in lawsuits against the sheriff's office. Most of these were dismissed because of government immunity to such lawsuits, but the sheriff's department settled out of court for $1.5 million in the death of teacher Dave Sanders. The sheriff's department allegedly wouldn't allow paramedics to go inside and attempt to save the teacher, even though they reportedly knew that Harris and Klebold were already dead. In addition, the families of thirty victims of the Columbine High School mass murder sued the families of Harris and Klebold and two of the people who had supplied guns and ammunition to the two shooters. The victims' families received a settlement of about $2.5 million, paid mostly by the homeowners' policies of those sued.

* * *

Naturally, after an incident of this magnitude, one of the major questions asked was "Why?" What could have driven these two young men to want to commit such a heinous act? What had happened to them that could drive them to such extreme behavior? Initially, and with very little evidence, a number of theories from police officials, forensic experts, psychologists, and others came to be printed or broadcast about the motivations of Harris and Klebold.

Within days of the Columbine High School mass murder, claims that Harris and Klebold had been relentlessly bullied by the school jocks and other popular students, that they were part of a Goth subculture at school, that they had been influenced by violent video games, that they were part of the Trench Coat Mafia at Columbine, and that they were social outcasts with no friends and no spot in the teenage hierarchy of the high school circulated widely throughout the news media. The two mass murderers were made to look like victims themselves, who only struck back because they had been oppressed and tortured to the point where they felt they had no other recourse. To most people this at least made some sense out of the brutality of the Columbine mass murder. However, after careful investigation, none of these reasons proved to be 100 percent true.

There were, for example, reports of Harris and Klebold being bullied at Columbine High School. In one of the videos Klebold made, he remarked, "You've been giving us shit for years."[5] An incident several students talked about after the mass murder involved members of the football team and others confronting Harris and Klebold and spraying them with ketchup and mustard. This is likely why the two young gunmen tried to identify the boys with the white hats in the library. The group also accused Harris and Klebold of being homosexuals. But interestingly, other students would say that Harris was the perpetrator of bullying much more often than he was a victim.

Bullying, regardless of whether Harris and Klebold actually were victims of it, is still one of the main motivators of many other school mass murders. Bullying students until they have finally had enough and want to strike back has been a motivation for mass murder numerous times. The US Secret Service in 2000 released a research report of thirty seven school shootings. They found that being bullied played a large role in more than two-thirds of them.[6] But of course readers have to remember that even if bullying is a cause for mass murder, there are many other variables affecting the desire to murder people. Otherwise, how do we explain the millions of students who are bullied but never resort to mass murder?

While Harris and Klebold's motivations, as we will see, had less to do with the school itself and more to do with their personalities, there have been mass murders at schools that took place because of the school itself, or rather the student environment there. Individuals who find themselves excluded from activities at school, who can't attract the people they would like to date, and who are bullied can sometimes strike back in a murderous way. In these cases, which mostly involve males,

the individuals feel that their masculine identity has been severely damaged by their treatment at school.

"Analysis suggests that boys' social status in middle and high school
is determined in a great part by peers' acceptance of them as 'appropri-
ately masculine,'" says an article in *Science Daily*.[7]

The only way to regain their full masculine identity, these individuals
often feel, is by doing something tremendously masculine. And what
could be more masculine than shooting up the school?

"These kids often feel very powerless," says psychologist Peter Langman. "The only way they can feel like they're somebody, that they're a
man, is to get a gun and kill people."[8]

Many mass murderers, in particular school mass murderers, also feel
powerless and left out when it comes to sexual activity. They see others
who seem to have no problems with the opposite sex, and they grow to
hate them because they don't have that success. An article in *Psychology Today* noted, "It turns out that killing people is an effective way to
elicit the attention of many women: virtually every serial killer, including Ted Bundy, Charles Manson, and David Berkowitz, have received
love letters from large numbers of female fans."[9]

Many people afterward theorized that being excluded from social
events in high school was one of the driving motives behind Harris and
Klebold's mass murder. Like bullying, there is some evidence for this,
but there is also evidence that counters it. In one of Harris's journals he
wrote, "I hate you people for leaving me out of so many fun things. And
no don't . . . say, 'Well that's your fault,' because it isn't, you people had
my phone number, and I asked and all, but no. No no no don't let the
weird-looking Eric KID come along."[10] However, as an argument
against this reason, both Harris and Klebold were involved in theater
productions and had a circle of friends at the high school. They were
also very good students academically. So, the final verdict was that,
rather than being victims striking back, both young men instead took
part in the Columbine mass murder to satisfy very selfish reasons.

"Most of the initial reporting was wrong," wrote Dave Cullen, author
of *Columbine*. "We were so anxious to answer that burning question for
you that we jumped to conclusions on tiny fragments of evidence in the
first days, even hours."[11]

Eric Harris, forensic scientists revealed after studying the writings
and videotapes he left behind, did not suffer from feelings of oppres-

sion and inferiority, but rather the opposite. He instead felt that he was a sort of superman who stood towering over the sheep that made up the majority of society. He felt disgusted when he saw the commonness of the people around him. To him they were nothing but insects scurrying around. As a consequence of this thinking, he didn't see any need to feel anything for them. He could step on them like he would ants. Harris suffered from what I discussed in a previous chapter: pathological narcissism. And so, to realize and prove his superiority, Harris knew that he had to do something truly huge that would firmly establish him as a hero and a step above all others. While some people might think this would mean becoming a star athlete, perhaps a crime-busting police officer, or maybe a scientist who makes a discovery vital to the survival of mankind, these ideas didn't fit into Harris's personality.

In Harris's mind and in his writings, he worshipped people like Timothy McVeigh, and he wanted to prove his superiority by doing something similar, but on a grander scale. Harris laughed at and mocked school shooters who only killed a dozen or so people. He wanted to do something much more deadly and dramatic. On one of the videos he made, Harris bragged about inflicting "the most deaths in US history."[12]

Forensic scientists who studied Harris also determined that he was a psychopath. Psychopaths, by definition, don't suffer from delusions or breaks from reality. They are most often very clear-headed and know exactly what they are doing, which is usually manipulating people for their own advantage. But while acting polite and helpful when manipulating people, they often actually feel contempt and hatred for these same people and many times the world at large. In Harris's journal the first line reads, "I fucking hate the world."[13]

Psychopaths also typically have no conscience, no empathy for others, and are pathologically narcissistic. They can hurt or even kill people with absolutely no regard for them, and can even enjoy doing it, as we saw in the above narrative. At the Columbine High School mass murder, Harris would shoot people, laugh at them or mock them as they lay injured, and then shoot them again and kill them. However, even though vicious and without conscience, one of the major traits of psychopaths is their ability to con others into believing that they are actually very nice people. To do this they can lie very convincingly, and Harris said in his journal that he lied constantly to fool people into seeing him differently than he really was. Harris was very successful at this because, before the mass murder, he was seen by many people, including his teachers, as a nice, polite young man.

As further evidence of his real personality, some months before the Columbine High School incident, Harris and Klebold had been caught breaking into a van and stealing computer equipment. The two weren't prosecuted because they took part in a diversion program that involved community service. Harris managed to convince the leaders of the diversion program that he was truly repentant, so repentant that the leadership of the diversion program released him and Klebold from the program several months early. Harris even wrote a letter to the owner of the van telling him how much he regretted his act and how sorry he was. In his journal though, Harris wrote of how stupid the owner of the van had been for leaving his valuable items in plain sight inside the van. He also wrote that he couldn't believe he had been arrested for taking advantage of the victim's ignorance and stupidity. Rather than feeling sympathy for the victim and regret for his act, as he wrote in the letter, he felt contempt. And, as we saw in the incident above, he relished his role as a mass murderer and loved being in the position of deciding who lived and who died. Harris liked hurting people because it gave him a sense of power over them.

Klebold, on the other hand, wasn't a psychopath or a narcissist, but rather a young man who felt that his life was meaningless and a failure. According to forensic scientists who also studied the writings and videos he left behind, Klebold suffered from depression and thought often about suicide, even though he came from a loving family who supported him emotionally. And yet, even though he felt his problems were his own fault, Klebold still harbored an intense anger. He had occasionally allowed this anger to take over and would fly into a rage at other students and teachers. Adding to his depression, Klebold in his journals would talk about his failure with females, and his consequent lack of sex. He would call it an "infinite sadness."[14] As discussed earlier, this problem can have devastating effects on young men who see other young men seemingly having great success with females and consequently, they believe, lots of sex.

"Indeed, sexual frustration is a theme running through the writings of many male mass shooters," says Adam Lankford, a criminal justice professor and author of a book on mass shooters. "Many shooters leave manifestos explicitly detailing their hatred of women and men who seemed to navigate relationships with women with ease." [15]

In his journals Klebold also talked a lot about wanting to commit suicide, how that would finally take away the pain. In his final video-tape, he said, "Just know I'm going to a better place. I didn't like life too much." [16]

The murder spree at Columbine High School was just what Klebold needed because it would end in his suicide. But much more important-ly, he could kill himself in a way that wouldn't look cowardly and weak. If he killed himself without some act like the Columbine High School mass murder, he feared people would see him as a weak, sick person. But to die in a dramatic way at the end of a famous act like what he and Harris had envisioned would make him a hero to many. He wouldn't look weak. He would look strong. The fact that he and Harris fell together in their plans became a recipe for an hour of brutality and savagery. Harris and Klebold were opposites in personality, but still their personalities fit together well when it came to how to solve their problems.

"Klebold was hurting inside while Harris wanted to hurt people," says FBI agent Dr. Dwayne Fuselier, who studied the Columbine mass murder. [17] He also says, "Eric went to the school to kill people and didn't care if he died, while Dylan wanted to die and didn't care if others died as well." [18]

However, because of Klebold's enthusiastic participation in the Columbine mass murder, some people have expressed doubt that Klebold just wanted to die. Instead, they asked if his personality might have been similar to Harris's. No—many people who have studied Columbine believe Klebold participated so enthusiastically because he knew that after doing what he did there would be no turning back. Suicide would be a necessity.

Another reason or motivation for mass murder can be revenge. There was speculation that part of the reason for the attack at Columbine High School was revenge for Harris and Klebold's arrest after breaking into the van and stealing computer equipment. Klebold reportedly wrote to Harris during their planning for the Columbine High School mass murder about how much fun they would have getting revenge on the police by killing them, and that his wrath over the arrest would be earth-shaking. Mass murderers, researchers have found, often feel that they have been wronged by society, the government, some group, or an individual. Consequently, they want revenge. However, with most revenge mass murders, the wrongs the perpetrators feel they have suffered are actually just imagined or involve blaming others for problems brought on by themselves. Harris and Klebold, for example, apparently felt that the police had wronged them by their arrest, even though they had been caught committing a crime. However, as we will see in the following narrative, occasionally mass murderers are seeking revenge for a genuine wrong.

※ ※ ※

A yellow Ryder rental truck sat parked in front of the Alfred P. Murrah Federal Building in Oklahoma City at 9:00 a.m. on April 19, 1995. The truck didn't raise any suspicion. After all, this was America's heartland. Bad things didn't happen there. They happened in New York City or Los Angeles or Miami. Not there.

A man using a South Dakota driver's license, which would later be found to be phony, and who had identified himself as Robert Kling, had rented the truck two days earlier at Elliot's Body Shop in Junction City, Kansas. What no one knew at 9:00 a.m. that day was that the truck contained 4,800 pounds of the explosive compound ammonium nitrate/fuel oil (ANFO).

Farmers regularly use ammonium nitrate as a fertilizer, but it can also find use as a very powerful bomb if someone with explosives knowledge can pair it with a powerful detonation device, powerful enough to cause the ammonium nitrate to decompose and explode. Ammonium nitrate, however, while an excellent fertilizer, really doesn't make a very efficient bomb by itself because it has a tendency to absorb moisture, which consequently makes it very difficult to detonate. Therefore, someone wanting to make a bomb with it must add a very precise amount of fuel oil to the ammonium nitrate, which then stops the moisture absorption and turns it into an ANFO bomb, which is easier to ignite but still requires a fairly powerful detonation device.

Unfortunately for the people inside the federal building in Oklahoma City, the 4,800 pounds of ANFO in the Ryder rental truck had been mixed perfectly. Also, it had been fitted with a very powerful detonation device.

At 9:02 a.m., the truck bomb exploded with an incredible release of energy, so powerful that it destroyed most of the front of the Murrah Building and caused many of the interior floors to crash down onto each other. And yet, in spite of the force of the bomb, while many people died, many others inside survived the initial blast. Knocked down or slammed against the walls by the explosion, these survivors immediately faced a new threat: that the remaining parts of the building, severely damaged by the blast, could collapse on them at any second. They knew they had to get out of the building quickly.

Michael R. Norfleet, a Marine Corps recruiter in the building, survived the initial blast and tried to escape down a stairwell packed with large chunks of the building. "All I remember is following the blood trail from somebody before me," he said. "That was like the yarn leading me out of there." Norfleet, a decorated Persian Gulf veteran, lost an eye in the incident but survived. [19]

Florence Rogers had been in a meeting in the building at 9:02 a.m. "I had leaned back in my chair to kind of relax while one of them started talking when, literally, the whole building started to blow up. All of the girls who were in the office with me had totally disappeared." Florence would be the only one in the meeting to survive. [20]

When the final body count had been completed, 168 people died in the explosion, including three pregnant women whose yet-to-be-born babies also died. But what horrified America most were the children. Nineteen children died that day, fifteen of whom were in the America's Kids Day Care Center that had been on the second floor. They had been crushed when the floors above crashed down on them. The other four child victims just happened to be in the building that day.

"They started bringing our babies out in those sheets, and they laid them by my feet," said Helena Garrett, whose sixteen-month-old son lay under the sheets. "They started making a line of them." [21]

While most people recoiled in horror at the thought of these dead children, speculation later was that their presence in the building had been one of the reasons the location had been picked as a target. But why, people asked, would someone want to blow up a building that he or she knew contained young children? The answer was that the person who did this was seeking revenge for the killing of other young children.

As often happens in police work, a bit of luck helped the authorities catch the Oklahoma City bomber. About an hour and fifteen minutes after the mass murder, State Trooper Charlie Hanger stopped a vehicle on Interstate 35 near Perry, Oklahoma. The vehicle didn't have a license plate on it. The state trooper, when talking to the driver, noticed a bulge under twenty-six-year-old Timothy McVeigh's jacket. McVeigh, when questioned about the bulge, admitted to the trooper that he had a 9mm Glock semiautomatic pistol in a shoulder holster. Since McVeigh couldn't produce a license for the gun, the trooper arrested him. The trooper also discovered upon searching McVeigh that he carried a set of earplugs. These earplugs would later be found to contain residue from the detonation cord that had been used to set off the ANFO bomb, as would McVeigh's jeans and T-shirt. The T-shirt, incidentally, had a quote on it from Thomas Jefferson: "The tree of liberty must be refreshed from time to time with the blood of patriots and tyrants."[22]

Federal authorities quickly realized that they had their bomber. They took custody of him and flew McVeigh in a military helicopter to Tinker Air Force Base in Oklahoma City, where they arraigned him for the mass murder.

Following the arrest, the investigation into the bombing began in earnest. One of the main questions to be answered was what was McVeigh's motivation for killing all of these people.

The police were able to identify and trace the Ryder rental truck used in the mass murder by an identification number stamped on its axle. "I saw this humongous object coming straight at us, spinning like a boomerang," said Richard Nichols.[23] The axle of the truck, weighing 250 pounds, crashed into Nichols's car, and he and his family barely escaped death. Using the identification number on the axle, the police went to Elliot's Body Shop, and the personnel there identified Timothy McVeigh as the man who had rented the truck.

Investigating McVeigh's background, the authorities found that he had been a soldier who served honorably during the Persian Gulf War. After applying unsuccessfully for the Green Berets, McVeigh left the army and began wandering around the country. He soon became attracted to right-wing causes, but also began displaying symptoms of paranoia. He believed and told people that the army had secretly inserted a microchip in his buttocks to track him. He also became enamored with the book *The Turner Diaries*. This novel, published in 1978 and authored by William Pierce, the head of a neo-Nazi group, told the story of a group of people who started a revolution against the United

States. In the book, this group bombed the FBI headquarters in Washington, DC, using a truck loaded with an ANFO bomb. McVeigh reportedly read the book over and over, and recommended it often to his friends.

Because of his attraction to right-wing causes, McVeigh became very interested in the government siege of the Branch Davidian compound in Waco, Texas. McVeigh traveled to Waco during the fifty-one-day siege and sold right-wing literature to the crowds of people who had assembled there. When the federal government assaulted the compound on April 19, 1993, the result would be more than eighty deaths, including two dozen children. McVeigh became incensed at this needless bloodshed and began planning his revenge for the attack.

McVeigh soon recruited a former army buddy, Terry Nichols, who also felt attracted to right-wing causes, to help him with his revenge. The two needed money if they were going to carry out their plot, so they robbed an Arkansas gun dealer of $60,000 to pay for the parts of the bomb they planned to use. Together, the two men purchased nearly 5,000 pounds of ammonium nitrate from a co-op in Kansas and also burglarized a quarry for more explosives. McVeigh then did an exhaustive search and finally located someone who would sell him enough detonation cord to set off the ANFO bomb. After gathering all the ingredients, McVeigh and Nichols built the ANFO bomb in Geary State Park in Kansas the day before the actual bombing.

Why did McVeigh pick the target in Oklahoma City for his mass murder? One of the reasons was that the security was light and he found he could park the truck right in front of the building. But more importantly, for some reason McVeigh believed that the agents who carried out the attack against the Branch Davidian compound in Waco had come from Oklahoma City and that their offices would be in this building. Along with this, many people speculated that since McVeigh had cased the location carefully, he also picked this building because it contained a childcare center. These would be innocent victims just like the child victims in Waco.

McVeigh would eventually be sentenced to death by lethal injection for his crime. Officials executed him at the federal prison in Terre Haute, Indiana, on June 11, 2001. A court also sentenced Nichols to life in prison. Several other people involved in the planning of the mass murder would likewise receive prison sentences.

✾ ✾ ✾

In the narrative above, Timothy McVeigh committed mass murder because he wanted revenge. But unlike many mass murderers, whose revenge is for imaginary wrongs, McVeigh had several real-life incidents he wanted to avenge—not that this excuses his overreaction in any way. Still, the event in Waco, in which the people in the Branch Davidian compound, including children, died, really didn't have to happen. It only happened the way it did because of a gigantic government screwup.

Federal law enforcement officials had been planning the assault on the Branch Davidian compound for weeks and had brought in agents and equipment from across the country. One of the key elements of the government's plan, however, was that the assault would be unexpected by the Branch Davidians, so consequently the people inside the compound wouldn't have time to prepare. However, on the morning of the planned assault, the agents in charge of the operation learned that their secrecy had been compromised and that the Branch Davidians knew they were coming.

Common sense would seem to demand that the assault should be called off since the key factor in making it successful had been eliminated. However, there had been so much time, energy, and money spent in preparation for the assault that to call it off would mean that everything that had been done in preparation, all the weeks of planning, of coordinating, of acquiring agents and equipment, had been a waste of time. Consequently, the assault plan, rather than being canceled, became like a boulder rushing downhill. It had so much momentum that nothing could stop it. Rather than calling off the raid, the agents in charge went ahead and launched the assault anyway, and it ended in disaster.

But the incident at Waco wasn't the only thing McVeigh wanted to avenge. He also held a grudge against the government for its actions at Ruby Ridge, Idaho, the year before Waco. In this case, the FBI had been trying to arrest Randy Weaver, an ex–Green Beret and possible member of the Aryan Nations, on a firearms charge. Weaver lived in a cabin in a very remote area of Idaho. Federal agents conducting surveillance of the cabin got into a confrontation with Weaver's fourteen-year-old son Sammy and a family friend, and shots were exchanged after one of the agents killed a dog belonging to the Weavers. The agents shot

Sammy in the back as he ran away, killing him, and the family friend shot and killed one of the agents.

Weaver and his family collected Sammy's body and then barricaded themselves in their cabin. Apparently because of the dead agent, the FBI issued a "shoot to kill" order for any male seen carrying a weapon on the Weaver property. This order was not only against FBI policy but was also a violation of the law. Some of the agents at the scene saw the order as illegal and refused to follow it.

"My reaction was 'you've got to be kidding,'" said FBI agent Donald Kusulas when questioned about the incident by a Senate panel. "That's crazy; that's ridiculous," said FBI agent Peter King to the same panel when asked about the "shoot to kill" order. [24]

However, not every agent at the scene refused to follow the order, and a sniper fired a shot at Weaver when he came outside to look at the body of Sammy, which he had placed in a shed on the property. The sniper wounded Weaver in the shoulder, and he raced back to his cabin. Just as Weaver went through the front door of his cabin, the sniper fired again, missing Weaver but hitting his wife Vicki in the face, killing her. She had been holding their ten-month-old daughter.

Negotiators finally talked Randy Weaver and his family into coming out of the cabin and surrendering. The government then charged Weaver and the family friend with murder and demanded the death penalty. A jury, however, believing that the government had instigated the shootout, found both men innocent. The federal government later agreed to pay Weaver $3.1 million to avoid a lawsuit.

The FBI, after an enormous blunder like this, went into cover-up mode. Top officials began accusing each other of fault in the "shoot to kill" order. Before anyone could find out exactly who gave the order, senior FBI official Michael Kahoe destroyed all the documents that could reflect badly on the FBI. He later pled guilty to obstruction of justice and received a sentence of eighteen months in prison.

As can be imagined, both of these incidents inflamed right-wing supporters. Timothy McVeigh, however, rather than just being incensed, decided to strike back.

Timothy McVeigh's case, however, is not isolated. There are other examples of mass murderers or would-be mass murderers committing or attempting to commit their crimes as revenge for some actual event, not just some imagined wrongs. For example, on March 26, 1993,

James Ray Holloway, a former law enforcement officer who served for eighteen years on the California Highway Patrol, and also served as an agent for the California State Board of Alcohol Beverage Control, disarmed a security guard at the California State Board of Equalization Building in Sacramento. He then handcuffed the guard to a parking meter and fired a shot at his feet with a .357 Magnum revolver when the guard tried to reason with him.

Carrying a bag that contained a 30-30 rifle, a twelve-gauge shotgun, and two .357 Magnum revolvers, Holloway tried to enter the building with a group of employees. When stopped by another security guard, Holloway pulled the shotgun from his bag and began blasting away at the glass doors of the building. Racing inside, Holloway then fired several shots from the shotgun at the glass-walled security station, which caused the crowd of people in the building's lobby to panic and run for the exit.

Holloway would eventually go to the eighteenth floor and take a number of people hostage there. The local police SWAT team arrived and eventually shot and killed Holloway. In his pocket they found a list of fifteen people he had intended to kill that day. As it turned out, none of the fifteen were in the building.

What was Holloway's reason for his assault on a government building? He had been receiving tax bills for his deceased wife for some time, and no amount of calling or talking personally to people could stop the bills. Individuals would assure him repeatedly that the problem had been taken care of, but the bills would just keep coming.

Another mass murder for revenge that made worldwide news was the January 7, 2015, mass murder attack at the offices of *Charlie Hebdo*, a satirical newspaper in France. Two brothers forced their way into the newspaper's offices, killed twelve people, and wounded eleven others. Their reason? The newspaper had printed cartoon images of the prophet Muhammad, which is considered blasphemy by many believers of Islam, and as such is punishable by death.

Mass murderers often leave behind material that talks about how revenge drove them to kill, but much of it, contrary to the three preceding incidents, is not for real incidents, but rather blames others for their own failures. They want revenge for being fired, even though they brought it on themselves. They want revenge for not obtaining some goal, even though the reason they didn't obtain it usually involves some failure on their part. They want revenge for being a spurned lover, even though they drove the other person away. These mass murderers simply want to blame their failures on someone else.

The police see this blame-others motive quite often in people who commit mass murder at a place where they worked. This usually follows being laid off or fired, a job demotion, or being disciplined at the job. These individuals see their job either disappearing or lessening in importance. And while, when investigated, the reasons for these actions were usually legitimate, the individuals who become mass murderers rarely see it that way. Instead, it's someone else wronging them. Because of these job actions, mass murderers often see their worth as a person diminishing. Without a job, or with a lesser job, they feel worthless. Consequently, they become angry and want to strike back. This motive also occasionally inspires mass murders at institutes of higher learning, from individuals who can't obtain the degree or level of education they desire.

A motivation for mass murder very close to this is life failure. We saw this in the Jiverly Wong incident in chapter 2. Wong could never seem to fit into American society, had never mastered the English language, and as such could never hold a job of any consequence for very long. His choice of targets told his story. He attacked a location that helps individuals from other countries assimilate into the American culture, something Wong could never do.

"They're typically failing in academics, failing in the world of work, failing in the world of friendship, in romance, or sexuality," says Dr. Peter Langman in an article in *The Atlantic*. "Nothing is really going right in any major domain for them."[25]

Everything these people try seems to fail, and they always feel it's someone else's fault. "All the disappointments, all the failures, the broken relationships are because other people treated them wrong," says criminologist Alan Fox. "They don't see themselves as being inadequate and flawed."[26]

However, one of the strongest and most frightening motives for mass murder is that the perpetrators want to become famous. They want people worldwide to know who they are. While normal people do this through years of study and preparation to be an actor, a singer, or perhaps a distinguished scientist, a subgroup of disturbed individuals wants to do it through infamy. This method is a lot less work and almost certain to succeed if they can kill enough people. They want to gain fame by committing a crime so horrific that it will be reported worldwide.

"Seems the more people you kill, the more you're in the limelight," said Christopher Harper-Mercer, who killed nine people at an Oregon college in 2015.[27]

Like Harris and Klebold in the narrative at the beginning of this chapter, many mass murderers commit their crimes because they see the press coverage other mass murderers are receiving and it spurs them into action. In the Columbine mass murder, not only did the incident receive worldwide media coverage; it inspired books, movies, and hundreds of articles in popular magazines and scientific journals.

"On Internet fan pages Harris is compared to a god, and at a recent auction Klebold's old car fetched a price way over book value, almost as if it were a religious relic," says an article in *Scientific American*.[28]

What disturbed person contemplating a mass murder could resist that possible reward? Consequently, following any highly publicized mass murder, there will usually be copycat mass murders by those who were inspired to act by the extensive media coverage they saw. These copycat crimes often don't rise to the level of the highly reported ones, but still people die or are injured.

"Thus the media attention showered on previous school shooters such as the Columbine killers Eric Harris and Dylan Klebold often appeals greatly to would-be copycats, because the publicity may pass for esteem in their minds," says the *Scientific American* article.[29]

Dr. Park Dietz, a forensic psychiatrist, says, "When they watch the coverage of a school shooting or a workplace mass murder, it only takes one or two of them to say, 'That guy is just like me, that's the solution to my problem, that's what I'll do tomorrow.'"[30]

For example, a twenty-one-year-old man arrested recently in Toledo, Ohio, who was planning to attack a Toledo synagogue, told undercover FBI agents that he wanted to copy the October 2018 mass murder at a Pittsburgh synagogue. "I admire what the guy did with the shooting actually," he said.[31]

As might be imagined, several copycat mass murders took place after the Columbine High School mass murder, including one eight days afterward at W. R. Myers High School in Canada, and a month later at Heritage High School in Conyers, Georgia. Several years after Columbine, Charles Andrew Williams allegedly told his friends that he was going to "pull a Columbine" just before shooting up Santana High School in Santee, California.[32] One school shooter even wore a trench coat like the Columbine killers and named his shotgun Arlene, the same name Eric Harris had given to his shotgun. As he was taken away from the school by the police, the shooter yelled, "Columbine! Remember Columbine! Eric Harris! Dylan Klebold!"[33] Along with these examples, a number of other mass murderers have referred to Harris and Klebold as a motivation for their crimes, some seeing them as martyrs and others seeing them as heroes.

"Numerous post-Columbine rampage shooters referred directly to Columbine as their inspiration," says Ralph W. Larkin, a sociologist who has studied school shootings; "others attempted to supersede the Columbine shooting in body count."[34]

Sometimes, of course, a motivation simply can't be determined because the individual was so psychotic that no one knows what he or she was thinking. No one knows who the mass murderer thought the people he or she killed were. The mass murderer could have seen them as demons, assassins, aliens from another planet, etc.

While we have seen in this chapter that there are many motivations for mass murder, it is impossible to say exactly what percentage of mass murderers acted with what motivation. The reason for this is that very often the perpetrators either kill themselves or are killed by the police. This then puts their motivation in the realm of speculation, not concrete proof.

Finally, occasionally mass murderers can be striking back at a single individual whom they believe has wronged them. But in doing so, and as we will see in the next chapter, they can commit mass murder against individuals who had nothing to do with this wrong but just happened to be in the vicinity.

6

SECONDARY VICTIMS OF MASS MURDER

Richard Wade Farley had stopped in Laura Black's work area that day in July 1984 to talk to a friend who worked in the same department at ESL, Inc., a defense contractor located in Sunnydale, California. For Farley, the unexpected encounter with Black, a new employee, became breathtaking and electric, and after meeting her he began four years of a relentless, but unsuccessful, wooing of her. Sadly, it ended not like Hollywood, with the two of them rushing into each other's arms, but rather in a shooting rampage that would result in seven people being killed and Black herself badly wounded. However, the truly sad part about the ending was that not one of the seven people killed had anything to do with Farley's pursuit of and rejection by Black.

Shortly after his first encounter with Black, Farley had lunch with his friend and Black. They all had sandwiches at the Eat Your Heart Out Deli. Black saw this as a casual meal with fellow workers, where everyone paid for their own sandwich and drink. But Farley didn't see it that way. It was the opposite. He saw it as a first date for two future lovers.

"I think I fell instantly in love with her," Farley would testify at his trial for the mass murder at ESL, Inc. "I thought she was attractive. It was just one of those things, I guess."[1]

When he began his pursuit of Black, Farley held several important jobs at ESL, Inc., including computer programmer, software engineer, and test technician. Because ESL, Inc., held a number of government contracts for the Department of Defense, Farley additionally possessed a top secret clearance. And while he was a rising star at work, Farley also had a darker side: he collected firearms and had assembled a huge collection of literature about violence.

Farley's infatuation with Black soon became known at ESL, Inc., and most of the other employees saw it as just a silly crush that would never amount to anything. After all, Black was a pretty, athletic, twenty-two-year-old with lots of friends. Farley, on the other hand, was an overweight thirty-six-year-old man with just a few friends. He had been described in high school as a "wimp" and "nerdy."

Interestingly, Black seemed to be the first real love interest of Farley's life. "I don't think girls were attracted to him. And I don't think he had the guts to go after a girl," said a high school classmate of Farley's.[2] His mother would later say that Farley didn't have a girlfriend in high school or in his adult life as far as she knew.

Apparently, however, Farley felt that he had met the true love of his life, and he went after Black with a relentless energy. For an actual first date he asked her to go with him to a tractor pull, but she declined. Undiscouraged, he asked her repeatedly for other dates, but she continued to turn him down. He began baking blueberry cakes and continually dropping them off at her desk; he began buying her gifts and asking for her telephone number. Black continued to say no, but Farley simply wouldn't let up. Finally, after months of his pursuit of a relationship, Black, in an attempt to stop him, told Farley that she wouldn't go out with him "if he was the last man on Earth."

This enraged Farley, and he became even more aggressive. "I had the right to ask her out," Farley would later explain. "She had the right to refuse. When she did not refuse in a cordial way, I felt I had the right to bother her."[3]

Part of this bothering included flooding her with love letters. He would later say that it sometimes took him eight hours or longer to write her a letter. Farley felt the wording had to be perfect. Black tried repeatedly to get him to stop the dozens of love letters he sent her.

"She told me to stop writing the letters," Farley would later testify. "I tried. But when I stopped, she started ignoring me. By that time I was hooked on her. I had fallen madly in love with her and I had to see her, even if I had to make her mad."[4] Apparently, Farley would settle for any kind of contact with Black.

In one of his letters to Black, Farley told her that he felt it was his option to make her life miserable. In pursuit of this goal, Farley became a stalker and began showing up wherever Black went: softball games, her health club, when she went out on a date with other men, and when she went shopping. He also called her on the telephone relentlessly. As stalkers do, Farley began compiling all of the personal information he could find about Black. He pried into her computer files and her personnel file at ESL, Inc. In a real invasion of privacy, he went through her desk when she was out of the office. In it, he discovered her application for a security clearance, in which Black had included a huge amount of personal information.

Naturally, Farley's obsession with Black eventually came to the attention of the management of ESL, Inc. They ordered Farley to stop his pursuit of Black immediately or else he would be fired. Farley by this time had become far too obsessed to let that happen, and he doubled his efforts to woo Black. Interestingly, even though the two of them had never been on a date or shared a romantic moment, Farley's fantasies about them became real to him. He began doctoring photographs to make it look like they had been on a date, claimed that he had (but never produced) tape recordings of romantic conversations between them, and insisted that she had given him a key to her house (he had actually secretly copied the key when Black left her keys on her desk while out of the office). Farley even had a garage door opener that would open the door at her house. He had purchased an opener of the same brand Black had and spent hour after hour at her house running through combinations until he found hers. Farley did all of this even though management had threatened to fire him if he didn't stop.

But because he wouldn't stop his harassment of Black, the management of ESL, Inc., finally did fire Farley. They told him that he would not be allowed on their property any longer. This, Farley knew, would seriously limit his access to Black; it appeared to infuriate him. His thoughts began to turn to violence rather than love. "I feel capable of killing to protect myself, and to hell with the consequences," he wrote her. "I do own guns, and I'm good with them."[5] Strangely, even though Farley's letters became threatening, he still maintained the fantasy that they had an intimate relationship. He ended one of his letters to Black with "Call me Saturday morning," something a person in a real relationship would write.

Finally, after Farley let Black know that he had a key to her house and could come in any time he wanted, Black went to court and persuaded a judge to issue a temporary restraining order against Farley. According to the order, Farley wasn't allowed to come within 300 yards of her or any place she frequented. The judge set February 17, 1988, as the court date when it would be decided whether to make the restraining order permanent.

Farley received a copy of the temporary restraining order and knew that if the order became permanent he would never be able to fulfill his desire to have Black, because if he tried he would go to jail. If the order became permanent, Black would be forever forbidden to him.

Something in Farley's mind told him that he had to do something dramatic to show Black how much she meant to him. On the day before the hearing to make the restraining order permanent, Farley rented a motor home. He filled it with various firearms, piles of ammunition, a container of gasoline, and a set of handcuffs. He then drove the motor home to ESL, Inc. Farley would later testify that he had originally intended to show Black what a man he was by destroying the computers at ESL, Inc., finding her, and then making her witness him killing himself.

"I just felt she had to see the end result of what I felt she had done to me," Farley would later explain. "It was important that she see it and not just read about it."[6]

He parked the motor home in the ESL, Inc., parking lot at around 3:00 p.m., and then loaded himself up with almost one hundred pounds of guns and ammunition. Even though he said he had only planned to destroy computers and kill himself, Farley apparently changed his mind when he climbed out of the motor home. In the parking lot, he used a shotgun to shoot and kill Lawrence Kane, a former coworker. Farley then stormed into Building M5, where Black worked on the second floor, and began shooting both at computers and at anyone he saw close by. Farley obviously rethought his plan and decided that murdering all of these people would show Black even more clearly the consequences of what he felt she had done to him by rejecting his romantic overtures.

"Some people popped out from around corners," Farley said, "and I just shot them."[7]

Farley killed a former coworker by shooting through the door to his office, and then killed another who happened to be in the stairwell leading to the second floor. When he reached Black's office, Farley forced open the door and shot her with the shotgun, wounding her seriously. She fell to the floor but managed to push the door shut with her foot. Farley didn't go back in after her, but instead continued down the hallway, destroying computer equipment and shooting at anyone he saw. He would kill seven people that day and wound four others. Farley also destroyed $300,000 worth of computer equipment.

Black, even though seriously wounded and bleeding profusely, managed to escape the building. On her way out, she discovered three women hiding, and they bandaged her wound as best they could.

Naturally, dozens of calls were made to the local police department, and they immediately sent out their SWAT team. The SWAT team negotiator spoke with Farley, who said he wasn't ready to come out yet. "I want to gloat for a while," he told the negotiator.[8] However, the euphoria soon evaporated and Farley began to worry about the consequences of what he had done and his fear of going to prison. "I never wanted to hurt her," he told the negotiator. "All she had to do was go out with me."[9] The negotiator, after discussing the possibility of Farley teaching computer classes in prison, finally talked him into surrendering.

Between his arrest and trial, Farley refused to stop the stalking and continued to write to Black from jail. On October 21, 1991, a jury found Farley guilty of seven counts of first-degree murder. The judge afterward sentenced him to death. He presently awaits execution on death row in San Quentin prison.

✳ ✳ ✳

As this incident shows, even though Farley had gone to ESL, Inc., with the idea of making an impression on Black by shooting up the equipment and then killing himself in front of her, the incident instead became a mass murder. But interestingly, Farley didn't target the bosses who had fired him. He didn't target anyone who had tried to stop him from getting to Black on the second floor. He didn't target anyone who also had romantic ideas about Black. He simply shot anyone he saw.

This incident clearly shows the danger of suddenly finding oneself in the middle of a mass murder. In a later chapter I will describe what a person can do in such a situation to lessen the risk of being killed.

Individuals, readers will find, are not totally helpless and at the mercy of the mass murderer.

In the above mass murder there were clearly seven secondary victims, the seven innocent people who had absolutely nothing to do with Farley and Black's situation, yet were killed by Farley as he was trying to get to Black. But in all mass murders, in addition to the fatally injured victims like the seven above, there are also living secondary victims, who are often called covictims in the literature about mass murder. They are called covictims because, while the murder victims themselves certainly suffer the most grievous effects of the incident, living secondary victims can suffer from the effects of a mass murder for the rest of their lives. Covictims can be those injured in a mass murder, at the event but not injured, family and friends of the victims, and, as we will see, even those not connected at all with the event.

Any sudden death of a family member, a loved one, or a close friend can be traumatic, but in cases in which the death came from events such as an unavoidable accident, the survivors grieve but can usually move on within a year or so. However, to lose a family member, a loved one, or a close friend to a senseless mass murder such as the one above can make the grieving go on for years. A mass murder is not an accident; it is an evil, intentional act with no explanation. Survivors want an answer as to why it happened, but they rarely receive it.

Most people, psychologists say, want to believe in a fair, just world. Yet to lose a family member, a loved one, or a close friend in a senseless mass murder, particularly if the victims are children, simply doesn't fit into this philosophy.

"Simply by definition, mass shootings are more likely to trigger difficulties with beliefs that most of us have, including that we live in a just world and that if we make good decisions, we'll be safe," says Dr. Laura Wilson, coauthor and editor of *The Wiley Handbook of the Psychology of Mass Shootings*.[10]

Most secondary victims also want to believe that an explanation for the mass murder must be somewhere within the framework of whatever belief system they espouse. But it usually isn't, and this can cause some serious psychological problems. The world suddenly seems very, very unfair.

"The perception that one's situation is not fair diminishes personal control; the perception that the world is unfair diminishes one's belief in a just world," says social psychologist Melvin Lerner. "Neither perception is good for psychological well-being."[11]

How difficult can it be for secondary victims, particularly the parents of children killed in a mass murder, to come to terms with what happened? Extremely difficult and sometimes impossible. Forty-nine-year-old Jeremy Richman, the father of six-year-old Avielle Richman, a victim in the Sandy Hook Elementary School mass murder described in chapter 4, tried desperately to make sense of the tragedy that took his daughter's life. He founded the Avielle Foundation, which tried to develop ways to stop this kind of violence. But apparently he simply couldn't recover from the senseless loss of his daughter. On March 25, 2019, he was found in his office, dead from a suicide.

"This is a heart-breaking event for the Richman family and the Newtown community as a whole," said police lieutenant Aaron Bahamonde.[12]

Specialists who treat individuals suffering from post-traumatic stress disorder (PTSD), a condition often suffered by individuals who have witnessed unusually bloody, vicious, and unthinkable violence, agree that senseless deaths such as those that occur in mass murders can negatively affect living secondary victims. "Coping with loss is difficult, but when that loss is unexpected and due to senseless violence, it can compound the impact on those who are left behind," said Sheila A. M. Rauch, PhD, in an article about the Las Vegas mass murder discussed in chapter 3. "As people, we want to have a sense of control over our world and the people we love. When death due to violence occurs, that sense of safety and comfort is ripped away and leaves the people left behind feeling vulnerable and angry along with the deep sadness that follows loss."[13]

A study reported in the *Journal of Traumatic Stress* found that those who were most directly exposed to a mass murder—those who suffered injuries, who saw someone else get shot, who lost a friend or loved one, or who feared they would die next—had a much greater chance of developing PTSD and other psychological problems than those who were farther away from the violence.[14] The National Center for PTSD, according to an article by Amy Novotney in the American Psychological Association journal, estimates that 28 percent of the people who have witnessed a mass murder will develop PTSD, and about a third will develop acute stress disorder.[15] This kind of experience can also easily lead to anxiety, depression, and difficulty sleeping and concentrating. Additionally, and especially if someone important to them dies during the mass murder, these individuals can suffer from guilt over surviving the incident while loved ones or good friends died.

"Survivors of shootings may also experience 'survivor's guilt,' the feeling that they failed others who died, did not do enough to help them survive, or just because they survived," says Dr. Arash Javanbakht, a clinical psychiatrist. [16]

Researchers have found that serious psychological problems can result from this survivor's guilt. "People who engage in self-blame for the tragedy—believing they should have done more to try and save friends who died, for example—are at greater risk for long-term poor psychological outcomes," says Novotney. [17]

Other very important secondary victims of mass murders can be the families and loved ones of the victims of the crime. While these individuals may not have been there to experience the crime, their pain nevertheless can be intense. Most mass murders appear random and senseless. To lose a family member or loved one to such an event can have a traumatic effect on the family members and loved ones left behind. It can be even more traumatic if the victim is a young child. There can be no greater horror than a parent losing a child to a senseless act of violence—an innocent child's life ended for no apparent reason. Experiencing this can upset an individual's entire vision of how the world operates. People die every day from accidents and illness, but young children simply aren't murdered. The effects of this trauma can linger for years and lead to various types of psychological problems.

But even before that, who can imagine the horror of knowing that a loved one has been at the scene of a mass murder, yet not knowing whether this person survived or not? Sometimes it can be hours before notification is given to family members. Andrew Pollack's daughter had been at Marjory Stoneman Douglas High School when a mass murder occurred there on February 14, 2018. He waited for hours outside the emergency room at Broward Health North, wanting any news of his daughter. He wasn't notified until 3:00 the morning after the mass murder that his daughter Meadow had been one of the victims killed in the incident.

"Something is not right," he said that night. "I keep looking at my phone. I don't know where to go from here." [18] We can only imagine the horror Pollack went through that day. No one is so tough that this sort of experience won't leave deep scars.

Once the waiting for notification is over, then the grieving for the victims of the mass murder can begin. But there is something that can make this grieving much worse. If an arrest is made, the families, loved ones, and close friends of the victims must then deal with the criminal justice system.

Usually, if an arrest for a mass murder is made, it is made on the scene or very soon afterward, and consequently the identification of the perpetrator or perpetrators is known right away. This spares the family, loved ones, and close friends of the victims the anxiety of waiting for the police to solve the case and make an apprehension. But still, even when there is an immediate arrest, the criminal justice system afterward grinds very slowly. As you'll remember from the narrative at the beginning of this chapter, the trial for Richard Wade Farley didn't take place until three and a half years after his arrest, and he is still awaiting execution, twenty-eight years after his sentencing.

Also, secondary victims often find, usually much to their surprise, that the criminal justice system doesn't operate with or have compassion for the immediate or secondary victims. It instead operates mostly to protect the various rights of the mass murderer. Many secondary victims feel shut out of the process.

"While the criminal justice process grinds slowly, surviving family members must take the initiative to be kept in the communication loop," police chaplain Philip Bacon told me. "In a sense, survivors become outsiders to the system, merely looking on. They often feel victimized by the process. Although crime victim families have legal rights, many are not versed in these and must rely upon someone in the system to be their advocate."[19]

Unfortunately, even though victims' families do have certain rights, occasionally these are ignored in an effort to move the case forward. As a police officer, I have often heard secondary victims complain about not being notified of a plea deal or a proposed sentence. Often, secondary victims can feel neglected while maneuvering through the criminal justice system.

"There are rights in some states, but if a prosecutor doesn't follow [them], there's nothing to fall back on," says Nancy Ruhe-Munch, executive director of Parents of Murdered Children.[20]

Many times the first members of the criminal justice system with whom secondary victims come in contact will be the police. In many mass murders, family members, loved ones, and close friends of the victims come to the crime scene. They naturally are concerned about the victim and many times want to enter the crime scene. The police obviously can't allow this because it would contaminate the evidence at the crime scene and cause much of it to be thrown out of court. However, few of these secondary victims understand the importance of untainted evidence in getting a conviction in court.

"It's my daughter, not yours," said a mother at a crime scene. "They took possession of my daughter. . . . It was very, very upsetting to me that their criminal investigation took precedence over just letting me see her."[21]

While I, as a parent, can certainly understand this woman's disbelief that the police wouldn't allow her into the crime scene to see her daughter, as the former commander of the Indianapolis Police Department's Homicide Branch, I recall a number of times when my officers had to physically restrain family members from crashing through the crime scene tape to see a loved one. Many of them would later tell me that they just wanted to hug or kiss the victim one last time. Unfortunately, to allow this would likely result in extremely serious evidence contamination, which just cannot be allowed if a conviction for the murder is to be obtained.

Also, as commander of the Homicide Branch, I had to constantly remind my officers to maintain an appearance of professionalism and seriousness at any crime scene. Secondary victims are often thunderstruck when they see or hear officers laughing and joking at a crime scene. To laugh or joke about the victims of a mass murder is so outrageous that most secondary victims find it hard to believe. However, there is a reason for this behavior.

As someone who has been at the scene of hundreds of murders, I can state with complete confidence that the officers, though laughing or joking, are not laughing at the victims and don't see anything humorous in the situation. Almost daily, police officers witness the many horrible things that people do to each other, and mass murder is one of the worst. The laughing and joking, the graveyard humor, is what police officers must do to deal psychologically with the horror that they see constantly; the more horrible the event, the more likely the graveyard humor. If police officers didn't have some way to redirect the stress of the things they experience, burnout would soon empty a police department.

"[T]hese emergency response professionals laugh at things most of us would consider to be in bad taste," says Professor Paul McGhee about the police use of dark humor. "But they have all learned that they need to laugh, because it helps them adapt to the terrible things they are exposed to."[22]

However, because of the police use of dark humor or because of their very clipped, cold, and professional attitude (an attitude officers use sometimes rather than humor), many secondary victims come away thinking that the police are unsympathetic to their grief. This isn't the case. The police are just trying to separate themselves from it. If the police shared the grief of all the hundreds of secondary victims they encountered, they would be basket cases and useless in no time. Police officers must maintain a distance from it.

"Professionals, particularly detectives, use the avoidance strategy because they are not comfortable seeing the pain of the bereaveds' loss, and they recognize that there is not much that brings them comfort," say the authors of a report on homicide and bereavement. "Detectives along with prosecutors use counselors as organizational shields to create a buffer between them and the bereaved."[23]

The police investigation, however, is just a start for the secondary victims' contact with the criminal justice system. The situation often becomes much worse. In most cases of mass murder in which the perpetrators survive, they are usually arrested at the scene surrounded by the bodies of their victims. Because of this, most secondary victims believe that the court process should then be swift. However, secondary victims instead often find themselves waiting through the long process, sometimes years, of legal wrangling before the murderers finally go to trial. There is no closure during this time, and often the legal hearings before the trial just keep reopening old wounds.

When the trial for the mass murder finally does begin, secondary victims want to believe that this will at last bring them closure, but many times it does just the opposite. The secondary victims find, often to their surprise, that the perpetrators receive much more concern from the court than do their slain loved ones, and during testimony secondary victims can sometimes hear gruesome and disturbing details of the crime that they didn't know about. It can be just as disturbing when secondary victims hear defense attorneys attempting to mitigate the mass murder by trying to raise sympathy for the perpetrator. If the perpetrator came from a difficult family situation or had emotional or psychological problems, defense attorneys will often try to paint him or her as just another one of the victims, hoping to raise sympathy among the jurors.

"Many families and friends think that the court proceedings will somehow take care of their pain," says Reverend Wanda Henry-Jenkins, whose mother was murdered, "only to find after the trial that the grief has only just begun."[24]

Even if the trial ends in a conviction and an appropriate sentence, the frustration with the criminal justice system may not be over. These cases are quite often appealed, and if successful, the secondary victims must start the process all over again.

"It was hard for me for them to try it again and I wonder if there will be another trial," said the mother of a murdered son after a second trial when the original verdict for the murder was overturned on appeal. "Having to relive it during the first trial was bad and now I've had to relive it again."[25]

As might be expected, all of this frustration and anger at the criminal justice system can have negative effects on the psychological well-being of secondary victims, often resulting in depression. A study by Professors Sarah D. Goodrum and Mark C. Stafford found that the more contact secondary victims had with the criminal justice system, the worse their depression.[26]

Another study, this one conducted by Professor J. Scott Kenney, said in conclusion, "Generally, those survivors who had, or chose, *extensive* involvements with the criminal justice system, coroner's inquests, civil lawsuits, and Criminal Injuries Compensation tribunals reported faring *worse* than those who did not. This was chiefly due to their institutionalized powerlessness, the intensive *reliving* of what happened in these contexts, added to by negative outcomes, and frustrating bureaucratic delays such that survivors had to 'put their grief on hold' and 'live from hearing to hearing.'"[27]

And as if the frustration and anger secondary victims feel when dealing with the criminal justice system weren't bad enough, families and loved ones of the victims of mass murder also often find that they have to deal with a very aggressive news media. The news media, while performing an important public service, are also money-making organizations, and the more viewers or readers they have, the more they can charge their advertisers. Consequently, to increase numbers of viewers or readers, news media outlets will many times attempt to sensationalize a mass murder. This is particularly true if the event is especially gruesome or newsworthy because of the vulnerability of the victims. Everyone has seen news stories in which the news outlet has added the sound of gunfire, sirens, and other sound bites to perk up the story. Dr. Arash Javanbakht, quoted earlier in this chapter, refers to cable news as "disaster pornographers."

Unfortunately, because many news outlets try to sensationalize a mass murder, they will often show pictures or give details they really shouldn't, which only further wounds secondary victims. In addition to this, secondary victims will many times find themselves hounded by news media personnel, who are looking for video clips of their grief or new information to use.

"Co-victims are quickly thrust into public view and become fair game for public consumption," says an article about media harassment of secondary victims.[28]

The families and loved ones of the Oklahoma City bombing victims suffered tremendously from news media intrusion into their lives. "Since the nature of news is what is 'new,' the pace in which the media intrudes in the victims' families is uncanny and often quite ruthless," says an article in a scientific journal about the Oklahoma City bombing. "The press often try to sensationalize tragedy when the truth and facts alone are hard enough for the families to cope with."[29]

Another news media tactic that can be especially cruel and troublesome to secondary victims is when the media, like defense attorneys, tries to portray the perpetrators in a sympathetic light. The news media will dig up information about how the mass murderer may have had mental issues, came from a brutal home, had been tossed around in the foster care system, etc. They will then sometimes present this information as if the perpetrator were just another one of the victims. For secondary victims this appears to be an attempt to lessen the value of the lives of their slain loved ones.

By presenting all this information, I'm not trying to say that every member of the news media is a heartless news scrounger. There are also many caring, considerate, and compassionate people who work in the news media. When writing another book, I interviewed Bonnie Druker, who at the time was a reporter for the CBS affiliate station in Indianapolis. She told me, "When I cover a murder story I feel like I walk a fine line. My heart hurts when I see family members in shock, in pain, and in tears. But I always wonder—what do they know? Sometimes I get the opportunity to ask them, sometimes I don't. My mission is always this: get the story, meet the deadline, show compassion. I always ask myself: what would I do if this were my family?"[30]

While the families of mass murder victims clearly suffer from the crime itself, usually the families of the mass murderers do as well. Quite often, the families didn't see any signs of the mass murder happening, or even if there were signs the families didn't believe that whatever was happening with the perpetrators would end in a mass murder. Afterward, families of mass murderers can be consumed with guilt for not seeing the signs and stopping the crime, and often they must face a community hostile to them for the actions of their family members and for their failure to stop them. In addition, families of mass murderers many times face lawsuits from the victims' families and can also occasionally face criminal charges if the mass murderers used their weapons in the crimes.

Another group that few people would recognize as secondary victims are the emergency responders to mass murder scenes, including the police, medical personnel, and occasionally firefighters. These individuals can often suffer negative consequences from responding to such a scene. Police officers in particular like to think of themselves as tough and impenetrable, but this just isn't true. Law enforcement officers, especially at scenes where the victims are children, can be affected just as negatively as anyone else. As commander of the Indianapolis Police Department's Homicide Branch for a number of years, I responded to the scene of hundreds of murders. Most of the adult victims have faded in my memory because so very often they were involved in criminal acts that brought about their demise. Also, many of these adult victims were so deeply involved in the drug world, and consequently dealing with extremely violent people, that their murder was almost inevitable. However, I can still recall almost every detail when the murder victims were children. Children never deserve to be killed, and even seasoned officers are not so tough and impenetrable that they can just push these sorts of memories out of their mind.

Dr. Javanbakht points out that "another group whose trauma is usually overlooked is the first responders." He adds, "PTSD has been reported in up to 20 percent of first responders to man-made mass violence."[31]

As strange as it sounds, mass murder can also negatively affect people with no connection at all to the mass murderers or their victims, and who didn't witness the crime. They only saw a report about it on the news or read about it in the newspaper. These sorts of incidents, especially those that are totally random and in which the perpetrator had no connection to and didn't even know the victims, can affect an individual's feeling of personal safety. Just hearing or reading about how people shopping in a supermarket, attending church, or doing business in a bank were mercilessly slaughtered can make a person uneasy when away from home and taking care of ordinary business. My wife, who is also a retired police officer, regularly carries a firearm in her purse while attending church, something totally unheard of just a couple of decades ago. And the more incidents that occur, and the more that the news media reports endlessly on them, the less safe people feel.

In addition to this, according to Dr. Charles Figley, director of the Tulane University Traumatology Institute, as these types of incidents keep occurring at what seems to be an increasing pace, the public can develop what is called "compassion fatigue."[32] This means that as these events occur more and more often, the public is no longer shocked or surprised. They begin to think that these events are to be expected; they become desensitized to them. Events that would have shocked or stunned the public a few decades ago are now taken as a sort of business as usual. And unfortunately, mass murderers looking for fame and glory soon realize that to be thrust into the international spotlight, their crimes now must be extraordinarily gruesome.

Roger Chui, a software developer who lives in Lexington, Kentucky, showed this compassion fatigue in his response to hearing about a mass murder of twelve people in a bar in Thousand Oaks, California, in November 2018. "And I was like, 'Oh, that seems really soon after Pittsburgh and Louisville. I thought we'd get more of a break.'"[33]

Can these acts of mass murder be stopped so that people won't feel unsafe when they leave their homes? Yes, they can. In the next chapter we will look at the written and video warnings many mass murderers have given before their crimes—warnings that if taken seriously could have stopped them.

7

COMMUNIQUÉS AND MANIFESTOS

The 911 operator in Roseburg, Oregon, received the first emergency call from the campus at 10:38 a.m. on October 1, 2015. A student told the 911 operator that a shooting was happening right then in classroom 15 in Snyder Hall on the campus of Umpqua Community College. The police dispatcher immediately notified the uniformed officers in the vicinity. Two plainclothes Roseburg Police Department detectives, who happened to be near, also responded to the call.

A few minutes before this, Christopher Harper-Mercer, a twenty-six-year-old student at the college, had entered classroom 15, where he attended an introductory composition class. Harper-Mercer, armed with a Del-Ton DTI-15 semiautomatic rifle (an AR-15 type assault rifle) and five handguns, looked around at the students for a second before firing a warning shot. He then herded all of the terrified students to the center of the room, where he selected one student he would spare so that that student could deliver a package to the police for him. Harper-Mercer had that student sit at the back of the room.

Harper-Mercer then shot and killed the English professor and afterward began asking the students if they were Christians. He killed those who answered affirmatively after telling them that they would be in heaven soon (though some witnesses later disputed this, saying that even though he did ask them about their beliefs he didn't kill them because of their religion). He also shot and killed a female student after forcing her to beg for her life and killed another female student who was trying to climb back into a wheelchair as he had ordered her to do.

Whipped into an apparent frenzy, Harper-Mercer also shot a student who tried to reason with him and another student who had tried to hide behind a desk. In all, eight people would die in the classroom, and one would die later at the hospital. He also wounded eight other students.

The two plainclothes detectives arrived at the school just six minutes after the 911 call and cautiously approached classroom 15. Harper-Mercer, aware of their arrival, leaned out of the classroom and fired several shots at the detectives with a handgun, but missed. The detectives returned fire and struck Harper-Mercer in the right side. Harper-Mercer fired again at the officers, but once more missed. Now bleeding seriously from the wound, Harper-Mercer ducked back into the classroom. Knowing that escape was now impossible, Harper-Mercer put one of the handguns up to his head and killed himself.

Searching the classroom later, the police discovered that Harper-Mercer had brought along a flak jacket and enough ammunition to have lasted a long time in a firefight. The wound the detectives had inflicted, however, apparently evaporated his resolve. The police would find through their investigation that Harper-Mercer or a member of his family had legally purchased all the weapons he brought with him to the school.

Along with the detectives, there was another act of heroism that day. Chris Mintz, a ten-year army veteran who was attending the college to study fitness training, heard the screams and gunfire from the classroom next to his. He immediately used his body to block the connecting door to classroom 15, so that the students in his classroom could escape. After the students had safely gotten out, he went to the library to warn the students there to get out quickly. Following this, he returned to the hallway outside of classroom 15 and tended to a wounded student there. Harper-Mercer leaned out of the door to the classroom and shot Mintz five times because he said that Mintz was the one who had called the police. Mintz would survive his wounds.

✻ ✻ ✻

As part of their investigation, the police looked into Harper-Mercer's background. Laurel Mercer, Christopher's mother and a nurse, would later tell the police that her son had been "born angry" and had not changed in twenty-six years. "I mean, he was born angry, pretty much," she said. "I mean, even the doctor said this is one angry baby."[1] At times in his life, she recalled, he had flown into rages, had tantrums, and had even pointed guns at her. Mercer claimed that she had always managed to calm him down but had never reported any of the incidents because she feared Harper-Mercer would be arrested. Because of his moods, she said, Harper-Mercer had been prescribed medicine, but it didn't seem to help, and he stopped taking his medication when he reached eighteen. Mercer also told the detectives that Harper-Mercer really enjoyed trolling the internet in search of videos about killings.

Harper-Mercer, at the time of the shooting, lived with his mother, who was a firearms enthusiast. In 2008, Harper-Mercer joined the army, but they discharged him after only five weeks, reportedly after a suicide attempt. Following his release from the army, Harper-Mercer moved back in with his mother and lived with her until the mass murder. In 2009, Harper-Mercer succeeded in graduating from a school for students with learning and emotional disabilities. After this, he attended college for several years in California before he and his mother moved to Oregon, where he attended classes at Umpqua Community College.

Serving a search warrant as part of their investigation, the police found eight additional weapons in Harper-Mercer and his mother's apartment. The two of them, the police would find, often spent time together at firing ranges. The police would also discover that Mercer once told a patient of hers that she owned a lot of guns, was a firm believer in the Second Amendment, and that she wanted to buy as many guns as she could before Congress outlawed them. In addition, she told the patient that she regularly took Harper-Mercer to firing ranges and that he had mental problems.[2]

As a number of mass murderers before him have done, three days prior to the shooting at the college, Harper-Mercer posted a warning online telling students not to go to school that day. During their investigation, officers found that the package Harper-Mercer had given to the student he spared contained newspaper clippings about other mass murders the news media had reported extensively on, a report about the Sandy Hook mass murder, and Harper-Mercer's manifesto, titled "My Story." In his manifesto, Harper-Mercer opened by stating that he was the most hated person in the world and that the world had been set against him from birth. A couple of sentences from the first paragraph, though, told the real story of why he was always so angry.

"My whole life has been one lonely enterprise," he wrote. "One loss after another. And here I am, 26, with no friends, no job, no girlfriend, a virgin."[3]

Sexual frustration is a theme that runs throughout his manifesto. To be twenty-six and a virgin, with never a girlfriend, became a huge part of the reason for his anger at the world. He daily saw men who seemed to sail smoothly through the dating scene, and he felt furious because he couldn't.

In his manifesto, Harper-Mercer continued with a rant about how he and other school mass murderers had been denied the things others received but didn't deserve. He also stated he believed that after he died he would become a demon and return to the Earth to kill some more. He followed this with encouragement for people like him, with "no job, no life, no successes," to buy a gun and start killing people.[4]

Following this, Harper-Mercer spent several paragraphs describing how much he loved black women but hated black men because of their success with women. He said this even though, he stated in the manifesto, he himself was 40 percent black. He explained this by claiming that his 40 percent came from a black woman, not a black man. Harper-Mercer then wrote, "It would be better if all black women left the beast on the altar and dated a white man."[5] Harper-Mercer's obvious frustration at his lack of a sex life rings loudly throughout his tirade.

In the next paragraph, Harper-Mercer talked about why so many mass murderers in the past had failed to reach a death toll that was respectable. He claimed they failed because they didn't act fast enough and didn't aim properly. He also ridiculed past mass murderers for not taking on the police when they arrived (from what happened at the college, it doesn't appear that Harper-Mercer had considered that he might get shot himself when taking on the police).

Harper-Mercer then made a list of his favorite singers and bands, his favorite movies, food, and colors. He said that this was for the news media. Following this, he included an FAQ section in which he answered questions about his religion, whether he was gay, and whether he was mentally ill.

In his conclusion, Harper-Mercer wrote that he was committing the mass murder to become part of the group of mass killers who had made the news the last few years. He wrote: "For all those who never took me seriously this is for you. For all those who haven't made their stand I do this. I am the martyr for all those like me." The last sentence of his manifesto read: "Today I die like Jesus Christ."

At the bottom of his manifesto Harper-Mercer placed two pentagrams and the number 666. In between them were the words "For Satan I do this, for the Darkness I do this."[6]

As is obvious from Harper-Mercer's manifesto, he was a very disturbed young man. The frustration and anger he felt at never having had sexual intercourse rings loudly throughout his manifesto, particularly in his hatred of black men, whom he saw as being very successful with women, while he was not. The manifesto, although only a few pages long, at least gave police investigators a sort of motive for the mass murder. Because Harper-Mercer believed that he had failed at everything in his life, because he had no friends or romantic entanglements, because he felt that his situation was never going to change, he harbored an intense anger and rage that finally boiled over into violence.

Harper-Mercer's manifesto also mirrors the final words of other mass murderers in that he believed he had been cheated out of all the good things in life that other people enjoyed. In his manifesto, he wrote: "Just like me these people [other mass murderers] were denied everything they deserved, everything they wanted." Interestingly, nowhere in the manifesto does Harper-Mercer own up to the possibility that even the smallest part of his problems could be his own fault.[7]

But what is really interesting is how this manifesto is not unique or even close to it. Many mass murderers like to express their feelings in writing or videos before they commit the crime. As mass murderer Jared Lee Loughner, who severely wounded Congresswoman Gabrielle Giffords and killed six others at a political rally, said, "Of course, I kept a journal. Don't people like me always keep a journal? It's part of the whole thing. It was me against the world."[8] And like Christopher Harper-Mercer in the narrative above, a number of these mass murderers who keep journals reveal that they are sexually frustrated young men looking to strike out violently because of their involuntary celibacy.

* * *

Before he began his mass murder, twenty-two-year-old Elliot Rodger made careful preparations. He purchased a Glock 34 semiautomatic pistol in November 2012. He noted in his manifesto that the Glock 34 was "an efficient and highly accurate weapon." Early the following year, he purchased two Sig Sauer P226 semi-automatic pistols, writing this time in his manifesto that they were "of a much higher quality than the Glock" and "more efficient."[9] Following these purchases, Rodger visited a shooting range several times so that he would know how to handle and shoot these weapons with reasonable accuracy.

Although at the time Rodger was seeing a mental health therapist and had serious psychological issues, he could still legally purchase the weapons and the ammunition for them because he had never been formally diagnosed as mentally ill, even though he had been seeing a mental health therapist since age eight and had been prescribed anti-psychotic medicine that he refused to take. A family friend said of Rodger: "I'm not a psychologist, but looking back now he strikes me as someone who was broken from the moment of conception."[10] Rodger also came from a very privileged background, wore expensive clothes, and drove a BMW. He used $5,000 from pocket money his parents and grandparents had given him to purchase the handguns.

Rodger's mass murder began on May 23, 2014, in his apartment on Seville Road in Isla Vista, California. Rodger lived there with two other men, twenty-year-old Weihan Wang and twenty-year-old Cheng Hong. Sometime around 6:00 p.m., Rodger lay in wait for them to return home. The roommates returned separately, and Rodger stabbed each one repeatedly with a knife as they came through the door. Along with his two roommates, Rodger also stabbed and killed nineteen-year-old George Chen, a friend of his roommates. The police would later recover evidence that Rodger had tried to clean up the blood from each attack, finding a blood-soaked towel and a pile of bloody paper towels in the apartment's bathroom. Rodger dumped his two roommates in their shared bedroom and tried to hide their bodies with blankets. He dumped George in the bathroom and again covered the body.

Following these three murders, Rodger went out to the apartment building parking lot and sat in his car, a BMW 328i coupe. At 9:17 p.m., he uploaded his written manifesto and a video communiqué titled "Elliot Rodger's Retribution." He then e-mailed these to thirty-four different people, including his mental health therapist, his parents, other family members, some childhood friends, and several teachers he'd had over the years. Afterward, he drove the BMW to the Alpha Phi sorority house near the campus of the University of California–Santa Barbara.

Rodger had formerly been a student at the university; he dropped out in 2012. At the sorority house, he tried to gain entry, but no one would let him in, so instead Rodger began firing one of the pistols at three female college students standing outside, who were members of the Delta Delta Delta sorority. He shot twenty-two-year-old Katherine Breann Cooper eight times and nineteen-year-old Veronika Elizabeth Weiss seven times, killing them both. Rodger also shot and wounded twenty-year-old Bianca de Kock.

Leaving before the police could arrive, Rodger drove to a coffee shop on nearby Pardall Road and fired a shot into the business. The coffee shop was closed and no one was inside. Next, Rodger drove the BMW to the Isla Vista Deli Mart. There, he fired several shots and killed twenty-year-old Christopher Ross Michaels-Martinez, who happened to be inside. Four police officers nearby heard the shots and raced to the scene. They saw Rodger's car leaving the area but didn't connect it to the shooting.

After that, Rodger turned his vehicle onto Embarcadero del Norte. Driving on the wrong side of the road, he rammed the BMW into a pedestrian and fired twice at two people standing on the sidewalk, but missed. Continuing on Embarcadero del Norte, Rodger shot his pistol at a couple leaving a pizza shop and wounded them both, then shot at a woman on a bicycle. As Rodger repeatedly fired his pistols at people, he eventually encountered the police. He exchanged gunfire with the officers and then sped away, striking two pedestrians with his car.

In his flight from the police, Rodger shot at and wounded three more people and used the BMW to ram a skateboarder and two people on bicycles. A little farther on, he rammed another skateboarder and shot two men standing on the sidewalk. However, he soon encountered more police officers and exchanged gunfire with them again. This time, Rodger received a bullet wound to his left hip. Speeding away after being shot, Rodger rammed his vehicle into another person on a bicycle and finally crashed the BMW into another car and then ended up on the sidewalk near the intersection of Del Playa and Camino Descadero. As the police warily approached his vehicle, Rodger shot himself in the head; he died at the scene. In a matter of less than twenty minutes, Rodger had killed three people and wounded fourteen others, not counting the three men he had killed at his apartment. All of the dead had been students at the University of California–Santa Barbara. They would receive posthumous degrees from the university.

* * *

By the nature of the crime, the police had a huge crime scene, amounting to seventeen locations. Inside Rodger's car, the police recovered the three handguns he had purchased, and in a backpack inside the car they found the two knives he had used to kill the three men at the apartment. Found lying on the front seat of the car were 548 rounds of ammunition already loaded into pistol magazines. The police also recovered fifty-five shell casings from the bullets Rodger had fired.

Immediately upon viewing Rodger's e-mailed manifesto, his mental health therapist called Rodger's mother, who went to the internet to watch the video her son had uploaded. Alarmed, she called Rodger's father, from whom she was divorced, and, after viewing the video, he jumped into his car and headed for Isla Vista, as did Rodger's mother. As they drove to Isla Vista, both called the police to warn them about Rodger, but it was too late.

Rodger's manifesto bears a striking resemblance to Christopher Harper-Mercer's manifesto in the earlier narrative, as does the video communiqué. Rodger titled his manifesto "My Twisted World: The Story of Elliot Rodger." It was 107,000 words long.

In his video communiqué, Rodger said, "For the last eight years of my life, ever since I hit puberty, I've been forced to endure an existence of loneliness, rejection, and unfulfilled desires all because girls have never been attracted to me. Girls gave their affection, and sex, and love to other men but never to me. I'm twenty-two years old and I'm still a virgin." He also talked about how much he envied sexually active men. "And all of you men," he said in the video, "for living a better life than me, all of you sexually active men, I hate you. I hate all of you."[11]

Rodger then ranted about how he had never even kissed a girl, and that it just wasn't fair. He claimed that he was the "supreme gentleman" and that he would punish those who had rejected him.

In his written manifesto, Rodger went on a tirade about interracial dating, and how his being half Asian made his life more difficult than if he had been fully white. He wrote: "How could an inferior, ugly black boy be able to get a white girl and not me? I am beautiful and I am half white myself. I am descended from British aristocracy. He is descended from slaves."

In his writing Rodger also told of his hatred of Asian men. He wrote: "Full Asian men are disgustingly ugly and white girls would never go for you." He then went on a racist tirade against Asians and ended with, "I suggest you jump off a bridge." [12] This part of his manifesto obviously presents a motive for killing the three men at his apartment, all of whom were Asian. Also, he said that he had come to hate the three men because he found out that they had lost their virginity years before.

As part of his revenge for never having had a girlfriend, and for "starving him of sex," Rodger declared in his manifesto that he would wage a "war on women." He decided that his revenge would start at the hottest sorority at the University of California–Santa Barbara. Apparently Rodger thought this was the Alpha Phi sorority. He said, "I will slaughter every single spoiled, stuck-up, blond slut I see inside there. All those girls I've desired so much." [13]

In his writing Rodger also ranted about his vision for a perfect world. In it, all women would be rounded up and put into concentration camps, where the majority would be starved to death. A few would be spared for procreation. As is obvious, much of Rodger's anger centered on his sexual frustration at not being able to connect with females.

Some of Rodger's problems also came about because he felt so socially intimidated and isolated that he withdrew into a fantasy world where he saw himself as standing above the human race, a superior being. In his manifesto he wrote, "I am more than human. I am superior to them all. I am Elliot Rodger. . . . Magnificent, glorious, supreme, eminent. . . . Divine! I am the closest thing there is to a living god." [14]

Interestingly, while Rodger blamed everyone else for his loneliness and rejection, he didn't see any of it as his own fault. A number of people said that they tried to be friends with Rodger, but that he rejected their attempts. A family friend once tried to help Rodger in his interaction with women by giving him a few tips on how to meet them, compliment them, and strike up a conversation with them. Rodger rejected all of this advice because he said he thought that women ought to compliment him.

As more evidence of his lack of self-blame, Rodger wrote in his manifesto about an incident that occurred in July 2013. Apparently feeling rejected by several girls at a party, he tried to push them off a ten-foot-high wall. He failed, and several boys at the party instead threw him off the wall. Hurting his ankle severely, Rodger tried to get away, but then returned to the party to retrieve a pair of expensive sunglasses. The boys who had thrown him off the wall saw him return and dragged him out to the parking lot and beat him. Rodger swore that he was going to kill the boys who assaulted him but attribted no blame to himself for trying to shove the girls off the wall.

"Rodger simply could not accept that his personal shortcomings were responsible for his failures; he could only project the blame onto women," says Dr. Peter Langman in an article in the *Journal of Campus Behavioral Intervention*.[15]

Unfortunately, after Rodger's mass murder, many men in his situation began to see him as a hero. Alek Minassian, who committed a mass murder in Toronto in April 2018, posted on Facebook before his attack, "The Incel Rebellion has already begun! We will overthrow all the Chads and Stacys! All hail the Supreme Gentleman Elliot Rodger!"[16] The word *incel* stands for "involuntary celibate."

Scott Paul Beierle, who killed two women and injured four others at a yoga studio in Tallahassee, Florida, in November 2018, posted online, "I'd like to send a message now to the adolescent males . . . that are in the position, the situation, the disposition of Elliot Rodger, of not getting any, no love, no nothing."[17]

In addition, a number of websites devoted to those suffering from involuntary celibacy highly praise Rodger and blame women, not him, for his mass murder. One of these sites says, "All violence, random attacks, and terrorism are done by men who cannot find GFs [girlfriends], and thus women are DIRECTLY responsible for all of it. The ONLY way to fix this problem is to take away women's rights and adopt a system of equal distribution of women."[18]

Thousands and thousands of people visit these websites every day. This is not to say that all these people are going to become mass murderers, but still it is rather frightening to see these people blaming women for their own problems. It's also frightening to know that among these thousands of people a few could be thinking about copycatting Rodger.

A number of people have studied the writings of mass murderers and find the thinking and logic of the writers to be frightening, especially because they intend to act out their anger against groups they feel have wronged them. "Mass murderers who leave diaries or Internet entries leave clues to their thinking, and it's very disturbing," said Professor Don Dutton of the University of British Columbia in an interview. "It shows a lifelong sense of grievance and perceived injustice, and often generalizes to current groups who may have only incidental contact with the perpetrator, but who serve a huge symbolic significance."[19]

This lifelong sense of grievance often figures prominently in written communiqués and manifestos to explain why individuals felt they had been forced into committing a mass murder. For example, sixteen-year-old Luke Woodham, on the morning of October 1, 1997, stabbed and beat his mother, fifty-year-old Mary Anne Woodham, to death. He then drove his mother's car to Pearl High School in Pearl, Mississippi, wearing a long trench coat to hide the Marlin 30-30 rifle he carried. He entered the school, where he shot and killed seventeen-year-old Lydia Kay Dew and sixteen-year-old Christina Menefee. Woodham had previously dated Christina, but she had broken up with him. He also wounded seven others during the gunfire.

In the manifesto he left behind, Woodham wrote, "I am not insane! I am angry. This world has shit on me for the final time. . . . I killed because people like me are mistreated every day."[20] Later in his manifesto he wrote, "It was not a cry for attention, it was not a cry for help. It was a scream in sheer agony, saying that if I can't pry your eyes open, if I can't do it through pacifism, if I can't show you through displaying of intelligence, then I'll do it with a bullet."[21]

Interestingly, this attitude from Woodham was not just a recent development. He had felt this way for a long time. In a writing assignment for school two years before the mass murder, he had been asked to assume the role of his teacher and tell what he would do with his day. Part of the assignment he handed in read, "Then I would go crazy and kill all of the other teachers. Then I would slowly and very painfully torture all of the principals to death."[22]

On the day of the mass shooting, Joel Myrick, an assistant principal at Pearl High School, heard Woodham's gunfire coming from the school commons. He ran to his truck, where he kept a Colt .45 caliber pistol. Racing back to the school commons, he confronted Woodham, who saw the gun in the assistant principal's hand, ran and jumped into his mother's car, and tried to get away. Myrick chased Woodham and confronted him with the pistol after Woodham's car spun out of control and got stuck. Woodham surrendered, and Myrick held him at gunpoint until the police arrived. Woodham presently resides in the Mississippi State Penitentiary, where he is serving a life sentence.

Eric Harris and Dylan Klebold, the two young men who committed the mass murder at Columbine High School, both left behind lengthy journals and other writings detailing their innermost feelings about how they saw the world. Anyone reading these before the Columbine High School mass murder should have been alarmed enough to intervene. For example, Harris wrote, "You all better fucking hide in your houses because I'm coming for EVERYONE soon, and I WILL be armed to the fucking teeth and I WILL shoot to kill and I WILL fucking KILL EVERYTHING!" Later, he wrote, "But before I leave this worthless place, I will kill whoever I deem unfit for anything at all."[23]

Demonstrating his pathological narcissism, Harris wrote, "My belief is that if I say something, it goes. I am the law. If you don't like it, you die." In addition, he wrote, "I am fucking armed. I feel more confident, stronger, more God-like."[24] Harris additionally complained in his journal about his inability to "get any sex" and how much he hated pretty, stuck-up girls. He also wrote that he hated the other students at his school who appeared to have money. Harris additionally devoted a section in his writing to his fantasies about rape and sadism, describing in detail how he would brutalize any woman he could trick into being alone with him. He also ranted about his dislike of gays and blacks.

Toward the end of his writings, Harris talked about the preparations he and Klebold had been making for the mass murder at Columbine High School. He told about obtaining the guns and ammunition they would use. He also wrote about their plans to leave bombs all around the campus. There were no hesitations, no misgivings in Harris's writings. He didn't seem to have any second thoughts or concerns. He appeared determined to commit the mass murder.

Klebold's writings, on the other hand, dealt a lot with his depression, his insecurities, and how much everything in the world was against him. He wrote, "I don't fit in here. Suicide gives me hope that I'll be in my place wherever I go after this life." He also wrote, "The routine is still monotonous, go to school, be scared and nervous, hoping that people can accept me."[25]

Not having a girlfriend also deeply upset Klebold. In one part of his writing he told about meeting a girl and how much he was in love with her. However, she apparently didn't share those emotions, and Klebold was devastated and wrote, "Oooh god I want to die sooo bad . . . such a sad, desolate, lonely, unsalvageable [life]. . . . Not fair, NOT FAIR! I wanted happiness! I never got it." He added, "I have no happiness, no ambitions, no friends, and no LOVE!" Klebold then wrote repeatedly about getting a gun and killing himself.

After the failed attempt at romance, Klebold's thoughts began turning to mass murder. He wrote, "Will get me a gun, I'll go on my killing spree against anyone I want."[26] Klebold began to see mass murder as the only solution. He would have to die if he went through with it. It was the only outcome possible.

Sexual frustration, pathological narcissism, and social isolation, however, are not the only factors driving mass murderers who leave manifestos behind. Life failure can often be a factor. Forty-one-year-old Robert Flores was a licensed practical nurse, but he wanted to be a registered nurse, so he signed up at the University of Arizona's Nursing School in Tucson. However, he eventually found himself flunking out. But that wasn't the only negative thing happening in his life. Flores's wife had divorced him and taken the children; he had also taken out large student loans that he couldn't make payments on, and he had fallen behind on his child support and other bills. All these problems pushed Flores into a deep depressive state that manifested itself as anger.

"He came across as very aggressive and mean and seemed to have a lot of issues with being angry," said Lori Schenkel, a fellow nursing student.[27]

One of the reasons Flores found himself flunking out of nursing school was that he had a habit of falling asleep during his clinical training. In addition, he apparently wanted attention in class. He would constantly raise his hand and then ask the instructors inappropriate questions. According to other students, he also enjoyed challenging his professors in class. Following numerous complaints from his professors, Flores was counseled about his behavior at school several times, but he wouldn't change.

Once Flores received the official notification that he was flunking out of nursing school, he realized that all his other problems were just going to become worse because now he wouldn't be able to find work that paid enough to cover all his bills and expenses. He decided to end it all.

At around 8:30 a.m. on October 28, 2002, Flores walked into the College of Nursing carrying five handguns and 200 rounds of ammunition. He headed up to the second-floor office of fifty-year-old professor Robin Rogers, where he shot and killed her. Following this, he went up to the fourth floor, where two more of his professors were teaching a class. In the classroom, he confronted forty-four-year-old Cheryl McGaffic, who taught ethics.

He told McGaffic "he was going to give her a lesson in spirituality," said one of the students in the class.[28]

Flores shot her twice in the chest and then walked over and fired a shot into her head, killing her. The other professor, forty-five-year-old Barbara Monroe, had hidden behind a desk. Flores walked over and asked her if she was ready to meet God, then shot her three times, killing her.

The students in the classroom, of course, cowered in fear, figuring that they would be next. Reportedly, Flores pointed to two students and called them by name. He told them they could leave. The remaining students figured that this meant he was going to kill the rest of them. If that had been Flores's plan, he apparently reconsidered. After the two students had left, he put one of the handguns up to his head and pulled the trigger, killing himself.

The day before the mass murder at the nursing school, Flores had mailed a letter to the *Arizona Daily Star* newspaper. In the envelope, the people at the newspaper found a twenty-two-page letter from Flores titled "Communication from the Dead."

The letter turned out to be Flores's last communiqué; in it he tried to tell his side of why he committed the mass murder. As might be expected, most of the letter consisted of Flores trying to justify what he did, along with his explanation of why he was flunking out of nursing school. Nowhere in the letter did Flores take any of the blame for what happened. For example, in response to his being counseled several times about inappropriate questions, he said he simply saw himself as an inquisitive student who wanted to ask questions in class to clarify the subject being discussed. He didn't see his questions as being hostile or inappropriate. However, other students in his class said that his questions and comments were almost always either highly inappropriate or aggressive. Flores, of course, didn't see it that way. Once when the professor wouldn't recognize his raised hand he got up and left the class and went to the assistant dean of students' office to complain about the teacher. In his letter, Flores also talked about a time when a professor finally called on him after he had had his hand raised for ten minutes. "When she finally called upon me I stated that I would appreciate her calling upon me before she change [sic] the subject as I felt I could add something to the class."[29]

Flores also had the habit of falling asleep during important parts of his schooling. In his letter, he blamed this behavior on how strenuous and time-consuming the schoolwork was, along with his need for employment outside of school. Apparently he felt that, because of his life situation, he should receive special consideration from the school. But he didn't get it, and instead he received notification that he was flunking out. This notification then set his plans for mass murder into action.

"The College of Nursing has burned all caring from my being," he wrote in the letter. "I find no joy in the future." Later in the letter he wrote about why he was going to commit the mass murder. "I guess what it is about is that it is a reckoning. A settling of accounts. The university is filled with too many people who are filled with hubris. They feel untouchable. Students are not given respect nor regard."[30]

As with most of the manifestos and communiqués from mass murderers, Flores saw none of the blame for the situation as coming from himself. It was other people who had it in for him. He was totally innocent.

* * *

Charles Joseph Whitman, the twenty-two-year-old University of Texas student who became infamous as the Texas Tower Sniper, killed sixteen people and wounded thirty-one others. He too left behind communiqués attempting to explain his behavior. And like Robert Flores above, he didn't see himself as doing anything wrong. For example, before he climbed up to the top of the clock tower on the campus of the University of Texas–Austin, he stabbed his mother and his wife to death. However, he didn't see this as evil or bad. He saw it as a good thing.

In a letter addressed to "Whom It May Concern," Whitman wrote, "I have just taken my mother's life." He then wrote a paragraph about what a miserable person his father was, how badly he had treated his mother, and how he had made her suffer. His father apparently was a physical and emotional abuser. At the bottom of the letter Whitman wrote, "I am truly sorry that this is the only way I could see to relieve her sufferings, but I think it was best."[31] Interestingly though, Whitman's parents at this time had been separated for several months, and his mother didn't have contact with his father.

After stabbing his wife to death, Whitman left another letter. "It was after much thought that I decided to kill my wife, Kathy, tonight after I pick her up from work at the telephone company," he wrote. "I love her dearly, and she has been as fine a wife to me as any man could ever hope to have." Explaining the reason he decided to kill her, Whitman wrote, "At this time, though, the prominent reason in my mind is that I truly do not consider this world worth living in, and am prepared to die, and I do not want to leave her to suffer alone in it."[32]

Nowhere in his communiqués did Whitman express guilt for his actions. He also didn't even consider the possibility that the two women may have very much wanted to live. Like many other mass murderers, Whitman had a god complex and felt that he should be the one to decide who lives and who dies.

A team led by Professor Don G. Dutton of the University of British Columbia in Vancouver studied the writings of a small group of mass murderers. They found that the mass murderers suffered from extreme paranoia. The subjects they studied seemed to be obsessed with a group that had rejected them, even though the mass murderers saw the group as superficial and receiving benefits they didn't deserve.

"They become and remain fixated and obsessed with rejection by what they see as an elite in-group, whom they see as having unfairly achieved success," says the study. "Instead of transcending the rejection, they formulate plans to annihilate the transgressors, which they justify as vengeance for the transgressions made against them."

The authors of the study also concluded, "[Such people are] thin-skinned or hypersensitive to perceived slights [and they] have closed information processing systems that preclude corrective information which is inconsistent with their worldview from being received."[33]

Another study of the writings of mass murderers concluded, "Common themes within mass killers' manifestos included envy, entitlement, paranoia, revenge, hopelessness, and revenge." This study also makes another very important observation: "In addition, verbalizing one's violent intentions in some ways makes them real, increasing their likelihood of occurrence."[34]

However, a more important observation of this study, and the reason for this chapter, is that "multiple acts of mass murder have been prevented because people reported hearing or observing oral or written threats of violence. In examining 57 cases of threatened or attempted mass murder in the United States, [another researcher] found manifestos were prevalent among would-be offenders who made threats deemed highly credible."

And since researchers have found that there is often leakage (letting others know of the intention to commit mass murder, often expressed through communiqués and manifestos) from potential mass murderers, these bits of information should never be ignored, but rather acted upon immediately. This action can stop mass murderers and save lives.

However, the police must eventually deal with those mass murderers who are not stopped. As stated in the first chapter of this book, mass murders have been increasing in number over the last few decades. Consequently, police departments have had to devise new ways to resolve these incidents. As we will see in the next chapter, police departments have often struggled to develop the necessary strategies and tactical plans for dealing successfully with mass murders.

8

POLICE RESPONSE TO MASS MURDER SCENES

Seventeen people died and seventeen were wounded. That was the toll at Marjory Stoneman Douglas High School in Parkland, Florida, on February 14, 2018. And unfortunately, as we will see, this toll didn't have to be that high, and it likely only was because the staff and police response to an active shooter at the school turned out to be much less than exceptional.

At 2:19 p.m. on February 14, nineteen-year-old Nikolas Cruz, who had taken an Uber, got out of his ride at the high school campus in Parkland, an upscale community about thirty miles north-northwest of Fort Lauderdale. He carried a backpack and a rifle bag. A baseball coach acting as a security monitor had been unlocking the campus gates in preparation for school dismissal when he saw Cruz walk through one of the gates carrying the rifle bag. The security monitor recognized Cruz as a person who had been identified as a threat to the campus. He immediately radioed to another staff member that he saw Cruz heading toward Building 12, a three-story building that usually housed about 900 students, but neither person ordered a Code Red lockdown. The staff member the security monitor had radioed saw Cruz inside Building 12 going into a stairwell. A few moments later, a freshman at the high school encountered Cruz in the first-floor stairwell as he was loading an assault rifle. Cruz warned the student to leave because things were going to get crazy. The freshman ran from the building and informed a staff member that a person with a gun was in Building 12, but still no one called a Code Red lockdown.

Cruz came out of the stairwell and back onto the first floor, where he shot and killed three students in the hallway. Upon hearing the gunfire, the staff member who had seen Cruz going into the stairwell raced up to the second floor and hid in a janitor's closet. Although possessing a radio, he still didn't call for a Code Red lockdown. Cruz continued walking along the first-floor hallway, not entering any of the classrooms but simply shooting at anyone he could see through the windows in the doors, killing six more students. He also shot and killed two staff members who confronted him on the first floor.

The first call to 911 came in a minute after the shooting started. The 911 operator could hear gunfire in the background and immediately notified all nearby officers. Either Cruz tripped the fire alarm or the smoke from the gunfire did, and because no Code Red lockdown had been implemented, the students started coming out of the classrooms to leave the building, as is required if the fire alarm goes off.

The high school had an armed Broward County sheriff's deputy on campus who acted as the school resource officer. Two minutes after the shooting started, he arrived at Building 12, drew his service weapon, but didn't enter the building. On his police radio he reported hearing possible gunfire coming from inside Building 12.

Meanwhile, Cruz, after killing eleven people and wounding thirteen others on the first floor, went up the stairs to the second floor but found the hallway empty. Several of the teachers, hearing the gunfire, had taken the precaution of covering the windows in the doors to their classrooms, and also moving the students out of the line of fire. While Cruz fired the assault rifle into several of the classrooms, he didn't hit anyone. During this time, the school resource officer still didn't enter the building, but instead radioed that a nearby intersection should be closed off.

Moving up to the third floor, Cruz found plenty of targets. Students leaving the building because of the fire alarm filled the hallways, and Cruz began shooting at them. At about this time, a sheriff's sergeant arrived at the campus. However, rather than heading for Building 12, he stopped far away and began blocking traffic. Also, after several minutes of gunfire, a Code Red lockdown was finally activated.

After killing six people and wounding four others on the third floor, Cruz moved into the teachers' lounge. He intended to shoot through the windows at the students and staff fleeing the building below. However, the windows, he found, were made of hurricane glass and the bullets wouldn't penetrate them.

Still no armed police officers had entered Building 12, but rather stayed outside. Four additional sheriff's deputies had arrived at the campus, but they stopped well north of Building 12. They could hear Cruz trying to shoot through the hurricane glass, but rather than heading toward the sound of the gunfire, they stayed near their police cars. The training the deputies had received taught them that they should get to the shooting site as quickly as possible and stop the shooter, by deadly force if necessary. But none of the deputies did. Later it was found that the sheriff of Broward County had amended the active shooter policy to give officers a choice of whether or not to confront an active shooter. All of the deputies could hear the gunfire, but none of them headed for Building 12. Instead, one of the deputies got on the air and told the others to stay at least 500 feet from Building 12.

A sheriff's captain arrived at the scene several minutes after the shooting ceased. She didn't set up a command post, but after seven or eight minutes in the school's administration building, she headed for Building 12 and took cover behind a car with other deputies. A command post wouldn't be set up for another thirty minutes. The captain ordered the deputies to establish a perimeter around the building but not to enter it. A sheriff's lieutenant would eventually arrive at the scene and take over command because he said the captain had a "dream-like" nature to her speech and "was not engaged with the problem."[1]

Several minutes after the shooting stopped, and believing that the shooter was still in the building, four Coral Springs police officers entered Building 12 looking for the shooter. They would later say that their training told them they should go in and confront the shooter.

Coral Springs officer Raymond Kerner would later say, "Basically, what we're trained to do is just get right to the threat as quick as possible and take out the threat because every time you hear a shot go off it could potentially be a kid getting killed or anybody getting killed for that matter."[2]

The Coral Springs officers, while clearing the building, eventually made it up to the third floor. There they found a bulletproof vest and an assault rifle that Cruz had dropped. The reason Cruz stopped shooting after six minutes of firing at helpless students and staff, unimpeded by any law enforcement officers, was reportedly because he found that the assault rifle he used had jammed. So he simply dropped it and his bulletproof vest in the third-floor hallway and joined the students fleeing the building. He left the campus unimpeded. The police would later find not only the gun and bulletproof vest but also a number of empty bullet magazines with swastikas carved on them.

Cruz, apparently surprised that he got away, and seemingly having no plan for what to do afterward, walked to a nearby mall and purchased a soft drink, then visited a nearby McDonald's and hung around there until 3:00 p.m. After he left the McDonald's, Cruz walked to nearby Coral Springs, Florida, where at 3:40 p.m. a Coconut Creek police officer stopped and arrested him. Security video from the high school, along with multiple eyewitnesses, would positively identify Cruz as the shooter, and he would be charged with seventeen counts of first-degree murder and seventeen counts of attempted first-degree murder. The prosecutor later announced that his office would seek the death penalty for Cruz.

Regardless of the less-than-adequate police response to the shooting, there were still heroics that day at Marjory Stoneman Douglas High School—but not from police officers. Cruz shot and killed a geography teacher, thirty-five-year-old Scott Beigel, after he had unlocked a room for students to hide in.

"I'm alive today because of him," said Kelsey Friend, a freshman at the high school.[3]

Cruz also shot and killed thirty-seven-year-old assistant football coach Aaron Feis as he used his body to shield two students.

"That's Coach Feis," said Colton Haab, a junior at the high school. "He wants to make sure everybody is safe before himself."[4]

The school's athletic director, forty-nine-year-old Chris Hixon, died when he ran toward the gunfire in an attempt to help the students escape the building. Fifteen-year-old Peter Wang, a member of the Junior Reserve Officers' Training Corps, held a door open so that students could quickly flee the building. Cruz spotted him and killed him with fire from the assault rifle. (Wang would later be posthumously admitted to West Point.) Eighteen-year-old Meadow Pollack, although shot four times, used her body to protect fourteen-year-old Cora Loughran. When Cruz saw this, he shot and killed them both. Fifteen-year-old Anthony Borges received five gunshot wounds as he placed himself in front of a door to a classroom containing twenty students. He was attempting to barricade it from the carnage. Anthony would survive his wounds.

Once the shooting had stopped and the building cleared, police detectives took over the case. Looking into Nikolas Cruz's background, investigators found that he had been adopted by a couple who had both died before the mass murder, the mother just a few months prior. Because of this, Cruz had been staying with various family members and friends. The detectives also found that Cruz had previously attended Marjory Stoneman Douglas High School, but that the school had expelled him before he could graduate. He had then enrolled in a GED program. Although Cruz had been part of the Junior Reserve Officers' Training Corps in high school and had received awards from them, he had also had serious disciplinary problems that eventually forced the high school to expel him. While attending the school, Cruz had reportedly made threats against other students, and the school administration had sent an e-mail to the teachers warning them about him.

The detectives discovered that when Cruz was fourteen, psychiatrists had recommended that he be involuntarily admitted to a mental health facility. He had cut himself on both arms and made claims that he intended to buy a gun. Although a number of people agreed with the psychiatrists' recommendation, a state mental health facility disagreed. They said that even though he had cut his arms, he "was at low risk of harming himself or others."[5]

In the following years, Cruz began making online postings that became increasingly disturbing. He posted pictures of himself holding a number of weapons and made racial slurs against blacks, Muslims, gays, Mexicans, and Jews. He also threatened police officers and said that he wanted to copycat the clock tower mass murder of Charles Whitman. Because he had never been admitted to a mental health facility, even though Cruz had obvious mental problems, he could still legally buy the assault rifle he used in the mass murder. A number of students who knew him said that he often talked about weapons and "shooting up establishments."[6]

As might be expected, before the mass murder Nikolas Cruz had come to the attention of law enforcement a number of times. Reportedly, the Broward County Sheriff's Office had received forty-five calls relating to Cruz, including a tip that he intended to shoot up the high school. The detectives investigating the mass murder found that on September 24, 2017, a person using the name Nikolas Cruz commented on YouTube that "Im [sic] going to be a professional school shooter."[7] Although a viewer of these comments reported it to the FBI, amazingly the FBI said that they couldn't track down whoever this Nikolas Cruz was who made the comment. Later, a month or so before the mass murder, the FBI received another warning about Cruz. The FBI would, after the mass murder, release a statement about this tip that said, "The caller provided information about Cruz's gun ownership, desire to kill people, erratic behavior, and disturbing social media posts, as well as the potential of him conducting a school shooting."[8] For some reason, according to the FBI, this information died with the tip line and never made it to the FBI's Miami office.

The fallout over the poor police response at Marjory Stoneman Douglas High School went beyond just the retirement of the Broward County Sheriff's Office resource officer and the resignation of the sheriff's captain who came to the scene. On January 11, 2019, Florida governor Ron DeSantis suspended Broward County Sheriff Scott Israel from his job because of his department's lack of action at the high school. The governor appointed a former Coral Springs police officer to take over the sheriff's position. The governor said that Sheriff Israel "has repeatedly failed and has demonstrated a pattern of poor leadership."[9]

The *South Florida Sun Sentinel* printed a detailed analysis of the police response to the Marjory Stoneman Douglas High School mass murder. They concluded, "A gunman with an AR-15 fired the bullets, but a series of blunders, bad policies, sketchy training, and poor leadership helped him succeed. Information reported over 10 months by the *South Florida Sun Sentinel* reveals 58 minutes of chaos on campus marked by no one taking charge, deputies dawdling, false information spreading, communications paralyzed, and children stranded with nowhere to hide."[10]

✤ ✤ ✤

Obviously, the police response to the mass murder at Marjory Stoneman Douglas High School was terribly flawed. The first armed police officer arriving on the scene but then failing to enter the building to confront the shooter likely cost lives. Of course, the idea of entering a building and confronting an armed adversary who has demonstrated a willingness to kill is certainly frightening. As a police officer for thirty-eight years, I can attest to that. But police officers have a sworn duty to protect the public, and that duty includes taking part in frightening situations and putting ourselves in harm's way. We don't have the luxury of "opting out."

A public safety commission set up to look into what caused all the mishaps at the high school had some harsh things to say about the response of Broward County sheriff's deputies to the mass murder scene. They noted that the law enforcement efforts had been hindered by the school resource officer's inaction. They also criticized the six other deputies who arrived at the scene but didn't take any action against the shooter. They said that a video of the scene showed the deputies taking excessive time, while the shooting was still going on inside Building 12, to change into their tactical gear. Other deputies, the commission said, arrived but stayed by their cars rather than going in after the shooter.

The final report issued by the public safety commission stated, "None of the Broward County Sheriff's deputies immediately responded to the gunshots by entering the campus and seeking out the shooter. Deputy Sheriffs who took the time to retrieve vests from containers in their cruisers, removed certain equipment they were wearing so that they could put on their vests, and then replaced the equipment they had removed all while shots were being fired, or had been recently fired, is unacceptable and contrary to accepted protocol."[11] The report also added, "Other deputies arrived at the road near the school, heard the gunshots, and remained on the road rather than going after the attacker."[12] The report additionally was critical of how law enforcement had ignored the many warnings it had received about Cruz. The commission believed that law enforcement should have acted on them.

Also, in September 2018, the Florida Department of Law Enforcement announced that it was conducting a criminal investigation into the actions or inactions of the police officers at the Parkland, Florida, mass murder scene. Pinellas County Sheriff Bob Gualtieri, who is in charge of the investigation, said that the criminal investigation "involves the response and [the school resource officer] and a number of things."

"We do not know what the potential charges could be until the evidence is presented," said Constance Simmons, spokeswoman for the state attorney.[13]

On June 4, 2019, the police arrested school resource officer Scot Peterson and charged him with eleven offenses, including neglect of a child, culpable negligence, and perjury. A criminal trial could have serious ramifications for Mr. Peterson. Under Florida law he could lose his pension if convicted of a felony.

Although the Parkland incident certainly didn't reflect it, the police response nationally to active shooters has changed radically since the Columbine High School mass murder. At that time, the standard police procedure was to secure the scene and wait for the SWAT team officers to arrive and go in. However, after serious review, experts determined that this could easily cost the lives of people still inside the crime scene; it might take precious minutes before the SWAT team could arrive. Following Columbine, police officers started being trained to forget about waiting for SWAT if the shooting was still going on, and instead to enter the crime scene and neutralize the suspect, by deadly force if necessary.

The aftermath of the Columbine High School mass murder inspired the creation of the Advanced Law Enforcement Rapid Response Training (ALERRT) Center. The ALERRT Center was formed in 2002 as a joint effort between Texas State University and two local police departments. In the years since then it has grown tremendously. The center has now trained more than 130,000 law enforcement officers and has partnered with the FBI, whose agents both teach and train there. "We teach that the first priority when you come on the scene is to stop the killing," said Pete Blair, executive director of the ALERRT Center at Texas State University. "The number one driving force is gunfire. If there's gunfire, we teach the officers to isolate, distract, and neutralize. We want [officers] to go directly to the sounds of the gunfire."[14]

James Gagliano, a retired member of the FBI's Hostage Rescue Team, agrees. "You're going to the sounds of the guns. The No. 1 goal is to interdict the shooter or shooters." He added that previously the police would enter a building and clear one room at a time, but now the emphasis is on getting to the shooters quickly and stopping them. This is a tactic known as "rapid deployment."[15]

* * *

While Columbine and Marjory Stoneman Douglas High Schools were examples of poor police responses to mass murder scenes, there have been a larger number of successful police responses using the new approach. For example, at the Fifth Third Center, Fifth Third Bank's corporate headquarters in downtown Cincinnati, it appeared to be business as usual on the morning of September 6, 2018. People inside the building were conducting their business and nothing looked out of the ordinary. At about ten minutes after nine, a man wearing business attire and carrying a briefcase suddenly pulled out a 9mm semiautomatic pistol and began firing at the people standing in the lobby. Within a minute the first call came in to 911 about the shooting.

The shooter, twenty-nine-year-old Omar Enrique Santa Perez, didn't seem to have any specific targets in mind, but rather shot randomly at anyone he could see. He shot and killed sixty-four-year-old Richard Newcomer, a construction superintendent; forty-eight-year-old Luis Felipe Calderon, an executive at Fifth Third Bank; and twenty-five-year-old Prudhui Raj Kandepi, a computer programmer. He also wounded two women, who would both survive.

Whitney Austin, a product manager at Fifth Third Bank, said she was in the middle of an important conference call on her cell phone that morning as she walked up to the Fifth Third Center building. She said she noticed a spiderweb pattern of broken glass on the revolving door to the bank, along with several people waving frantically for her to stop and not enter the building. But she didn't stop, and instead walked into the lobby. Santa Perez shot her twelve times, and she fell to the floor just inside the revolving door. Miraculously, none of the bullets hit vital organs. Police officers would eventually carry Austin out of the line of fire.

"A bunch of cops were coming in with guns," said Michael Richardson, who witnessed the shooting. "I saw a lady down. A Cincinnati police officer dragged her out of the bank. She was talking. She was bleeding. Her shirt was red."[16]

"There's no logical explanation for why I survived and others didn't," Austin said. "If you survived, you have a responsibility to move forward with your story and do everything you can to make a difference with gun violence."[17]

The police arrived at the scene less than four minutes after the first 911 call. One of the arriving officers had been working on a nearby traffic detail when the gunfire broke out. He got on his radio and advised the dispatcher of his location, then removed his reflective vest and headed to the bank, where he would be joined by other officers. Santa Perez was still shooting when the police got there. Several of the officers rushed into the building's lobby, distracting Santa Perez, while another officer stayed outside and fired his weapon through a plate glass window, striking Santa Perez and killing him. Santa Perez had fired a total of thirty-five rounds, including some at the officers, and had brought another 200 rounds with him in the briefcase. Five minutes after the first 911 call came in, the officers declared the scene safe.

"They did everything we wanted them to do and more," said Lieutenant Colonel Mike John, chief of the Cincinnati Police Department's Investigations Bureau, about the officers' actions.[18]

"The police saved lives," said Cincinnati Mayor John Cranley. "We owe them all a huge debt of gratitude. Trust me: It would have been a lot worse if those officers hadn't rushed in when they did."[19] The Hamilton County Prosecutor's Office would later find the officers' actions totally justifiable.

Investigators who took over the case couldn't find any connection between Santa Perez and Fifth Third Bank. He had filed a lawsuit the previous year against CNBC and Ameritrade. However, a judge dismissed the suit because he said that Santa Perez was obviously delusional. Detectives also discovered that Santa Perez's family had previously appealed to a judge to have Santa Perez involuntarily committed to a mental health facility because of a series of violent outbursts and periods of delusional behavior.

As to Santa Perez's motive, Lieutenant Colonel John said, "There are no red flags. I don't think we'll ever know."[20]

* * *

In another incident, this one in Pittsburgh, at 9:50 a.m. on October 27, 2018, forty-six-year-old Robert Bowers stormed into the Tree of Life Congregation Synagogue. Screaming "All Jews must die!" he fired the AR-15 type assault rifle he carried at the people inside.[21] He had additionally brought along three Glock semi-automatic pistols, which he also fired. Until this moment, Bowers had never come to the attention of the police as a danger to the community.

Bowers first killed two brothers who stood just inside the entrance to the synagogue. Most of the people inside the building heard the gunfire but didn't recognize it for what it was. The first 911 call didn't come in until 9:54 a.m. A minute later, Bowers shot a man coming out of a closet in the basement, then went into the synagogue's kitchen and killed two people there. A physician who heard the gunfire rushed in to see if anyone needed medical attention, and Bowers also shot him.

At 9:57 a.m., Bowers left the basement and went upstairs, where a service had been under way. Several of the people attending the service escaped out a side door, but eight people remained. Bowers killed seven of them and wounded the other.

By 9:59 a.m., the first police officers arrived at the scene and immediately confronted Bowers, who was attempting to leave the building. They exchanged gunfire with him, and Bowers wounded one of the officers in the hand, then ran back inside and up to the third floor. The police officers took up strategic positions to make certain Bowers could not escape and was not a threat to anyone.

When the SWAT team went in after Bowers, he again exchanged gunfire with them, wounding two of the officers, but also getting wounded himself. He had barricaded himself in a room on the third floor of the synagogue but eventually came out and surrendered.

Investigators would later find various racial and anti-Semitic rants on Bowers's social media accounts, including that "Jews are the children of Satan."[22] A few months before the mass murder, Bowers began posting anti-Semitic slurs against the Hebrew Immigrant Aid Society. He had become convinced that the Jewish community was sponsoring the caravans of immigrants coming up from South and Central America. Just before the attack at the synagogue, Bowers posted on social media, "I can't sit by and watch my people get slaughtered. Screw your optics. I'm going in."[23] The *optics* refers to a fight among white nationalists about the most effective way to spread their message.

Bowers would end up facing dozens of charges, in both state and federal court. These charges include murder, aggravated assault, ethnic intimidation, obstructing exercise of religious beliefs, and others. If convicted, he faces either the death penalty or hundreds of years in prison.

"This was the single most lethal and violent attack on the Jewish community in the history of the country," said Jonathan Greenblatt, CEO and national director of the Anti-Defamation League.[24]

In both of these last two incidents the first police officers to arrive at the scene immediately confronted the mass murderer and were able to put an immediate stop to the loss of life. This has been shown to be the most effective way to deal with mass murderers, although of course it takes great bravery on the part of the police. Four officers suffered injuries in the gunfight with the mass murderer at the synagogue.

* * *

Prior to the Texas clock tower sniper incident in 1966, practically no police department in the United States had a SWAT team. There had simply been no need for one. While occasionally an incident would occur where a SWAT team would have been useful, these events didn't occur often enough to justify a specialized unit such as SWAT. In the Texas clock tower incident, Charles Whitman fired from the top of the clock tower down at innocent people on the ground for an hour and a half. Civilians and police officers on the ground fired back at Whitman, but they only succeeded in chipping the sandstone face of the clock tower.

The police knew they had to stop Whitman, that they had to somehow get to the top of the tower and confront him, but no one could approach the tower above ground because Whitman would simply pick them off from above, as he had been doing for ninety minutes. Finally, several officers came up with a plan. They had discovered that there were a series of underground tunnels under the campus and that one of these tunnels ran to the clock tower. The officers used this tunnel, got into the clock tower, went to the top, and shot and killed Whitman.

Following the Texas clock tower incident, which for an hour and a half no one knew how to solve, costing many lives, police departments all across the country realized that they needed to be ready for such incidents and couldn't continue their fly-by-the-seat-of-their-pants approach. Consequently, police departments all across the United States began forming SWAT teams. These were specially trained and equipped police officers who could be called to handle special and highly dangerous incidents such as the Texas clock tower incident.

Therefore in any incident that appeared to need the SWAT team, the standard procedure was for first responding police officers to surround and secure the scene, then wait for the SWAT team to arrive. The SWAT team, with its highly trained and properly equipped officers, would take over and either negotiate a surrender or go into the scene and force one. This procedure seemed to work well for thirty years or so.

However, in the 1999 Columbine High School incident, this procedure failed miserably. The two gunmen killed innocent students and staff while the police waited outside for the SWAT team to arrive. Police departments simply weren't ready for the new norm in American crime: kill as many people as possible in a very short time. This new paradigm made the old SWAT team approach obsolete.

"Active shooter incidents create a time problem for innocent victims and emergency responders trying to save lives," Todd Fletcher, a police officer and firearms instructor at Combative Firearms Training, told me in an interview. "The traditional response of forming perimeters, waiting for other officers, and calling in SWAT no longer applies to active shooter incidents. These murderers intend to terrorize and kill as many people as possible in a short time period. If officers wait even a single minute for additional personnel to arrive, more innocent people will be hurt or killed."[25]

In 2014, Sergeant A. J. DeAndrea, a police team leader at Columbine, spoke about how the old SWAT team concept didn't work there. "We realized that that's not the answer," he said. "Active shooters are now seen as a patrol dilemma. We needed to get resources into that building immediately to stop the threat. That is the biggest lesson from Columbine, and since then we've seen our tactics evolve in ways that are designed to produce a faster response."[26]

As Sergeant DeAndrea pointed out, police departments quickly realized that in order to save lives with this new type of mass murderer they needed to come up with new and different procedures. At first, to face this new threat, police departments used a procedure called Immediate Action Rapid Deployment. Rather than securing the scene and waiting for the SWAT team to arrive, the new procedure was for the first three or four police officers who arrived on the scene to form a team and go in after the mass murderers. However, this, like the SWAT team concept, didn't reduce the loss of life. Although the first police officer at a mass murder scene often arrives while the incident is still going on, most often within a few minutes of the first 911 call, it usually takes several precious minutes more to get a team of police officers there, and many innocent lives can be lost during these precious few minutes.

"Then we started to realize that waiting for four or five people could mean waiting several minutes, so we started authorizing smaller teams to enter," said Pete Blair. "From four to three to two, and now we are in an era where departments authorize a single officer to make entry."[27]

Consequently, police departments have come up with the solo officer plan. This means that the first police officer at the scene of a mass murder that is still ongoing must enter the scene, find the mass murderer or murderers by going toward the sound of gunfire, and then use whatever means necessary to neutralize the threat. Is this dangerous? Of course it is. But it is part of the job police officers are sworn to do and must do if we are to save lives and stop the rise of mass murders.

"Recent instances of mass murder in our society have dictated that policy, tactics, and training for an active shooter incident need to be ongoing and evolve as law enforcement assesses the actions and outcomes of past incidents," Michael Gerard, a former police officer and now police practices and premises security expert at Robson Forensic, said in an interview. "Because active shooter incidents are generally of a short duration, law enforcement must respond and neutralize the threat as quickly as possible. This means it may be necessary for a properly trained lone officer to immediately intervene when such an incident occurs."[28]

What is the level of danger using the solo officer plan? Experience has shown that the appearance of the police at the crime scene often forces the mass murderers, who realize that the killing spree is over, to surrender or commit suicide. Notwithstanding, a number of mass murderers have also shot at the police, so solo officers must be cautious and prepared for that possibility. A study reported in the Police Executive Research Forum's *The Police Response to Active Shooter Incidents* found that in 44 percent of the cases studied the mass murderer either surrendered or committed suicide when confronted by the police, but in 56 percent of the cases the mass murderers resisted and the police had to shoot or physically subdue them. Also, in a third of these cases, officers were wounded.[29]

An important point to make, though, is that the solo officer procedure is only implemented if the killing is still going on. If not, the officer or officers, as they did in the past, are trained to secure the scene and wait for the SWAT team. The solo officer procedure, while dangerous, has nevertheless been deployed successfully a number of times.

For example, on March 20, 2018, a student at Great Mills (Maryland) High School, seventeen-year-old Austin Rollins, came to school carrying a 9mm Glock semiautomatic handgun owned by his father. At 7:50 a.m., he walked through the main entrance to the high school. A few minutes later, he encountered his ex-girlfriend, sixteen-year-old Jaelynn Willey; he shot her in the head, killing her. Fourteen-year-old Desmond Barnes received a gunshot wound to the back of his thigh.

Barnes crawled into a nearby classroom and called 911. "I was just shot in my school," he told the dispatcher. A teacher also called 911. "There's a girl outside my door bleeding on the ground," she reported.[30]

As Rollins continued down the hallway after killing Willey, he suddenly found himself facing Sheriff's Deputy Blaine Gaskill, the school's resource officer, who had not waited but responded to the call of shots fired. He ordered Rollins to drop the gun; when he didn't, but instead raised it to his head, Deputy Gaskill shot Rollins in the hand, but too late. Rollins had time to fire a bullet into his brain. He died later at the hospital.

Several years before this, in Newton, Kansas, thirty-eight-year-old Cedric Larry Ford fired a gun from his car at two other cars, wounding one of the drivers. Ford then headed for US Route 81 and shot at oncoming traffic, causing a car to crash into his. Getting out of his wrecked vehicle, Ford shot the other driver and stole his car.

Using the stolen vehicle, Ford drove to Excel Industries in Hesston, Kansas, where he worked. Armed with an AR-15 type assault rifle, he first shot a woman in the parking lot, then went inside the building and began firing randomly at the workers. Reportedly, more than 200 people occupied the building at the time. Three people would die and fourteen would be wounded during Ford's rampage.

The first police officer to arrive at the scene, Hesston Police Chief Doug Schroeder, entered the building alone looking for the gunman.

When Ford saw Chief Schroeder, he fired the assault rifle at him; the chief returned fire. Ford fell to the ground, mortally wounded. The reason for this mass murder? Ford had been served by a deputy earlier that afternoon with a restraining order forbidding him from having any contact with his ex-girlfriend.

Kansas Governor Sam Brownback would later credit Chief Schroeder's actions and say that he "saved a lot of lives."[31]

In September 2016, this time in St. Cloud, Minnesota, twenty-year-old Dahir Adan went on a rampage at the Crossroads Center Mall. Earlier, he had told his family that he was going out to buy a new iPhone, so no one thought anything of it. At the mall, dressed in a security guard's uniform from a former job, Adan flashed two knives and began stabbing and slashing anyone within reach, injuring ten people. Reportedly, he had been shouting "Allahu Akbar" (God is greatest) and had asked several people if they were of the Muslim faith.

An off-duty Avon, Minnesota, police officer, Jason Falconer, happened to be at the mall shopping for a gift for his son. He said he heard screaming and saw people running from a man in a security guard's uniform. Not worrying about backup, Officer Falconer identified himself as a police officer and approached Adan. Adan asked Falconer if he was a Muslim, and the officer answered no. At that moment, Adan fled into the nearby Macy's store, and Officer Falconer could see the two knives in Adan's hands. He chased after Adan, and, with his weapon drawn, he ordered Adan to drop the knives and get down on the floor. It appeared that Adan was obeying him as he got down on the floor. However, he didn't drop the knives.

"I didn't hear it," Officer Falconer would later say, "but witnesses said he counted down 3, 2, 1 and jumped up and charged at me."[32]

At this point, the officer fired his weapon at Adan, striking him several times. Adan fell to the floor, but after a few moments got back up and again charged at the officer with the knives poised to strike. Officer Falconer shot him several more times, and Adan, shot six times, fell once more to the floor; he would die from his wounds.

In addition to the solo officer procedure, demonstrated so well above, another important change that has developed in the law enforcement response to mass murder scenes concerns the medical treatment of the victims. The first officers on the scene are now trained to bypass any injured victims, no matter how badly injured, and deal with the mass murderer first if the mass murder is still ongoing.

A model policy for active shooter scenes, developed by the International Association of Chiefs of Police, states, "The contact officer or team shall locate the suspect(s) in the most expeditious manner possible in order to stop the threat. In doing so, officers should not stop to render aid or assistance to victims."[33]

This may sound cold and heartless, but if the officers do stop to give aid, more innocent people can become victims of the mass murderer, and of course the officers also stand a good chance of being surprised and killed by the mass murderer while they are attending to a wounded victim. Bypassing wounded people is a very difficult thing to do, particularly if the victims are children or they are pleading for help, but it must be done.

My own police department had an incident that demonstrates the danger of helping the wounded before finding the shooter. The first officer at a shooting scene went into a house, saw a victim bleeding on the floor, and stopped to tend to the victim. The shooter was hiding behind some curtains in the same room; he shot and killed the officer while his attention was drawn to the wounded victim.

On the other hand, Columbine and other mass murders have shown that many of the victims at mass murder scenes need medical attention as soon as possible. Therefore, police departments are now equipping their officers with special medical equipment that can stabilize victims until medical help arrives in the event there are enough officers at a mass murder scene that one of them can stay behind to protect the officer giving aid to a victim. These medical kits contain tourniquets, fast-clotting combat gauze, self-clinging bandages, plastic Halo Seals to go over open chest wounds, and other items needed to stabilize severely injured victims until they can be moved.

Also, as happened at Columbine, for years EMS personnel were not allowed into a mass murder scene until the police were positive that no threats remained and an "all clear" had been given. This practice has led to many unnecessary deaths of victims who needed immediate medical attention. Consequently, another new development in the response to mass murder scenes, called Rescue Task Force, has been implemented. EMS personnel equipped with ballistic helmets and bulletproof vests are now being trained on how to enter a "warm zone" and assist victims. A "warm zone" is an area where there is not an active threat, but there is still danger elsewhere at the mass murder scene. EMS personnel, with a police escort, can then administer life-saving aid and also transport those victims who need to be at a medical facility as soon as possible.

As can be seen in almost all of the incidents in this book, even if the police receive notification immediately about a mass murder in progress and respond quickly to the scene, there is still usually a four- or five-minute gap before they can arrive and do anything to help the victims. Many things can happen and many people can die during these four or five minutes. This is just a fact. Consequently, people finding themselves caught up in a potential mass murder situation can't just wait and hope that the police will rescue them. They must take action on their own if they want to be certain to survive. As we will see in the next chapter, individuals caught up in such situations are not powerless; they have a number of life-saving options.

9

HOW TO SPOT AND SURVIVE A MASS MURDER

It was a little after 9:00 p.m. on April 4, 1991, and the Asian youths gave ice-tinged smiles to the two groups of hostages that sat tied up in front of them. One of the young men then flipped a quarter into the air.

"[They] then began to flip coins deciding which persons were going to be shot first," says Sacramento County Sheriff Glen Craig.[1]

The two groups were forty hostages, all of whom sat around in the appliance store showroom tied up in bunches of three and four. The hostages watched in terror waiting to see which of the two groups was going to die first. They knew that the young men were deadly serious. The four Asian men who had taken them captive had already shot two of the hostages. It all seemed like a nightmare—a nightmare that had now been going on for almost eight hours—eight hours that seemed to have stretched into an eternity. But they all feared it was about to come to a gruesome end, likely for all of them. The police had rejected the hostage takers' demands, so something very bad seemed almost certain to happen.

Earlier, at around 1:30 p.m., the Good Guys Electronics Store, located in the Florin Mall in Sacramento, California's south side, had been buzzing with business. Customers were spread out all over the huge store looking at the merchandise and picking out purchases.

All at once, four Asian youths, ranging in age from seventeen to twenty-one, burst into the store and, armed with three pistols and a shotgun, started firing their weapons into the ceiling. Most of the people in the store froze in shock, and before they could recover, the four men began rounding them up and herding them into a group at the front of the store. However, because Good Guys Electronics was such a huge store, several people managed to slip out during the first moments of gunfire. They immediately called 911 and reported what had happened. The Asian youths positioned the hostages in front of the large glass entry doors to discourage an assault by the police from that direction.

Uniformed police officers arrived quickly, and since no more gunfire had taken place and no hostages had been harmed, they surrounded the building and called for the SWAT team. Within thirty minutes, the SWAT team had set up a command post in a nearby bank and had positioned several snipers who had a clear view of the front of the showroom, where the gunmen and hostages were. Since no one had been shot, and at the moment it didn't appear anyone was in grave danger of being shot, the SWAT team's hostage negotiators attempted to start a dialogue with the four hostage takers to see if they could negotiate a peaceful surrender. While this was going on, the officers in the command post began talking with the customers who had escaped, trying to get an idea of how many hostage takers there were and what kinds of weapons they carried. The officers also interviewed a store manager; he got them a floor plan of the building.

A serious problem with the news media quickly developed, however. A whole wall of the store contained television sets, and they were now showing live broadcasts of the area and the police movement around it. The SWAT team commander persuaded the press to limit their on-air coverage to the front of the store only, so that the hostage takers couldn't gain intelligence about what the police were doing.

The SWAT team, while the hostage negotiators talked with the hostage takers, began formulating a plan to storm the business and rescue the hostages if it suddenly became necessary. What the police didn't know at that point was that this wasn't just a robbery gone wrong, as everyone thought. Rather, it was a planned hostage taking. But even so, it wasn't an ordinary hostage taking. The four young Asian men didn't have any serious demands, as most hostage takers do. There were no estranged spouses or lovers to bring to the scene. There were no former bosses to demand an apology from. The four had become hostage takers because they believed it would make them media stars.

"[The gunmen] went there with the idea of taking hostages," said Sheriff Craig.[2] "They were attempting to gain notoriety."[3]

After a bit of intelligence gathering, the SWAT team commander became even more worried about the possible outcome of the event. The four young men, the police discovered, belonged to a street gang known as the Oriental Boys. The members of this gang had a reputation for being extremely vicious and had no problem spilling blood.

The hostage negotiators also soon began to fear for the lives of the hostages because the demands of the hostage takers didn't appear to be serious or reasonable. At first, they demanded $4 million in cash, then various firearms (a completely nonnegotiable item), a fifty-passenger helicopter, and even some 1,000-year-old ginger root. Following this, the demands became even more bizarre. The four talked about wanting to be flown to Southeast Asia, where they would fight the Vietcong.

Since the negotiations didn't seem to be going anywhere, the SWAT team began finalizing a rescue plan for the hostages. Examining the floor plan given to them by the store manager, they found that they could slip into the building undetected through a freight door in the back. Seven members of the SWAT team did so, and after moving silently down an inside hallway, they found themselves at a door that led to a storeroom for the electronics store.

After slipping into the storeroom and wanting to know what was happening in the showroom where the hostages were being held, the SWAT officers inserted a pinhole camera into a wall that looked toward the showroom. They could see that the door leading out of the store-room had been blocked with large boxes, but that two metal roll-up windows on either side of the door were clear. The SWAT officers decided that these windows would be their entry points into the show-room if the SWAT team commander decided an assault had become necessary.

During the time the SWAT team was setting up, the hostage nego-tiators had managed to gain the release of several hostages for the promise of four bulletproof vests. However, the police had only given them one vest so far. Consequently, the four hostage takers decided to send a hostage out with their demands. The hostage takers selected a store employee as the person who would give the police their demands. They told the employee that they would let him go if he'd promise to give a message to the police. But it wasn't going to be that easy. First, they told him, they were going to have to shoot him in the leg.

Seeing that this was his best option to get out of the store alive, the store employee reluctantly agreed. One of the hostage takers then shot him in the leg and forced him to crawl out the front door and over to the police line.

"They want three bulletproof vests, a helicopter, and firearms," the store employee told the police. "That's it. That's all they want."[4]

Apparently not happy with the length of time it was taking for the police to respond, the hostage takers decided that they needed to shoot another hostage to show the police how serious they were. The four turned and looked at the hostages, who all cringed and tried not to meet their eyes. At this moment, one of the hostages began having a diabetic attack.

The four hostage takers laughed among themselves. "Well, it looks like he has just decided who is going to be our next person to be shot," one of them said.[5] They then shot the hostage in the leg and threw him out the front door.

After the second shooting, the SWAT team commander decided that an armed assault on the hostage takers appeared to be the best option. The four hostage takers were obviously unstable and had no qualms about shooting the hostages. A wholesale slaughter, the commander knew, could suddenly erupt, and it would be too late to do anything to save the hostages. The plan they decided upon involved coordinating the surprise entry into the showroom with shots from the snipers the SWAT team had positioned. What the police didn't know at that moment was that since the hostage takers had not yet received any of their demands other than one bulletproof vest, they decided that they needed to up their game and, rather than shoot one of the hostages in the leg, kill one of them. The hostage takers decided that a coin flip would pick the victim.

However, just as one of them flipped the coin, the police dropped off another bulletproof vest in front of the store. The SWAT team hoped that one of the hostage takers would expose himself to get it. The snipers would then take him out, and the assault team in the storeroom would burst out into the showroom. The hostage takers, though, didn't go out to get the vest. Instead, they tied a long tether to a female hostage and sent her out to retrieve it. One of the hostage takers held the door open for her as she went out to get the bulletproof vest, exposing himself to the snipers as he did so. A sniper took the shot. But at that instant, for some reason, the hostage taker let the door shut and the sniper's bullet smashed into the door frame instead.

The hostage takers, at first stunned and then infuriated, turned to the hostages, and one of them began shooting at the hostages with a shotgun. At the same moment the sniper fired, the SWAT officers in the storeroom charged out and split into teams. The first hostage taker the SWAT team encountered would be the one shooting at the hostages with the shotgun. They quickly killed him. The SWAT officers were using weapons equipped with sound suppressors, so even though the other hostage takers saw their comrade fall, they didn't know where the shots had come from. One of the hostage takers ran directly into the line of fire of the SWAT officers, and they also shot him. Within a few seconds the other two hostage takers also fell to the floor, shot. Three of the hostage takers died at the scene, and the other, though critically injured, lived to be sentenced to multiple life terms in prison.

※ ※ ※

Fortunately, the SWAT assault team had entered quickly enough that the hostage takers had only managed to kill three of the hostages before being shot themselves. However, rather than seeing this as a victory, the police came under heavy public criticism because they didn't save everyone. Of course, it is possible that had the sniper hit his mark there would have been enough confusion among the hostage takers that the SWAT assault team could have lessened the death count among the hostages. But it didn't happen that way, and much of the public felt that the police had let them down.

The sister of one of the deceased hostages complained that she didn't think the police coming out of the storeroom had acted quickly enough. "If they had rushed, my brother wouldn't be dead now," she told the *Los Angeles Times*.[6] But SWAT team members are specifically trained not to just rush into a scene willy-nilly, shooting their guns in a "spray and pray" action. They are trained to go forward as a unit, identify a threat, and only then to shoot. To do otherwise is to invite disaster.

The Sacramento County sheriff, Glen Craig, answered the public criticism of his department's actions. He told the press that he felt they had made the right decision under the circumstances, and that if they hadn't moved in when they did, many more people would have died.

The problem with this incident is that the public only saw the three hostages killed, not the thirty-seven saved. This was actually an excellent police action that prevented what could have been a massive tragedy. If the same incident happened today, the police would likely follow the same procedures. What the public forgets is that in these types of incidents the people the police are dealing with are desperate, extremely dangerous, and occasionally delusional. There is no way to guarantee a 100 percent perfect ending. Unfortunately, the police often find that the public is conditioned by television and the movies, which almost always end with the bad guys dead or in handcuffs and all the innocent victims rescued safely. Real life, however, is never that simple. In real life people get killed in these types of incidents, and the police can only do so much to save them.

But the real point to the incident above is that individuals caught up in these types of situations should never fail to immediately—I repeat, immediately—take some sort of action that will save them. For example, the people at the beginning of the incident above who fled the store the moment the shooting began didn't have to worry about putting their fate in someone else's hands. Too many people who could have fled didn't, but just froze at the sound of gunfire or waited to see what was happening, and consequently became hostages. A lot of people don't recognize the sound of gunfire (or don't want to believe that's what it is). All that's needed to correct the first part of this problem is a short visit to a firing range to become aware of the sound that gunfire makes. And while the police will do everything possible to rescue the people who didn't react immediately, as the incident above clearly demonstrated, there is never a guarantee as to the outcome of these incidents.

Another fact demonstrated by the above incident is that there are many people in this world who have absolutely no qualms about hurting or killing innocent people in order to carry out whatever plan or agenda they have. But very importantly, readers should remember that, at best, in these types of incidents, it will take the police four to five minutes to reach the scene, and many dangerous and deadly things can happen in that short period. That's why individuals should never have the mindset that "I don't need to do anything. The police will save me," or "Good, the police are here. Everything's going to be okay." This may be true or, as in the incident above, it may not. According to the FBI study of 160 active shooter cases referenced in chapter 1, two-thirds of the cases they studied ended before the police arrived.[7] While the police will do everything they can to save victims, these minutes before the police arrive are extremely dangerous.

"Four minutes is not slow," says Mike Rehfeld about the police response time. "It's just not effective in reducing casualties." Rehfeld owns a company that specializes in active shooter solutions.[8]

Dr. Pete Blair, who works with the ALERRT program at Texas State University, agrees that the police often cannot get there in time to stop casualties. "When it comes to dealing with active shooter incidents, the focus has been on increasing the speed of the law enforcement response," he said. "However, even when officers reach the scene quickly, casualties have still been high, which shows the importance of training civilians to do what they can to delay the shooter and prevent casualties."[9]

As Dr. Blair says, since the police can't be there instantly, people should be prepared to take action on their own to lessen the possibility of being involved in mass murder incidents, or take action that can save their lives if caught up in one. What actions? For public businesses, schools, and commercial establishments worried about the safety of customers, students, or employees, there are several training courses available that will give these individuals the best chances of surviving a mass murder attempt. At one time, many schools' primary action in an active shooter incident was to lock down the school and call the police. As seen many times, however, this doesn't work if the mass murderer is already inside. Therefore, these training courses show the best strategies to use if the mass murderer has already gained access to the facility.

One of these training courses is known as ALICE training, which stands for Alert, Lockdown, Inform, Counter, Evacuate. This program began in 2001 because of the Columbine incident. Another of these courses is known as CRASE training, which stands for Civilian Response to Active Shooter Events. The CRASE training course, developed by ALERRT trainers in 2004, came about because of the huge demand on law enforcement for instruction and presentations on the best actions to take if confronted by a mass murder event. There are three defenses that the CRASE course teaches in the event of a mass murder incident. CRASE teaches "Avoid, Deny, Defend." There are also similar courses that teach "Run, Hide, Fight," which are pretty much the same thing.

"Run" or "Avoid" means that at the first sign of a mass murder event, such as the sound of gunfire, screams, people running, public announcements, etc., the best option is to attempt to get away from it. If the gunfire or screams are coming from the south, for example, head in any other direction that is clear and get as far away as possible from the incident. Individuals should try to put as much distance and as many barriers as possible between them and the mass murderer. As was shown by the incident at the beginning of this chapter, too many people simply freeze when something violent and unexpected happens. The individuals in the Good Guys Electronics store who didn't freeze managed to escape before the mass murderers could take them hostage; they spared themselves the eight hours of terror the hostages went through. The best advice, therefore, is at the first sign of a possible mass murder event, react immediately! And as discussed in the previous chapter concerning police response, fleeing individuals must also run past any injured victims. Individuals stopping to help injured victims could easily become the mass murderer's next victims. Instead, fleeing individuals should remember the injured victims' location and alert the authorities about them as soon as they are safely away.

The second part of the training, "Hide" or "Deny," should be used only if there is no chance of escape. Escaping is the best option, but it's not always possible. For example, in the Jiverly Wong incident in chapter 2, Wong had blocked the rear door of the American Civic Association and then came in the front door, thereby eliminating the possibility of escape. Ten people, however, fled to the basement and hid. They were not harmed. Therefore, the next best option to escaping is for individuals to find a spot where the mass murderer won't have access to them or be able to find them. Also, hiding individuals should try to devise a way for rescuers to find them, through texting, e-mail, or even a sign in the window. They should also let the rescuers know whether they have anyone injured hiding with them.

The reason escaping is the better option is that if the perpetrator does find out where individuals are hiding, as we've seen several times in this book, the consequences can be deadly. The best place to hide is in a location that will deny the mass murderer access or entry. In a classroom, for example, lock or barricade the door, turn off the lights, block the window in the door, and pick a spot out of the line of fire in the event the perpetrator fires some rounds through the door. Also very important: silence any cell phones! Mass murderers usually know that they only have a few minutes before the police show up and stop them, so unless they are after a specific target, they won't waste a lot of time trying to get into a location they believe is vacant or will take a lot of effort, but instead will move on to softer targets.

Hiding, however, doesn't mean under a table or desk. As has been shown several times in this book, it's not really much of a hiding place if a perpetrator can see a person without a lot of effort. In the Columbine incident, the shooters easily saw the individuals hiding under tables and desks; they killed several of them. If hiding is the option decided upon, then it should be in a closet or storeroom, somewhere not immediately visible if the mass murderer does gain entry into the room. As said above, most mass murderers are on a tight schedule and often won't waste time on a prolonged search if the room appears to be empty.

Also with regard to hiding, there comes a time when the police will reach individuals who have successfully hidden from a mass murderer. A word of caution, though: individuals should be certain it is the police before opening a door or making their presence known. It could be the mass murderer trying to trick his or her way in. An effective way to do this is to call 911, explain the situation, ask for the names of the SWAT officers responding, and then ask the person wanting admittance for a name. In addition, once the police have rescued hidden individuals, those rescued should make sure their hands are visible and that they always follow the instructions of the officers.

Readers might wonder about the idea of playing dead if wounded or in the line of fire. The CRASE course says, "Whether you live or die while playing dead is a matter of chance. In many events, the shooters shoot people who are down in order to make sure that they are dead. We never advise it as a primary strategy."[10]

Finally, the last part of the training, "Fight" or "Defend," is the least favorable, but can become necessary if individuals find themselves confronted in the open by a mass murderer or the mass murderer discovers the individuals' hiding spot. Individuals caught in these situations must attack instantly and viciously. They must try to seriously injure the perpetrator. This is not a time to be concerned about fighting fairly. Strike out violently. This is also not a time for talking, bargaining, or begging.

It won't work. As we've seen so far, most mass murderers just want to get as high a body count as possible. Therefore, if hiding was the choice made, individuals should try to find a weapon to take with them when they hide, something solid and heavy. Keys held between the fingers and thrust at the eyes can also be a potent weapon.

Again, if confronted or discovered, don't hesitate—strike out quickly and viciously. Mass murderers pick soft targets for a reason. They do it because they don't want, or expect, to run into any opposition. Therefore, a violent attack can often shock and confuse the perpetrator, providing individuals precious time to escape or to overpower the mass murderer. For example, Jared Loughner, who shot Congresswoman Gabrielle Giffords and killed six others, was tackled by bystanders who reacted quickly with violence of their own. As more evidence that this works, SWAT teams regularly employ the tactic of "Shock and Awe" when taking on hostage takers and others. What this means is that before they enter a room, they throw in flashbang grenades (grenades that explode with tremendous noise and a blinding flash) and then come in immediately with their guns ready. SWAT team members know that it is human nature to be stunned for a few moments by acts of extreme and unexpected violence. And even though potential victims of mass murderers don't have flashbangs, they can still use "Shock and Awe" by striking out suddenly and violently.

Of course, there will be those who will say that they just couldn't hurt someone like that or that they fear if they do so it will just infuriate the mass murderer. This is foolishness. At the moment when a mass murderer confronts a possible victim, it is all about raw survival, about staying alive. Mass murderers usually don't have a conscience and will kill without any qualms. If individuals feel they can't strike out violently, then they will likely die. That's just a fact. And as for the idea of infuriating the perpetrator, so what? This person means to kill innocent victims, angry or not. Take action and stay alive!

There has been, not surprisingly, considerable blowback on these strategies, particularly the "fight or defend" strategy for potential school mass murders. Critics argue that society shouldn't encourage violent actions from young people. They believe that advocating violence is sending the wrong message to youngsters. Critics also argue that it would be impossible to train young people to simultaneously attack a mass murderer. However, the courses that teach fighting as an option are not talking about a team effort or a wrong message. They are talking about worst-case scenarios and survival. They are talking about suddenly being face to face with someone who has killed others and wants to add to the death toll. All the criticism of these programs sounds good while having coffee with friends, but it is not quite as good when it is their child face to face with a mass murderer. If they want their children to survive, they must be prepared.

"The idea behind CRASE is that the shooters at Columbine, at Virginia Tech, at Fort Hood, at Sandy Hook, in San Bernardino, and in scores of other horrific events across the country since the late 1990s aren't like muggers," said a speaker on a CNN program. "They don't want your wallet or purse. They want a body count, blood, and headlines."[11]

Along with the three actions described above, there are numerous other things people can do that will help them avoid or survive a mass murder incident. The first, and most important, defense individuals can use is to always be aware of their surroundings. Far too often people are so involved in some task that they don't pay any attention to things happening around them. Readers will recall the mass murder incident discussed in chapter 8 that occurred in Cincinnati, where one person became a shooting victim because she was so wrapped up in a conference call on her cell phone that she walked right into the mass murder scene, despite the fact that people all around her were trying to warn her. The point is that individuals should never walk blindly or be oblivious to their surroundings, but instead be observant of them. This can alert them to clues that a bad event is about to happen.

If readers ever have the opportunity, watch a police officer as he or she enters a room. Notice how the officer immediately scans the room for any signs of a threat, and how the officer will usually pick a chair that gives a full view of the room. These are excellent habits to pick up. They can give a person an advantage that might mean the difference between life and death.

Individuals should also be aware of information leakage by possible mass murderers. In the FBI study of sixty-three active shooters referenced earlier, more than half had told someone of their plans.[12] These warnings should always be taken very seriously and acted upon immediately, particularly if it is a family member. While many people are reluctant to report a family member to the police or others, keep in mind that a number of mass murderers have first killed family members before going on their rampage.

Also, no matter where individuals happen to be, they should always be aware of the location of at least two exits, because one of the exits could be blocked by a mass murder event (this would also apply to a fire or another emergency). The few seconds saved by knowing where the exits are could mean a successful escape. According to a CNN program, "when a fire engulfed The Station nightclub in Rhode Island, where the band Great White was performing in 2003, 100 people died—58 of them in the main entryway or just outside it, despite there being three other exits in the club."[13]

In addition, and very importantly, always be suspicious of people who appear extremely nervous, who seem to be sweating or breathing heavily for no reason. It could mean nothing, or it could be extremely important. Along with this, a very interesting article in the *Journal of the American Academy of Psychiatry and the Law* posted this warning: "Hempel et al. were among the first to note that mass murderers with a 'warrior mentality' may convey their central motivation in a psychological abstract, a phrase or a sentence yelled with great emotion at the beginning of the mass murder."[14] If this occurs, try to get as far away as possible, in particular if the phrase shouted is "Allahu Akbar," which is often shouted by Islamic terrorists. This means the situation has just turned critical.

If readers, however, despite all precautions, do find themselves in the middle of a mass murder and there is nowhere to run, the best advice is to get low and if possible find a thick and heavy barrier to get behind. Mass murderers in open places, such as shopping malls, often simply target the people they can see. Don't be an easy target.

As we saw in the incident at the beginning of this chapter, mass murder events can occasionally involve hostage taking. One has only to remember America's worst mass murder, 9/11, to realize how dangerous such a situation can be. Being a hostage can be just as terrifying and just as dangerous as being in the middle of a mass murder event while it is occurring, because hostage incidents can often end in mass murder.

The first thing individuals must keep in mind if they do find themselves in such a situation is that the hostage takers are usually desperate individuals caught up in a no-win situation. This makes them extremely dangerous. The events of 9/11 aside, many of the hostage-taking incidents over the last thirty years or so in our country have involved either criminals in a botched crime, such as an unsuccessful robbery, or someone who has found themselves in an untenable romantic or domestic situation, such as a marriage or relationship breakup. The hostage takers hope that they can force the police to let them escape or that they can repair a marriage or relationship by forcing a person to come and talk to them, and the hostages are the bargaining chips. These situations usually happen on impulse and are unplanned, which makes them incredibly dangerous.

While some people might believe that they can persuade or bargain with the hostage taker to let everyone go or to give up to the police, this is seldom advisable. The most likely result will be an increase in the stress the hostage takers are already under, which is never desirable. Hostage takers usually quickly realize the hopelessness of their situation and consequently become even more dangerous. Unless a hostage taker talks to a hostage, it is best to remain silent. Hostage takers really don't want advice or criticism from a hostage. A veteran hostage negotiator who worked for the Indianapolis Police Department once told me, "The most important thing for any person who is taken hostage to remember is that seldom are hostage takers rational, clear-thinking individuals with a plan. Most have no plan at all. Most have gotten themselves into a really bad situation and now don't know how to get themselves out of it."[15]

There are important things, however, to know about a hostage situation that can increase the chances of surviving it; one of these is that the first half hour of a hostage incident is the most dangerous time. The hostage takers are usually very tense during this time and can become upset easily, which can lead to violence. If there is not a good chance of escaping or overpowering the hostage taker, hostages should remain quiet and appear submissive. A troublesome or hysterical hostage can often infuriate the hostage takers.

If hostage takers are in negotiations with the police, then in most cases—not all, but most—the odds are favorable for a good outcome for the hostages. Therefore, it is best to leave the talking to the police hostage negotiators and not interrupt the negotiations or offer advice. If, on the other hand, a hostage is legitimately ill or in need of medicine, informing the hostage takers of this can be wise. Ill hostages are often the first traded during negotiations with the police.

As a hostage, individuals should try to be very observant of the location where they are being held and of the hostage takers themselves. Note their fortifications, their descriptions, weapons, and attitudes. This information can be extremely valuable to the police on the chance that a hostage is released before the others. However, don't stare at the hostage takers. This can make them nervous.

Hostages can occasionally have a certain amount of mobility at a hostage scene. Hence, unless ordered there, as in the incident at the beginning of this chapter, hostages should stay away from windows and doors. These may be used by the SWAT team if a rescue attempt is made. And if a rescue attempt does occur, hostages should immediately drop to the floor, lie flat, and stay that way until the rescue is over.

Whether to escape from a hostage situation if the opportunity presents itself depends totally on the facts of the situation. If an opportunity to escape does present itself and it appears that there is a very good chance of success, it should certainly be considered. Historically, hostage situations several hours old in which the hostage takers are negotiating with the police usually indicate a good chance of being released, but not escaping when a good opportunity presents itself leaves a person in the hands of desperate, unstable people. Readers have only to recall the events in the incident at the beginning of this chapter, or of 9/11, to know how these events can end for hostages passively allowing hostage takers to be in control. Therefore, if the chances of escaping appear very good, it probably should be attempted—but be aware that failure can often have disastrous and possibly fatal consequences. The decision therefore must be based on the prevailing circumstances.

Notwithstanding, the following narratives illustrate another type of mass murder that has increased significantly over the last few decades. Like the events described above, these are incidents into which innocent people can find themselves suddenly thrust, so they must be prepared to take immediate action in order to survive them.

✻ ✻ ✻

The Henry Pratt Company in Aurora, Illinois, a little more than forty miles west of Chicago, manufactures valves for industrial use. Forty-five-year-old Gary Montez Martin had worked there for fifteen years and had just been fired for violating various company rules. Martin apparently felt that the rules didn't apply to him.

"He'd just kind of look at you like you were stupid for telling him not to do something," one of Martin's former bosses said.[16]

Unknown to many of his fellow employees, Martin had a long history of violence. He had served two and a half years in prison in Mississippi for aggravated assault on a girlfriend.

"All I can remember is him hitting and kicking me, I can remember fighting and screaming for help," the victim, Martin's girlfriend, told the police. "I remember him pushing my head into that brick wall outside the apartment and thinking that he was going to kill me."[17]

The police in northern Illinois also knew Martin. He had been arrested six times for assorted charges, including domestic violence, disorderly conduct, and criminal damage to property.

Since Martin had a felony conviction in Mississippi, the laws of the state of Illinois did not allow him to own a gun. Despite this, he applied for an Illinois Firearm Owner's Identification card (FOID), and the state police granted it, apparently not performing a fingerprint check. With his FOID card, Martin purchased a Smith and Wesson .40 caliber semiautomatic pistol. After purchasing the handgun, he then applied for a concealed weapon permit. This time, however, the state police did perform a fingerprint check and discovered his felony conviction in Mississippi. The Illinois State Police rejected his application for a concealed weapon permit and also canceled his FOID card. In addition, the state police sent him a letter saying that he was required to surrender the weapon he had purchased. He didn't, and apparently no one followed up on it.

When Martin was fired from the Henry Pratt Company, he apparently decided that he had been treated unfairly and needed to seek revenge. On the afternoon of February 15, 2019, at 1:24 p.m., Martin entered the plant with his handgun, which had a green laser sight, and began shooting. He killed five people at the plant and wounded another. The police arrived four minutes after the first 911 call, and Martin began shooting at them. He wounded five police officers before they killed him. The individuals killed at the plant included a human resources officer, a machine operator, a stockroom attendant, a plant manager, and a college student intern.

❊ ❊ ❊

The type of incident described above in Aurora is certainly not an isolated event, but, like school shootings, has become part of a growing epidemic in America. For example, in Orlando, Florida, on June 5, 2017, forty-five-year-old John Robert Neumann Jr. returned to the place where he had worked but from which he had been fired two months before. He entered through the back door of the Fiamma Company, which manufactures awnings for motor homes. Armed with a handgun and a knife, he killed five employees. When the police arrived at the scene, Neumann shot himself in the head. The Fiamma Company had fired Neumann because he constantly started fights with other employees.

In September of 2012, in Minneapolis, an incident took place at Accent Signage Systems. Thirty-six-year-old Andrew John Engeldinger had worked for the company, but they had fired him. According to his fellow employees, Engeldinger didn't associate with the other people at work, refusing to eat or take breaks with them. Apparently a supervisor at the company had told Engeldinger that he was going to be fired and said he should report to the executive offices. Before going to the company's executive offices as instructed, however, Engeldinger first went to his car and retrieved a Glock 9mm semiautomatic pistol. At his termination meeting, Engeldinger shot two people, left the office and killed the company's founder, and then went into the factory, where he shot and killed four more people. Engeldinger then killed himself when the police showed up.

Interestingly, even people who wouldn't be suspected of being violent can surprise other employees with gruesome mayhem if they feel they have been mistreated. At the Connecticut Lottery Headquarters in Newington, thirty-five-year-old Matthew Beck worked as an accountant. Earlier, Beck had had a disagreement with his employers. He had been ordered to assume some duties that were not a part of his job description and were supposed to be performed by someone who made more money than he did. Consequently, Beck filed a grievance, expecting that he would be promoted to this higher position. However, while Beck was off on medical leave, management gave the higher-paying job to someone else. Beck, of course, felt cheated; apparently this was not the first time he had been passed over for a promotion.

"He was always angry about not being promoted," Beck's supervisor said. "He used to talk about how they treated him unfairly."[18]

At 8:30 a.m. on March 6, 1998, Beck walked into a meeting at the lottery headquarters. Using a handgun and a knife, he killed the lottery's chief financial officer, the vice president of operations, and an information specialist. The lottery president, seeing what had happened, tried to run away. Beck chased him out of the building and across a parking lot before the man being chased stumbled and fell. Beck stood over him and shot and killed him. The local police arrived just as Beck had killed the man in the parking lot. As the police approached him, Beck shot himself in the head.

What all these narratives show is that the workplace today can be a ripe territory for mass murders. The measures individuals need to take to escape one of these events are simple. Most employees know which coworkers are troublemakers, are always in conflict with management, or are likely to be or have already been fired. Individuals should also listen to other employees to stay informed about such persons; seeing one of these individuals at the workplace, and particularly in the work area, after they have been fired should raise red flags. Upon seeing this, aware employees should quickly leave the area if possible, but if not, at least be ready in an instant to race to the nearest exit. On the other hand, if shooting starts unexpectedly, don't, as many people have done, freeze or look around to see what's going on. Instead, immediately get low and preferably behind something heavy and solid. Hurry to an exit as quickly as possible. Call the police.

For the individuals doing the firing or discipline, even more caution should be exercised. If management has any cause at all to believe that violence might erupt at a disciplinary or termination meeting, they should have at least one armed security guard present at the meeting. If there are none employed at the business, management should call the local police and explain the situation. Many police departments will send a uniformed officer to ensure that no violence occurs. When I was a uniformed police officer, I did this a number of times.

In this chapter, I have discussed what individuals can do when faced with a mass murder incident. In the next chapter, I am going to discuss what society at large can do that will stop our country's growing epidemic of mass murder.

10

THE FUTURE: WHAT CAN WE DO?

Noblesville, Indiana, is an affluent suburb northeast of Indianapolis where few bad things happen. The crime rate there is 50 percent lower than the national average, and violent crime seldom makes an appearance. Consequently, the people living in Noblesville don't worry about many of the things that other people in the country see daily. That is why the events of May 25, 2018, so violently shattered the tranquility of Noblesville.

On that day, at a little after 9:00 a.m., at Noblesville West Middle School, a thirteen-year-old student asked to be excused to go to the restroom during a science test. He told the teacher he had finished the test. When he returned to the classroom, he carried several weapons: a .22 caliber and a .45 caliber handgun and a knife. The teacher, twenty-nine-year-old Jason Seaman, said another student opened the door for the thirteen-year-old. Seaman's attention was focused elsewhere; he was assisting a student, Ella Whistler, with a test question. Suddenly, without warning, the returning student shot Seaman three times: in the right forearm, right hip, and abdomen. The student also shot thirteen-year-old Whistler seven times.

Seaman, though at first shocked by the violence, threw a miniature basketball he was holding at the assailant, which distracted him, and then wrestled the thirteen-year-old to the ground and disarmed him. All the while he was doing this, his white shirt soaked red with blood, Seaman yelled for the students to get out of the classroom and call 911. Although seriously injured, Seaman held the boy down until the police arrived. He would later say, "I want to make it clear that my actions on that day, in my mind, were the only acceptable actions I could've done given the circumstances. I deeply care for my students and their well-being."[1]

The students in the room also reacted right away. "He tackled him to the ground; we were all hiding in the back of the classroom behind some desks, then he was yelling to call 911, to get out of the building as fast as we could, so we ran down the stairs," a student in the classroom told reporters.[2] Several of the students barricaded themselves in a storage room. "One of my friends, Zane, he tied a rope around the inner door so if it was opened it couldn't open," said a seventh grader who witnessed the shooting that day.[3]

Another student in the class later talked about the teacher's actions: "He knocked the gun out of his hand and tackled him to the ground. If it weren't for him, more of us would have been injured for sure, and who knows what would have happened."[4]

Ella Whistler, the seventh grader shot seven times and severely injured, had to be airlifted to Riley Children's Hospital in Indianapolis. She had received gunshot wounds to her face, her neck, her hand, and her chest, causing a collapsed lung, a broken clavicle and jaw, damage to her neck vertebrae, and other injuries. Although at one time listed in critical condition, she recovered enough to return to school. The teacher, Jason Seaman, though suffering three gunshot wounds, also recovered and returned to school.

The assailant, since he was only thirteen years old, couldn't be charged as an adult under Indiana law. A person must die before that can be done. Because of the heinousness of the act, the inability to try the young assailant as an adult caused an uproar in the community. The Hamilton County prosecutor put out a statement that read, "As a Prosecuting Attorney, I do not make the laws applicable to criminal or juvenile cases. . . . Under current Indiana law, this case is not eligible to be heard in adult court despite the heinous or aggravated nature of the alleged acts and despite the serious harm caused."[5] The thirteen-year-old assailant, described by his classmates as friendly and open, had never come to the attention of the authorities. At a hearing in Juvenile Court the first week of November 2018, he apologized for his actions in a written statement read in court. However, at the hearing, the court played a video the thirteen-year-old had made just before the shooting.

In it, he said, "I'm not killing myself. I have to take other people's lives before I take mine."[6] In the video he showed the weapons he would take to school, which belonged to his parents. While he was at the juvenile facility awaiting trial, the staff there had to take away some Lego blocks because he had made a rifle out of them.

Investigators later found that before the shooting the assailant had searched the internet for information on the Columbine and Sandy Hook mass murders, on "school shooting memes," and on "what was the largest mass shooting in America?" He also searched for blueprints of Noblesville West Middle School. Because he was only thirteen at the time of his crime, the maximum sentence he can receive is to be confined to a juvenile detention facility until he reaches adulthood.

Following the shooting, a student at Noblesville High School, whose little sister attended Noblesville West Middle School, said, "I never thought it would happen here." A parent of a student at the middle school said, "Never thought that this would happen. Not in Noblesville."[7]

Later that year, in December 2018, in another city in Indiana, this time Richmond, another mass murder was averted through quick action. Richmond, with a population of just a little more than 35,000 people, sits off of Interstate 70 on the eastern edge of Indiana. On December 13, 2018, at around 8:00 a.m., fourteen-year-old Brandon Clegg kidnapped a male relative at gunpoint and forced the relative to drive him to Dennis Intermediate School in Richmond, where he intended to commit a mass murder. Clegg carried a pistol and a rifle. He had been, but was not at that time, a student at the school.

Fortunately, Clegg's mother knew of his plot and his intentions. As soon as he left, she immediately notified the police and told them where Clegg was heading and what he intended to do. The school immediately went into lockdown, and the entrance doors and all doors inside the school were locked. Because of his mother's notification, the police arrived at the school as Clegg was getting ready to unload something from his car. Clegg, seeing his plans foiled, raced to the north entrance to the school and shot out the glass in the door, the police close behind him. Because all of the doors inside the school were locked, Clegg couldn't get into any of the classrooms, likely saving many lives, and instead he fled to a stairwell, where he exchanged gunfire with the police. The young man, apparently seeing the futility of his position, then shot and killed himself. No one else suffered any injuries. The police later said that Clegg had Molotov cocktails in the car and that this was apparently what he was trying to unload when the police officers arrived.

A parent of a student at the school said, "I'm still shaking. I can see it on the news, but it's scary when it's your own baby."[8] Another parent added, "This is insane. You don't expect it to happen in your little town. . . . I mean, it's small town USA."[9]

* * *

The above two incidents show very clearly that potential mass murders can be prevented and that they can be stopped. But this can only happen when citizens take action. Stopping mass murders takes citizens who don't just wait for the police to show up but who take action themselves. These two incidents clearly show that quick action by citizens can stop mass murders.

Since so many schools in the last few decades have suffered mass murders, a suggestion put forward by those looking for ways to stop this increasing trend of violence is to arm some of the school staff. Naturally, these would be only staff members who volunteered and had met strict training standards. Many mass murderers choose schools for their crimes because they see schools as soft targets. The mass murderers know that they will have five minutes or so to carry out their crime before the police arrive, and that they will run into little, if any, resistance from the victims during that time.

According to an article on the *Police One* website, "The time between the start of killing and the arrival of police represents the most lethal period in most active shooter events as the attacker operates unopposed."[10]

However, by arming some of the school staff, these locations are no longer soft targets, and the mass murderers no longer feel confident that they will be unopposed. If potential mass murderers knew that they could be met by gunfire in any classroom they entered, and they didn't know which ones, then the attractiveness of schools for mass murder events would diminish greatly. It's the same type of advice the police give for most other crimes. Make yourself or your property look like a tough target and criminals will move on to an easier, softer target.

The Marjory Stoneman Douglas High School Public Safety Commission, formed to look into the mass murder there and make recommendations that would prevent a reoccurrence, said in its preliminary report in January 2019 that they recommended allowing teachers to be armed. The report said that the state should allow teachers "properly selected, thoroughly screened, and extensively trained to carry concealed firearms on campuses for self-protection, and the protection of other staff and students in response to an active assailant incident."[11] A program of this type would, of course, have to be on a strictly voluntary basis. Demanding that all school staff be armed wouldn't work and really wouldn't be necessary. Just a few at each school would be enough to sow doubt in any potential mass murderer's mind.

A clear example of where this idea would likely have saved lives was in the Santa Fe, Texas, incident, described in chapter 2. The school had a detailed safety plan in place for just such an incident, they had run drills to be certain that it worked, they had two armed police officers at the school, and they had even won a statewide award for their plan. "We can never be over-prepared," said J. R. Norman, president of the school district's board of trustees. "But we were prepared."[12] Yet still, it took several precious minutes for the armed police officers to arrive as planned, and during this time ten people died. An armed teacher could likely have stopped this tragedy.

As might be expected in society today, there has been considerable resistance to the idea of arming teachers. A number of politicians and teacher organizations have resisted it. Randi Weingarten, president of the American Federation of Teachers, told the *Washington Post*, "We don't want to be, and would never have the expertise needed to be, sharp shooters; no amount of training can prepare an armed teacher to go up against an AR-15."[13] This statement is wrong on several points. Most confrontations with any potential mass murderers would be within five or six feet of each other, so being a sharpshooter isn't important, and a handgun can immediately stop someone, no matter what weapon that person carries, be it an AR-15, a shotgun, a rifle, etc.

Many people have also opposed the idea of arming teachers because they feel that it sends the wrong idea to the students. And it probably would if the teachers wore the guns openly, but that is not the idea. To resist out-of-sight guns in schools is similar to the thinking of the residents of Noblesville and Richmond: that this sort of thing couldn't happen in their community. This is the worst way to bury one's head in the sand. All of the talk about nonviolence only works on others who believe in nonviolence. Violent people, such as mass murderers, feed off it and use it to make others their victims. I've found a number of times in my nearly four decades as a police officer that all of the rhetoric about peace, love, and nonviolence comes to a screeching halt when a person or that person's loved ones are in extreme danger. It's great to talk about such things over coffee or at a party, but when faced with reality, when faced with probable severe injury or death, these ideas quickly evaporate. Then, as I saw numerous times, for these people, any measure, absolutely any measure at all, would be okay to use to resolve the threat. Sometimes people forget that there are no do-overs in real life.

In support of the idea of arming teachers, in March 2019, a judge in Ohio threw out a lawsuit filed by parents against a proposal approving teachers and school staff being armed. The parents wanted the teachers to have no less than 700 hours of training (nearly the amount of total training needed to be a police officer), but the judge said that this was far too excessive. The school district required thirty hours.[14]

The incidents described in this book, particularly those involving schools, have shown that the entrances to these facilities and the doors to the interior rooms have been much too easy for mass murderers to get through. A number of corrections to these facilities need to be made. Too often the entrance doors or panels on either side of the entrance doors are made of glass, so the mass murderers simply shoot out the glass and walk through. Entrance doors and their panels should either have metal grating over them or be made of hurricane glass that will stop bullets. All interior doors must be solid and have heavy locking mechanisms that lock from the inside. There should also be a shade that can be pulled down over any windows in the doors. In addition, classrooms must have hard corners where students can gather, hard corners that will not allow bullets to penetrate the room. These corners must, without exception, always remain free of obstructions. The final report on the Parkland, Florida, mass murder says, "Cruz only shot people within his line of sight and never entered any classroom. Some students were shot and killed in classrooms with obstructed or inaccessible hard corners as they remained in Cruz's line of sight from outside the classroom."[15] As discussed, a mass murderer has only a few minutes of freedom to kill before the police arrive, and denying or slowing access to a building and its interior rooms will consume a lot of this time.

Additionally, teaching students emergency first aid could prove life-saving in any violent incident. Students need to know how to stabilize a victim until medical help can arrive. This training would also serve the students well in the event of a serious automobile accident, injuries in the home, etc.

As we have seen in many of the narratives reported in this book, mass murderers often commit their crime because they want the huge media coverage that other mass murderers have received. Many readers will wonder, "Yes, but who would want that kind of media coverage? Who would want to be portrayed as a murdering psychopath?" The truth is that there are many disturbed people in the world for whom this type of media coverage is like a treasure they have always been seeking. Suddenly, rather than being an unknown loser, their picture is on every television set, and their story is on the front page of every newspaper. Readers have only to recall the incredible news media glut the Columbine mass murder brought about. Every news channel ran coverage for hours on end, and the story sat on the front page of every newspaper and numerous news magazines. Books have been written and movies have been made about Columbine. To many people, Eric Harris and Dylan Klebold became demigods to be worshipped and imitated.

Harris and Klebold, however, are not the only ones worshipped for being mass murderers. As described in chapter 7, an online post by Alek Minassian, who killed ten people by ramming them with his van, stated, "The Incel [involuntary celibate] Rebellion has already begun. . . . All hail the Supreme Gentleman Elliot Rodger!"[16]

Unfortunately, in order to garner this kind of news media interest, most potential mass murderers realize that they must be even more violent and bloodier than Columbine and the mass murders that followed it. The body count must be higher, there must be more blood, and the gore of the incident must be stunning. This has led to some terrible incidents brought about for media coverage. Also, wanting the world to know who they are is the reason so many mass murderers leave behind communiqués and manifestos that the media will often report on word for word.

There is a solution for this. I visited the Lorraine Motel in Memphis, Tennessee, several years ago. This is the spot where, on April 4, 1968, an assassin struck down Dr. Martin Luther King Jr. They have since turned the location into a monument to Dr. King, but interestingly, nowhere in all the displays is there a mention of Dr. King's murderer by name. I found this both interesting and innovative. Why give any notoriety at all to a criminal?

Other people have also followed this trend. Twenty-four-year-old Alex Teves died in the 2012 mass murder at a movie theater in Aurora, Colorado. In his memory, his parents started a "No Notoriety" campaign to persuade the news media to stop glamorizing mass murderers, and instead to shift their focus to the victims. Of course, the problem is that the news media is a money-making business, and crime and gore sell well. Cable news channels recorded some of their biggest viewer numbers ever during the around-the-clock coverage of the mass murder at Columbine High School.

Regrettably, this type of massive news media coverage can't help but spur unbalanced minds into wanting to copycat the crime and share in what they see as the glory of their face and name on every news media outlet around the world. This kind of news media coverage lifts the perpetrators to heroic status in the eyes of the unbalanced. But, as mentioned above, because the news media is in the business of making money, it is a hard sell to convince them to downplay the acts of the perpetrators in these types of events.

Time magazine, in its May 3, 1999, issue, had pictures of Eric Harris and Dylan Klebold on the cover, as did the December 20, 1999, issue. *Newsweek*'s May 3, 1999, cover story reports on Columbine with the byline "Portraits of the Killers." *People* magazine, *New York* magazine, and others also had cover stories about Columbine. In addition, there were television specials made about Harris and Klebold, dozens of articles in newspapers and magazines, and even movies made about them. To disturbed individuals with simmering grievances, this incredible amount of publicity about Columbine raised Harris and Klebold to demigod status.

There is a large group of individuals who spend a considerable amount of time online discussing true crime, and of these there is a sizable subsection who call themselves "Columbiners." These are individuals who are fascinated by Harris and Klebold. There are even websites dedicated to the Columbine killers, and on some of them the killers are the subject of fan art, fan fiction, and more. The individuals who visit these websites spend countless hours discussing the crime and the two killers. To this group, Harris and Klebold are to be worshipped.

Interestingly, after the Columbine massacre, a carpenter from Illinois erected a memorial of eight-foot-high crosses on a hill near the mass murder site. He built and erected thirteen crosses for the victims of Columbine, but he also put up one each for Harris and Klebold, apparently feeling that they were victims too. This drew some very angry responses from the parents of the victims, and the crosses came down.

The quest for notoriety as great as Harris and Klebold received has shown itself in a number of mass murders since Columbine. For example, on December 5, 2007, nineteen-year-old Robert A. Hawkins killed eight people at a mall in Omaha, Nebraska. He had written a suicide note that said, "Just think tho [sic], I'm gonna be fuckin famous."[17]

According to author David Brin, "Western culture has also come to include a vast and powerfully influential value system devoted to celebrity and fame. In place of what should be profound shame, an aura of undeserved notoriety and infamy is often accorded to certain individuals who commit horrible crimes."[18]

In a 2015 article in the *New Yorker*, author Malcolm Gladwell explained that as more and more mass murder incidents occur, individuals' threshold for perpetrating these acts is lowered because through the media flood of reporting they see more and more people committing these acts. Therefore, these individuals realize that they are not alone, that what they're contemplating isn't really outside the sphere of acceptable behavior after all.[19]

As discussed earlier, huge amounts of publicity for mass murders can often spur copycat crimes. Dr. Sherry Towers of Arizona State University, whose specialty is statistics, studied the "contagious period" for mass murders. She found it to be thirteen days. That is, within thirteen days of a mass murder, the chances of another one become much more likely. Although she realizes that the news media can't just ignore such events, she believes they should focus on the victims, not the perpetrator or the grisly details.

"When I talk publicly, or to the media," Dr. Towers said, "I don't name the perpetrator unless there is a specific reason why."[20]

Dr. Pete Blair from the ALERRT program agrees with this, and consequently the ALERRT program has started a "Don't Name Them" campaign. "A lot of shooters—not all of them—are driven by this desire for notoriety," Dr. Blair said. "If we know that's one of the motivations, why are you giving them the reward?"[21]

After the Umpqua Community College mass murder described in chapter 7, Sheriff John Hanlin said that he would not name the shooter. "I will not give him credit for this horrific act of cowardice," he said. "Media will get the name confirmed in time . . . but you will never hear us use it."[22]

Dr. Jennifer Johnston, a psychology professor at Western New Mexico University, conducted a study similar to that of Dr. Towers and found that extensive news media coverage of mass murders led to an overall increase in such crimes. "I go to my three or four major mass media news organizations and see if they're leading with the shooter's name and the shooter's photo," Professor Johnston said about the Parkland, Florida, school shooting described in chapter 8. "Unfortunately, in this case, that's what I found."[23]

Professor Johnston and graduate student Andrew Joy wrote a paper in 2016 titled "Mass Shootings and the Media Contagion Effect." In this paper they recognize what an uphill battle they're fighting. "Indeed, any attempt to curb the flow of information is likely to encounter considerable resistance, as the coverage of these events is recognized to significantly increase viewership and boost advertising," the paper says. In their paper the authors reference another study that "expressed concern that extensive news coverage of mass shooters, their methods and motivations, inspires copycat killers because they essentially are given a blueprint to crime, and a glorified model with whom to identify and emulate in the pursuit of infamy." The paper suggests that the news media builds the mass murderer up to almost celebrity status, and, through this, encourages others who seek fame to follow their example.[24]

In an interview, Professor Johnston said, "We suggest that the media cry to cling to 'the public's right to know' covers up a greedier agenda to keep eyeballs glued to screens, since they know that frightening homicides are their No. 1 ratings and advertising boosters."[25]

The situation is not hopeless, however. In the 1990s, the news media voluntarily agreed to lower the emphasis when reporting on celebrity suicides because it had been found that intensive reporting on celebrity suicides sparked an increase in suicides among young people. Therefore, in an effort to stop copycat mass murders, much like copycat suicides, there are several efforts presently under way to convince the news media not to give the perpetrators of these acts so much exposure that they become media stars. But the only way this is going to work is through intense viewer pressure. Only if news media outlets see that glamorizing mass murderers will hurt their viewer numbers will anything change. This is a tall order, but it is up to the public to do this.

Along with what I've discussed so far, there are a number of other changes society can make that will decrease the number of mass murders every year. The following narratives illustrate very clearly one of these changes.

✿ ✿ ✿

Koeberie Bull, a widow living in New Jersey with three biracial children, received a disturbing message on Facebook from a man she had never met. It was October 2018, and she said, "[He was] basically repeating himself about hoping my children would die and be hung because they're black. It was definitely racially motivated, 'you and your monkey children' and using the 'n' word a lot."[26]

After doing some research because she feared the man might live in New Jersey, Bull discovered that instead he lived in Lawrenceburg, Kentucky. She also found that he was holding a gun in his profile picture. Bull didn't drop the matter or just brush it off because he lived so far away. "Something in the back of my head was like this isn't right, like something's not sitting well," she said.[27]

Knowing she had to do something, Bull called the Kentucky State Police and reported the incident. The police, after looking into her complaint, found that the message sender, twenty-year-old Dylan Jarrell, had previously been questioned by the FBI because he had used social media to make threats against a school in Tennessee.

The Kentucky State Police sent officers out to talk with Jarrell, and as they arrived at his home they found him in his vehicle just getting ready to leave. Upon talking with him, the officers said they found clear evidence of an imminent threat to local schools. In his vehicle, the officers reported, they discovered that Jarrell had an assault weapon with a hundred-round magazine, a bulletproof vest, and a detailed plan for attacking a school. The police arrested him for second-degree terroristic threatening and harassing communications.

"He was caught backing out of his driveway with the tools he needed to commit this heinous act," said Kentucky State Police Commissioner Rick Sanders. "This young man had it in his mind to go to schools and create havoc."[28]

Bull said that she had no idea how Jarrell came upon her Facebook page or why he targeted her. She had absolutely no connections to Kentucky. Naturally, Bull received praise for her actions, but she brushed it off. "I'm just a mom protecting my kids."[29]

The next month in Springfield, Kentucky, employees at the LB Manufacturing Company noticed a strange pickup truck parked on their property. The police later found that the occupant of the pickup truck, thirty-seven-year-old Matthew Smith, had been stalking a woman who worked at the plant. Two employees went out to the truck and told Smith to leave, but he refused, so they called the police.

When the police arrived and started to question Smith, he raised a handgun at the officers. "I opened the truck door, and at this time, he raised a Glock handgun toward my chest," says Officer Joe Templeman of the Springfield Police Department.[30] The officer was able to grab the gun out of Smith's hand. Then he and another officer wrestled Smith out of the truck and onto the ground, keeping him from getting to another handgun he had in his waistband. They also found that he had an additional handgun in an ankle holster.

After subduing and handcuffing Smith, the police officers searched his pickup truck. In it they found two additional handguns, a .308 hunting rifle with a scope, a shotgun, and an AR-15 assault rifle, modified to fire on full automatic. They also found more than twenty magazines for the weapons.

When the police later questioned Smith, he told them that he was looking for a woman and that he had "brought what he needed to get the job done."[31] He also told them that he was "going to do what he needed to do."[32]

The local chief of police praised the two employees who called the police and his two officers for doing the right thing in this situation. "Four people stepped up and prevented what we believe was a mass shooting," said Springfield Police Chief Jim Smith.[33]

✣ ✣ ✣

As seen above, reporting potential mass murderers to the authorities can save lives. Many mass murderers, it has been found, will tell someone or several people of their plans before they actually carry them out. In the FBI study of sixty-three active shooter cases, referred to earlier, researchers found that in all sixty-three cases at least one person in the mass murderer's life witnessed disturbing behavior but didn't report it.[34] Many potential mass murderers will even talk about their plans on social media.

Like the present "See something, say something" campaign to reduce crime, doing this for potential mass murders can not only reduce crime but save lives. Many times, it has been found, a potential mass murderer will tell a family member about his or her plans, but families often don't want to get other family members in trouble, so they don't do anything, or they try to handle it themselves. But as a society we must overcome this reluctance to involve the authorities. Not only are family members possibly saving lives by reporting such information; they are also possibly saving theirs and other family members' lives as well, because mass murderers sometimes kill family members first, and family members themselves are likely to die in the incident. In the FBI study of 160 mass shooting incidents, also referred to earlier, the researchers found that in around 10 percent of these events the mass murderer also targeted family members, resulting in twenty deaths.[35]

A study of mass murderers, according to Professor Mia Bloom of Georgia State University, found that 83 percent had at least hinted to others about their plans. "We need to find a way that if someone says they are planning to do something, that there are safe mechanisms for the individual to report without themselves becoming a suspect or a person of interest," says Professor Bloom.[36]

An article in *Scientific American* says, "Early on, troubled teenagers typically keep these fantasies secret, but they increasingly begin to leak their thoughts and plans to friends, chat rooms, and even media outlets. Recognizing the signs of such deadly thoughts, as opposed to harmless daydreaming, can enable parents, teachers, social workers, and other trusted adults to head off trouble before it begins."[37]

Sometimes the warnings from potential mass murderers are not verbal but instead are behaviors that alarm family and friends. These too must be reported. A study of mass murders conducted by the US Secret Service found that "the attackers who had elicited concern in others had a higher average number of total casualties . . . than attackers who had not elicited concern in others." The casualty rate was double.[38] An article that appeared in the *Journal of the American Academy of Psychiatry and the Law* sums it up: "Retrospectively, one may sometimes discover windows of opportunity that if taken advantage of, could have diverted the course of events leading up to the tragedy." It adds, "Thus, perhaps one hope of prevention ultimately falls to third parties who possess knowledge about the individual's behavior."[39]

The FBI's study of sixty-three active shooters found that the most common response from someone who witnessed disturbing behavior was to talk to the person about it, followed next by doing nothing, and the third most common response was to report it to the authorities.[40] One particularly disturbing and important sign of impending mass violence is when an individual constructs a "legacy token." This is some type of communication in which the person takes credit for an impending mass murder and often tries to explain the reasons behind it. Anyone discovering one of these should always report it to the authorities immediately.

As we have seen, potential mass murderers often leak information about their intended crime, sometimes even giving specific details. Nikolas Cruz, who killed seventeen people at Marjory Stoneman Douglas High School, posted numerous rants online. "The man did everything but take out an ad in the paper [saying], 'I am going to kill somebody,'" Senator Lindsey Graham said about the killings. Jarrod Ramos, who killed five people at the *Capital Gazette* office in Annapolis, Maryland, in July 2018, said in 2014, in a legal pleading, that he had "sworn a legal oath he would like to kill" a columnist he claimed had defamed him.[41] Even Dimitrios Pagourtzis, discussed in chapter 2, whom everyone felt didn't have the outward characteristics of a mass murderer, left behind warnings in a journal about what he was planning. "This young man planned on doing this for some time," said Texas Senator John Cornyn. "He advertised his intentions but somehow slipped through the cracks."[42] The list goes on and on, with potential mass murderers giving obvious clues ahead of time about their intentions. These simply must not be ignored.

While most mass murderers are not diagnosed before the mass murder as psychotic and possibly dangerous, a small number have been, including Major Nidal Hasan, who opened fire at Fort Hood Army

Base; Jared Loughner, who killed six people at a political rally for US Representative Gabrielle Giffords; James Holmes, who murdered twelve people at an Aurora, Colorado, movie theater; Aaron Alexis, who killed twelve people at the Washington Navy Yard; and others. Some have even told mental health professionals that they want to kill people. Mental health professionals are supposed to report individuals who are a danger to others, but obviously they don't always do this. When this happens, mental health professionals should be called to task and ordered to explain the reason for their nonreporting.

School personnel can also be involved in looking for clues to future violence. The schools in Noblesville, Indiana, for example, after the incident described earlier, began looking into the monitoring of students' social media accounts for threats of violence at their schools. There are a number of companies nationally that provide this service and claim it only costs a couple of dollars per student per year.

Of course, any program of this nature will always run into individuals who claim it is a violation of the students' privacy. But how can it be an invasion of privacy if the student has posted the information on a public social media platform that can be accessed by anyone? And as we have seen several times in this book, mass murderers have often posted information on public social media platforms about their plans and intentions for a public rampage. A company that provides this service, Social Sentinel, which has clients in education, sports, theaters, private companies, and others, makes it clear on their website that their service only monitors social media posts that can be seen by anyone, not private posts.

"Our service accesses only public social media, which can be seen by anyone, anywhere, anytime," says the website. "If the author's account is marked private, or they use a closed social network, our service does not have access."[43]

While this idea has received mixed reviews from parents, others see it as a valuable tool. "I truly believe this technology is a game-changer for both public and private safety," said former Porter County (Indiana) Sheriff David Lain. "And ultimately, it could save lives."[44]

Another idea gaining foothold is for schools to have anonymous tip lines that students can use to alert school officials about possible danger brewing. No one wants to be seen as a squealer, and this would remedy that. The same idea has worked well in law enforcement. The Crime

Stoppers Program allows citizens to anonymously report criminal activity, and it has been astoundingly successful.

Often after a heinous mass murder, people will ask why the perpetrator was allowed to possess deadly weapons. The person may have been in the possession of several deadly weapons yet had been acting weirdly and talking about mass violence. Why, people ask, was this person allowed to keep the deadly weapons? Why weren't they taken away? When I first became a police officer in the late 1960s, we had a method that often staved off violence in these types of incidents. If we went on a run where there was a person who appeared emotionally unstable and capable of violence, and who also had possession of deadly weapons, we would confiscate the weapons and put them in the police property room as personal property of the person we took them from. It would then take that person several days to be able to retrieve their property—long enough for the person to cool down. This wasn't actually legal then, but we did it anyway.

A lot has changed since my rookie days. Thirteen states now have laws that allow for the confiscation of deadly weapons, but in a much more formal procedure that requires a court hearing. California, for example, now has Gun Violence Restraining Orders, which allow the police to remove weapons from individuals who are emotionally unstable for some reason. These types of orders are issued usually by civil courts, so getting an order issued doesn't carry the heavy burden of proof that criminal courts do. This is a step in the right direction. Laws like this in every state could go a long way toward reducing a lot of violence.

Also, many times after a mass murder, people will view the history of the mass murderer and question why this person was allowed to walk around free. This person may have been violent in the past and seemed to have given clue after clue about his or her intentions. Why, the public asks, wasn't this person locked up? While the public's shock that a mass murderer was allowed to walk around freely is understandable, this is a situation where the authorities are looking at serious civil liberties problems. Professor Richard Cooter, chair of George Washington University's forensic psychology program, summed up the problem when he said, "There are a lot of people who have grievances, who are loners, who will never hurt anybody. And so if you said, 'There's your profile,' you'd end up . . . identifying all sorts of people who will never be dangerous to anybody."[45] Using these profiles, the police would end up arresting a lot of people who didn't deserve it. Nevertheless, it is still important to report people who seem to be contemplating mass murder, so that the police can speak to them (which will often defuse deadly desires) and check on whether they have access to deadly weapons they shouldn't have. There may also be a need for a temporary mental health confinement.

As seen on the news frequently, many mass murderers have used high-powered assault rifles in their crimes. I want to state right now that I am certainly not opposed to citizens having firearms. Being a law enforcement officer for many years, I know that the police have a four- to five-minute lag before they can get to any crime scene, and a lot of bad things can happen during that time. Citizens shouldn't be deprived of the means of protecting themselves until the police can arrive, but they don't need an assault rifle to do this. A handgun, a regular hunting rifle, or a shotgun will give them plenty of protection. Assault rifles are meant for one purpose: to kill lots of people quickly. And because bullets from assault rifles have high penetration capacity, using them in urban areas always presents the threat of hitting innocent people behind walls or in the next house. There is really no justifiable reason for private citizens to own or possess an assault rifle.

Senator Bill Nelson of Florida said, "I have hunted all my life . . . but an AR-15 is not for hunting, it's for killing."[46]

While many people want expanded background checks on assault rifles and other firearms purchases, there is a gigantic hole in this plan: gun shows. When I was writing a book on the Militia Movement, I went to several of these gun shows and saw thousands of weapons and pieces of equipment for sale, including assault rifles, bump stocks, and high-capacity magazines. None of the purchasers of these had to go through any kind of background check. They just laid down the cash and walked away with the products. The same applies to purchases from private individuals. This loophole in the law must be fixed because, according to a 2017 study, every year one in five firearms purchases in the United States doesn't involve a background check.[47]

Another serious problem we have seen several times in this book is individuals who shouldn't have possession of guns taking those legally belonging to someone else, usually teens taking their parents' guns, and using them in violent acts. A study reported in the *Los Angeles Times* found that of 239 school shootings examined in which the shooter was a minor, more than half of them acquired the weapons from their home.[48] Keeping firearms out of the hands of potentially violent individuals is the responsibility of every firearms owner; it can save families and others not only the shame of a family member being involved in a mass murder, but also serious financial blowback from the lawsuits filed by relatives of the dead and injured.

The police can also at times be at fault for mass murderers possessing guns. In the case involving Gary Martin, described in chapter 9, the Illinois State Police, after discovering that Martin had a felony domestic violence conviction in Mississippi, sent him a letter that revoked his Firearm Owner Identification Card and instructed him to turn in the firearm he had purchased. But no one followed up on this to ensure it was done. Police departments must be vigilant in ensuring that violent individuals, or those with serious mental health problems, don't possess firearms.

When I was a member of the police department in Indianapolis, there was a program in which any employee who felt the need to see a mental health professional could call and do so with no charge. The office for this service was not located at the police department, and all visits were confidential. Unless a person presented a clear danger to others, no one at the police department knew who was visiting the mental health service or for what reason. This would be an excellent idea for schools and large businesses.

Actually, an anonymous mental health support system should be available in every community for every citizen so that people at risk for community violence can get help. Many people don't want to see a mental health professional if they think others will know they are going. They fear others will see them as weak. But people who need help should have a place to get it.

This type of anonymous mental health care should especially be available to students. High school in particular can be a stressful time when a person's ego is the most fragile. There must be somewhere students can go to get help if they need it without fear of embarrassment for looking weak. Another idea that has been put forward is that schools should have a class each year that talks about the causes and warning signs of violent events at schools. This could lead some students to ask for help and other students to report troubling behavior seen in their peers.

As we have seen throughout this book, bullying has been at least partially to blame or used as an excuse for a number of mass murders. To remedy this, schools must act promptly against all complaints of bullying. When some students are bullied or excluded, eventually the hate and resentment caused by this can boil over into violence. Schools must stop believing that bullying is a "rite of passage" and aggressively tackle the problem.

A real must, however, if America is ever going to reduce the number of mass murders, or at least reduce the number of casualties, is for locations such as schools, public businesses, corporations, and other places where mass murders might occur to have a plan in place for what to do if such an event does occur: where is a safe location to go, who is in charge and will work with the police, how will the threat be communicated to those affected, what are the duties of certain employees, etc. As we have seen far too often, mass murder events can erupt into complete chaos because no one knows what to do. Of course, plans and training can never perfectly predict how an incident will turn out, but at least people will know where to go and what to do. The plans, though, once drawn up, need to be communicated clearly to employees and practiced often. Even though these plans may have to be modified on scene if a real incident occurs, the alternative of no planning is much worse. For schools that feel they need professional help in developing their safety plan, there are groups that can assist. A short list would include Safe Havens, International; National School Safety and Security Services; and others.

A number of communities have also adopted the "Sister School" concept. At the first notice of a school shooting or other emergency that affects the entire school, inevitably hundreds of fearful parents rush to the scene. This crowd of parents can greatly interfere with the resolution of the situation. Under the Sister School idea, parents are directed to the sister school, where they will be briefed about the situation and where the schoolchildren who have escaped from the incident will be taken for pickup.

Finally, along with schools making improvements to deal with mass murder incidents, police departments also must update their policies for dealing with them. There are many police departments, which other police departments should emulate, that now use social media and other community communications pathways to quickly alert the public to mass murder events so that citizens won't accidentally stumble into them. They also use these communication pathways to disseminate information to the parents and loved ones of those directly affected by a mass murder. Many parents at school shootings in particular complain about the dearth of information they receive. The police can correct this using social media. A number of police departments have even used these communication methods in the days after an event to correct the erroneous information that almost always follows a newsworthy event. Of course, there are certain facts that cannot be communicated while the event is ongoing, but I've found in my career that the police often keep things secret that should be released to the public.

The most important point, and the reason for this book, is that if mass murders are ever going to be stopped, the police and the public must work together as a team, as equal partners. Only as a team, with information flowing both ways, can society bring this terrible tragedy under control.

As we've seen and talked about many times in this book, mass murders have become a common occurrence over the last few decades, almost so common that no one seems surprised or stunned by them anymore. But they can be stopped. Airline hijackings became a common occurrence in the 1970s but are seldom heard of today. This happened because of a concerted police/public effort to combat them. The same effort must be made to stop mass murders. If it is, they too will become a rare event.

NOTES

1. MASS MURDERS IN THE UNITED STATES

1. "School Dynamiter First Slew Wife," *New York Times*, May 20, 1927, https://www.nytimes.com/1927/05/20/archives/school-dynamiter-first-slew-wife-charred-body-of-mrs-kehoe-is-found.html.

2. "Bath School Disaster," https://en.wikipedia.org/wiki/Bath_School_disaster.

3. "Massacre in Michigan—The Bath School Disaster," https://www.legendsofamerica.com/bath-school-massacre/2.

4. Monty J. Ellsworth, *The Bath School Disaster*, Bath School Museum Committee, 1991.

5. "The Story of the First Mass Murder in U.S. History," https://www.smithsonianmag.com/history/story-first-mass-murder-us-history-180956927.

6. "Veteran Kills 12 in Mad Rampage on Camden Street," https://longform.org/posts/veteran-kills-12-in-mad-rampage-on-camden-street.

7. "Rampage in Camden," http://murderpedia.org/male.U/u/unruh-howard.htm.

8. "Serious Mental Illness and Mass Homicide," Office of Research & Public Affairs, June 2018, https://www.treatmentadvocacycenter.org/key-issues/violence/3626-serious-mental-illness-and-mass-homicide.

9. *A Study of Active Shooter Incidents in the United States between 2000 and 2013*, US Department of Justice, September 16, 2013, 6.

10. "Serious Mental Illness and Mass Homicide."

11. "Quick Look: 250 Active Shooter Incidents in the United States from 2000 to 2017," https://www.fbi.gov/about/partnerships/office-of-partner-engagement/active-shooter-incidents-graphics.

12. "More Mass Shootings at US Schools in Last 18 Years Than Entire 20th Century: Study," https://www.straitstimes.com/world/united-states/more-mass-shootings-at-us-schools-in-last-18-years-than-entire-20th-century.

13. "Pearls Before Swine," *Indianapolis Star*, November 27, 2018, 3E.

14. *Study of Active Shooter Incidents*, 14–19.

15. Jen Viegas, "Mass Shootings in the US: Some Common Characteristics of the Men That Kill," https://www.seeker.com/culture/behavior/mass-shootings-in-the-us-some-common-characteristics-of-the-men-that-kill.

16. *A Study of the Pre-Attack Behaviors of Active Shooters in the United States between 2000 and 2013*, US Department of Justice, June 2018, 7.

17. Ford Fessenden, "They Threaten, Seethe and Unhinge, Then Kill in Quantity," https://www.nytimes.com/2000/04/09/us/they-threaten-seethe-and-unhinge-then-kill-in-quantity.html.

2. WHO ARE THE MASS MURDERERS?

1. Ngoc Huynh, "Jiverly Wong's Father: What Prompted Mass Killing in Binghamton Remains a Mystery," https://www.syracuse.com/news/index.ssf/2009/04/jiverly_wongs_father_our_son_w.html.

2. Associated Press, "Transcript of Letter Purportedly Sent by Binghamton Shooter," https://www.syracuse.com/news/index.ssf/2009/04/transcript_of_letter_purported.html.

3. Huynh, "Jiverly Wong's Father."

4. *A Study of the Pre-Attack Behaviors of Active Shooters in the United States between 2000 and 2013*, US Department of Justice, June 2018, 7.

5. Julie Turkewitz and Jess Bidgood, "Who Is Dimitrios Pagourtzis, the Texas Shooting Suspect?" https://www.nytimes.com/2018/05/18/us/dimitrios-pagourtzis-gunman-texas-shooting.html.

6. Dan Frosch, "Texas Shooter Spared Students He Liked, Court Document Says," https://www.wsj.com/articles/texas-shooter-spared-students-he-liked-court-document-says-1526735627.

7. Jake Harris and Melissa B. Taboada, "Santa Fe Student: Teacher Pulled Fire Alarm to Get Students to Safety during Shooting," https://www.statesman.com/news/20180518/santa-fe-student-teacher-pulled-fire-alarm-to-get-students-to-safety-during-shooting.

8. Evan Perez, Jason Morris, and Ralph Ellis, "What We Know about Dimitrios Pagourtzis, the Alleged Santa Fe High School Shooter," https://www.cnn.com/2018/05/18/us/dimitrios-pagourtzis-santa-fe-suspect/index.html.

9. Joe Marino and Ruth Brown, "Suspected Texas Shooter Was 'Weird' but Didn't Raise Red Flags," https://nypost.com/2018/05/18/suspected-texas-shooter-was-weird-but-didnt-raise-red-flags.

10. Perez, Morris, and Ellis, "What We Know about Dimitrios Pagourtzis."

11. US Secret Service, "Mass Attacks in Public Spaces—2017," March 2018, 2.

12. Interview by author, April 8, 2019.

13. Joe Navarro, "Identifying the Next Mass Murderer—Before It's Too Late," https://www.psychologytoday.com/us/blog/spycatcher/201506/identifying-the-next-mass-murderer-it-s-too-late.

14. Allen J. Frances, "The Mind of the Mass Murderer," https://www.psychologytoday.com/us/blog/saving-normal/201405/the-mind-the-mass-murderer.

15. Peter Langman, "Columbine, Bullying, and the Mind of Eric Harris," https://www.psychologytoday.com/us/blog/keeping-kids-safe/200905/columbine-bullying-and-the-mind-eric-harris.

16. Lindsay Carlton, "The Psychology behind Mass Shootings," https://www.foxnews.com/health/the-psychology-behind-mass-shootings.

17. *Study of the Pre-Attack Behaviors*, 12.

18. D. M. Weisbrot, "Prelude to a School Shooting? Assessing Threatening Behaviors in Childhood and Adolescence, *Journal of the American Academy of Child and Adolescent Psychiatry* 47, no. 8 (2008): 847–52.

19. George S. Everly, "'Profiling' School Shooters," https://www.psychologytoday.com/us/blog/when-disaster-strikes-inside-disaster-psychology/201803/profiling-school-shooters.

20. Kevin M. Carlsmith, Daniel T. Gilbert, and Timothy D. Wilson, "The Paradoxical Consequences of Revenge," *Journal of Personality and Social Psychology* 95 (2008): 1317.

21. Interview by author, April 9, 2019.

22. Alexia Cooper and Erica L. Smith, "Homicide Trends in the United States, 1980–2008," US Department of Justice, 2011, 10.

23. Stephanie Pappas, "Female Mass Killers: Why They're So Rare," https://www.livescience.com/53047-why-female-mass-shooters-are-rare.html.

24. "Tribal Shooting Suspect in California Killed 3 Relatives," https://www.seattletimes.com/seattle-news/tribal-shooting-suspect-in-california-killed-3-relatives.

25. "Cherie Lash Rhoades, Woman Arrested for Tribal Shooting, Known as Bully," https://www.cbsnews.com/news/cherie-lash-rhoades-woman-arrested-for-tribal-shooting-known-as-bully.

26. Elizabeth Janney, "Snochia Moseley: 5 Things to Know about Maryland Shooter," https://patch.com/maryland/belair/snochia-moseley-5-things-know-maryland-shooter.

27. Dan Frosch, "Woman in California Postal Shootings Had History of Bizarre Behavior," https://www.nytimes.com/2006/02/03/us/woman-in-california-postal-shootings-had-history-of-bizarre-behavior.html.

28. *Study of the Pre-Attack Behaviors*, 9–12.

29. "US Mass Shootings, 1982–2019: Data From *Mother Jones'* Investigation," https://www.motherjones.com/politics/2012/12/mass-shootings-mother-jones-full-data.

30. Dana Ford, "Who Commits Mass Shootings?" https://www.cnn.com/2015/06/27/us/mass-shootings/index.html.

31. *Study of the Pre-Attack Behaviors*, 9.

32. Interview by author, April 8, 2019.

3. WEAPONS OF MASS MURDERERS

1. Lynh Bui, Matt Zapotosky, Devlin Barrett, and Mark Berman, "At Least 59 Killed in Las Vegas Shooting Rampage, More Than 500 Others Injured," https://www.washingtonpost.com/news/morning-mix/wp/2017/10/02/police-shut-down-part-of-las-vegas-strip-due-to-shooting.

2. Nicole Chavez, "Security Guard Shot by Las Vegas Gunman Breaks Silence," https://www.cnn.com/2017/10/18/us/las-vegas-security-guard-jesus-campos/index.html.

3. Bui, Zapotosky, Barrett, and Berman, "At Least 59 Killed."

4. Joyce Anderson-Maples, "UAH Alum Recalls Fateful Night of Las Vegas Strip Shooting," https://www.uah.edu/news/people/uah-alum-recalls-fateful-night-of-las-vegas-strip-shooting.

5. Mitch Smith and Julie Turkewitz, "Las Vegas Gunman Shot Security Guard Before, Not After, Targeting Concertgoers," https://www.nytimes.com/2017/10/09/us/jesus-campos-las-vegas-shooting.html.

6. Sabrina Tavernise, Serge F. Kovaleski, and Julie Turkewitz, "Who Was Stephen Paddock? The Mystery of a Nondescript 'Numbers Guy,'" https://www.nytimes.com/2017/10/07/us/stephen-paddock-vegas.html.

7. "Weapon Types Used in Mass Shootings in the United States between 1982 and November 2018," https://www.statista.com/statistics/476409/mass-shootings-in-the-us-by-weapon-types-used.

8. Scott Pelley, "What Makes the AR-15 Style Rifle the Weapon of Choice for Mass Shooters?" https://www.cbsnews.com/news/ar-15-used-mass-shootings-weapon-of-choice-60-minutes.

9. "Weapon Types Used in Mass Shootings."

10. Patrick Winn, "Under Strict Gun Laws, Japan's Mass Killers Must Rely on Knives Instead," https://www.pri.org/stories/2016-07-26/under-strict-gun-laws-japans-mass-killers-must-rely-knives-instead.

11. "Knife Crime: Fatal Stabbings at Highest Level since Records Began in 1946," https://www.bbc.com/news/uk-47156957.

12. Alexandra Chachkevitch and Liam Ford, "Deaths of All Six Victims in Gage Park Ruled Homicides by Medical Examiner," http://www.chicagotribune.com/news/local/breaking/ct-gage-park-slayings-20160205-story.html.

13. "DNA, Phone Records Lead to Charges in Gage Park Massacre: Police," http://www.chicago.suntimes.com/news/sneed-gage-park-massacre.

14. Rummana Hussain, "Teen Massacre Victim Begged for Mercy: 'I Just Want to Live!'" https://www.chicago.suntimes.com/2016/5/20/18360438/teen-massacre-victim-begged-for-mercy-i-just-want-to-live.

15. Hussain, "Teen Massacre Victim Begged for Mercy."

16. Melissa Marino, "Middle School 'Satanists' Arrested for Mass Murder Plot in Bartow," https://www.wfla.com/news/polk-county/middle-school-satanists-arrested-for-mass-murder-plot-in-bartow/1546893810.

17. "Accused Driver Reported Feeling Suicidal at Time of Parade Crash," http://www.cnhinews.com/news/article_419426a8-7cac-11e5-931f-43709fb417d6.html.

18. "Adacia Chambers Sentenced in Deadly Oklahoma State Homecoming Crash," https://www.cbsnews.com/news/adacia-chambers-oklahoma-state-homecoming-crash-sentenced.

19. "Fire Kills 87 People at the Happy Land Social Club in the Bronx in 1990," http://www.nydailynews.com/new-york/nyc-crime/dozens-die-fire-illegal-bonx-social-club-1990-article-1.2152091.

20. Sam Roberts, "Julio Gonzalez, Arsonist Who Killed 87 at New York Club in '90, Dies at 61," https://www.nytimes.com/2016/09/15/nyregion/julio-gonzalez-arsonist-who-killed-87-at-new-york-club-in-90-dies-at-61.html.

21. Irene M. Kunii, "Engineer of Doom," *Time*, June 12, 1995, 45.

22. Nicholas D. Kristof, "Japanese Cult Said to Have Planned Nerve-Gas Attacks in U.S.," *New York Times*, March 23, 1997, 14.

23. Lawrence K. Grossman, "The Story of a Truly Contaminated Election," *Columbia Journalism Review* 39, no. 4 (January/February 2001).

24. Lawrence Sartorius, "The New Earth," https://www.thenewearth.org.

4. TACTICS OF MASS MURDERERS

1. Rick Anderson, "A Portrait of Violence Emerges of Suspect in the Washington State Mall Killings," http://www.latimes.com/nation/la/na-washington-shooting-20160925-snap-story.html.

2. Anderson, "Portrait of Violence."

3. Jody Allard and M. L. Lyke, "Washington Mall Shooting Suspect Confesses to Killings," https://www.washingtonpost.com/news/post-nation/wp/2016/09/25/after-day-long-manhunt-police-arrest-20-year-old-in-washington-state-mall-killings.

4. "Cancer Survivor Sarai Lara Identified as Victim in Cascade Mall Shooting," https://komonews.com/news/local/cancer-survivor-sarai-lara-identified-as-victim-in-cascade-shooting.

5. Hayley Hudson, "Becky Virgalla, Newtown Shooting Survivor, Says Principal, Others Saved Her in Sandy Hook Rampage," http://www.huffingtonpost.com/2012/12/24/becky-virgalla_n_2357284.html.

6. "6-Year-Old Survivor: 'Mommy, I'm OK but All My Friends Are Dead,'" https://washington.cbslocal.com/2012/12/17/6-year-old-survivor-mommy-im-ok-but-all-my-friends-are-dead/.

7. Ed Pilkington, "Sandy Hook Report—Shooter Adam Lanza Was Obsessed with Mass Murder," https://www.theguardian.com/world/2013/nov/25/sandy-hook-shooter-adam-lanza-report.

8. Matt Smith, "Sandy Hook Killer Took Motive to His Grave," https://www.cnn.com/2013/11/25/justice/sandy-hook-shooting-report/index.html.

9. "Sandy Hook Shootings: Four Things Revealed by FBI Files," https://www.bbc.com/news/world-us-canada-41749336.

10. James L. Knoll, "The 'Pseudocommando' Mass Murderer: Part I, The Psychology of Revenge and Obliteration," *Journal of the American Academy of Psychiatry and the Law* 38, no. 1 (March 2010): 87–94.

11. *A Study of the Pre-Attack Behaviors of Active Shooters in the United States between 2000 and 2013*, US Department of Justice, June 2018, 13.

12. Paula McMahon and Brittany Wallman, "Parkland School Shooter: Typical of Today's Mass Killers Studied by FBI," http://www.latimes.com/nation/la-na-parkland-mass-shooters-20180701-story.html.

5. THE MOTIVATION BEHIND
MASS MURDER

1. Brooks Brown, "Columbine Survivor with Words for Virginia Students," https:www.npr.org/templates/story/story.php?storyid=9658182.

2. Julie Cart, "Sheriff Releases Report on Columbine Shootings," https://www.latimes.com/archives/la-xpm-2000-may-16-mn-30573-story.html.

3. "Deputies on Scene," http://edition.cnn.com/SPECIALS/2000/columbine.cd/Pages/DEPUTIES_TEXT.htm.

4. Trevin Wax, "7 Myths about the Columbine Shooting," https://www.thegospelcoalition.org/blogs/trevin-wax/7-myths-about-the-columbine-shooting.

5. *Murderpedia*, http://murderpedia.org/male.H/h/harris-eric.htm.

6. US Secret Service, "The Final Report and Findings of the Safe School Initiative," https://www2.ed.gov/admins/lead/safety/preventingattacksreport.pdf.

7. "What Characteristics Do School Shooters Share?" https://www.sciencedaily.com/releases/2017/10/171019100756.htm.

8. Tia Ghose, "Mass Shooting Psychology: Spree Killers Have Consistent Profile, Research Shows," https://www.huffpost.com/entry/mass-shooting-psychology-spree-killers_n_2331236.

9. Ogi Ogas and Sai Gaddam, *A Billion Wicked Thoughts* (New York: Dutton, 2011), 98.

10. Greg Toppo, "10 Years Later, the Real Story behind Columbine," https://www.usatoday.com/news/nation/2009-04-13-columbine-myths_N.htm.

11. Abby Jackson, "Americans Look to Columbine to Better Understand School Shootings—but Myths about the Shooters Have Persisted for Years," https://www.insider.com/columbine-shooters-motives-2018-2.

12. Dave Cullen, "At Last We Know Why the Columbine Killers Did It," https://www.slate.com/news-and-politics/2004/04/at-last-we-know-why-the-columbine-killers-did-it.html.

13. Andrew Gumbel, "The Truth about Columbine," https://www.theguardian.com/world/2009/apr/17/columbine-massacre-gun-crime-us.

14. Peter Langman, "Dylan Klebold's Journal and Other Writings," https://schoolshooters.info/dylan-klebolds-journal-and-other-writings-transcribed-and-annotated.

15. Stephanie Pappas, "Female Mass Killers: Why They're so Rare," https://www.livescience.com/53047-why-female-mass-shooters-are-rare.html.

16. Dave Cullen, "The Reluctant Killer," https://www.theguardian.com/world/2009/apr/25/dave-cullen-columbine.

17. Cullen, "At Last We Know Why."

18. Daniel Wenger, "Pearl Jam's 'Jeremy' and the Intractable Cultural Script of School Shooters," https://www.newyorker.com/culture/cultural-comment/pearl-jams-jeremy-and-the-intractable-cultural-script-of-school-shooters.

19. Michael Fleeman, "Bombing Survivors Recall Horror of Blast," *Indianapolis Star*, April 26, 1997, A-3.

20. Michael Fleeman, "McVeigh Evidence Lacks Fingerprints," *Indianapolis Star*, May 16, 1997, A-16.

21. Fleeman, "Bombing Survivors Recall Horror."

22. Michael Fleeman, "FBI Chemist Testifies Explosive Residue Found on McVeigh's Clothing," *Indianapolis Star*, May 20, 1997, A-7.

23. Michael Fleeman, "Camera Tracked Truck's Movement," *Indianapolis Star*, May 15, 1997, A-3.

24. "SWAT Team Members: FBI Shooter Rules 'Crazy' at Ruby Ridge," http://www.cnn.com/US/9510/ruby_ridge.

25. Emily DeRuy, "The Warning Signs of a Mass Shooting," https://www.theatlantic.com/politics/archive/2015/12/the-warning-signs-of-a-mass-shooting/433527.

26. Olga Khazan, "Why Better Mental-Health Care Won't Stop Mass Shootings," https://www.theatlantic.com/health/archive/2017/10/why-better-mental-health-care-wont-stop-mass-shootings/541965.

27. DeRuy, "Warning Signs."

28. "Deadly Dreams: What Motivates School Shootings?" https://www.scientificamerican.com/article/deadly-dreams.

29. "Deadly Dreams."

30. "Dr. Park Dietz: Dangerous Minds," https://www.independent.co.uk/news/people/profiles/dr-park-dietz-dangerous-minds-412116.html.

31. "Man Arrested in Synagogue Plot Inspired by Pittsburgh Attack," *Indianapolis Star*, December 11, 2018, 1B.

32. Terry McCarthy, "WARNING: Andy Williams Here," http://content.time.com/time/magazine/article/0,9171,102077,00.html.

33. "Deadly Dreams."

34. Ralph W. Larkin, "The Columbine Legacy," *American Behavioral Scientist* 52 (May 2009): 1309.

6. SECONDARY VICTIMS OF MASS MURDER

1. Ann W. O'Neill, "Farley Testifies, Says Obsession Began with Love at First Sight," *San Jose Mercury News*, August 21, 1991, A1.

2. Kristin Downey and Jeanne Huber, "ESL Gunman 'A Nerdie Kid,'" *San Jose Mercury News*, February 20, 1988, A1.

3. Bob Trebilcock, "I Love You to Death," *Redbook*, March 1992, 103.

4. O'Neill, "Farley Testifies."

5. Trebilcock, "I Love You to Death," 112.

6. Trebilcock, "I Love You to Death," 112.

7. S. L. Wykes, "Judge Hears Tape at Farley Trial," *San Jose Mercury News*, July 15, 1988, B1.

8. Wykes, "Judge Hears Tape at Farley Trial."

9. Trebilcock, "I Love You to Death," 114.

10. Amy Novotney, "What Happens to the Survivors?" *Monitor on Psychology* 49, no. 8, http://www.apa.org/monitor/2018/09/survivorshttps://www.apa.org/monitor/2018/09/survivors.

11. Melvin Lerner, *The Belief in a Just World Hypothesis: A Fundamental Delusion* (New York: Plenum Press, 1980).

12. John Bacon, "Sandy Hook Victim's Dad Dies in Apparent Suicide," *Indianapolis Star*, March 26, 2019, 9A.

13. "The Psychological Ripple Effects of Mass Shootings," https://www.salon.com/2017/10/09/the-psychological-ripple-effects-of-mass-shootings_partner.

14. Cited in Novotney, "What Happens to the Survivors?"

15. Novotney, "What Happens to the Survivors?"

16. Arash Javanbakht, "What Mass Shootings Do to Those Not Shot: Social Consequences of Mass Gun Violence," https://www.medicalxpress.com/news/2018-11-mass-shot-social-consequences-gun.html.

17. Novotney, "What Happens to the Survivors?"

18. Alexandra Seltzer, "Parkland Victim's Dad: My Daughter Will Be the Last Kid Murdered in School," https://www.palmbeachpost.com/news/local/father-parkland-school-shooting-victim-pledges-meadow-movement/XLfH2mS07kq0uKa0JQfRNM/.

19. Interview by author, June 4, 2004.

20. Mike Ellis, "Call for Legal Protection Highlights Victims' Plight," *Indianapolis Star*, April 26, 2002, A1.

21. Sarah D. Goodrum and Mark C. Stafford, "Homicide, Bereavement, and the Criminal Justice System, Final Report," https://www.ncjrs.gov/pdffiles1/nij/grants/189567.pdf.

22. Paul McGhee, "Humor and Mental Health," https://www.nurseslearning.com/courses/nrp/NRPCX-W0009/html/body.humor.page7.htm.

23. Goodrum and Stafford, "Homicide, Bereavement, and the Criminal Justice System."

24. Goodrum and Stafford, "Homicide, Bereavement, and the Criminal Justice System."

25. Don Lowery, "Former GA Deputy Convicted of Slaying Boyfriend, Encasing Body in Concrete," *Savannah Morning News*, March 26, 2004.

26. Goodrum and Stafford, "Homicide, Bereavement, and the Criminal Justice System."

27. J. Scott Kenney, "Survivors of Murder Victims," paper presented at the X World Symposium on Victimology, Montreal, Quebec, August 6, 2000.

28. Ohio Crime Victim Services, "Co-Victim Grief," https://www. crimevictimservices.org/homicide.html.

29. M. Victoria Cummock, "The Necessity of Denial in Grieving Murder: Observations of the Victims' Families Following the Bombing in Oklahoma City," *NCP Clinical Quarterly* 5, nos. 2–3 (Spring/Summer 1995): 18.

30. Interview by author, July 19, 2004.

31. Javanbakht, "What Mass Shootings Do."

32. Rhitu Chatterjee, "Another Mass Shooting? 'Compassion Fatigue' Is a Natural Reaction," https://www.npr.org/sections/health-shots/2018/11/09/666150361/another-mass-shooting-compassion-fatigue-is-a-natural-reaction.

33. Chatterjee, "Another Mass Shooting?"

7. COMMUNIQUÉS AND MANIFESTOS

1. Rick Anderson, "Here I Am, 26, with No Friends, No Job, No Girlfriend," https://www.latimes.com/nation/la-na-school-shootings-2017-story.html.

2. Nancy Dillon, "I'll Be Joining You Soon," https://www.nydailynews.com/news/national/christopher-harper-mercer-planned-kill-witness-article-1.2384171.

3. "My Story," https://www.schoolshooters.info/sites/default/files/Christopher-Sean-Harper-Mercer-My-Manifesto.pdf.

4. "My Story."

5. "My Story."

6. "My Story."

7. "My Story."

8. Tom Junod, "Why Mass Shootings Keep Happening," *Esquire*, October 2017.

9. Alan Duke, "Timeline to 'Retribution': Isla Vista Attacks Planned over Years," http://www.cnn.com/2014/05/26/justice/california-elliot-rodger-timeline.

10. "How I Tried to Help Elliot Rodger," https://www.bbc.com/news/magazine-28197785.

11. "Elliot Rodger's 'Retribution' Video," https://www.schoolshooters.info/sites/default/files/rodger_video_1.0.pdf.

12. "Elliot Rodger Manifesto: My Twisted World," https://www.documentcloud.org/documents/1173808-elliot-rodger-manifesto.html.

13. "Elliot Rodger's 'Retribution' Video."

14. Peter Langman, "Elliot Rodger: An Analysis," https://www.schoolshooters.info/sites/default/files/rodger_analysis_2.0.pdf.

15. Langman, "Elliot Rodger."

16. Hailey Branson and Richard Winton, "How Elliot Rodger Went from Misfit Mass Murderer to 'Saint' for Group of Misogynists—and Suspected Toronto Killer," http://www.latimes.com/local/lanow/la-me-ln-elliot-rodger-incel-20180426-story.html.

17. Ben Feuerherd, "Yoga Studio Shooter Was a Racist Misogynist Who Found Solidarity with 'Incels,'" https://www.nypost.com/2018/11/04/yoga-studio-shooter-was-a-racist-misogynist-who-found-solidarity-with-incels.

18. Branson and Winton, "How Elliot Rodger Went from Misfit."

19. Interview by author, April 9, 2019.

20. Wensley Clarkson, *Driven to Kill* (London: John Drake Publishing, 2004), 35–36.

21. Katherine Newman, *Rampage: The Social Roots of School Shootings* (New York: Basic Books, 2004), 249.

22. "Luke Woodham's Writings," https://www.schoolshooters.info/sites/default/files/Luke%20Woodham%20Writings.pdf.

23. "Themes in the Writings of Eric Harris," https://www.schoolshooters.info/sites/default/files/harris_themes_1.7.pdf.

24. "Writings of Eric Harris."

25. Peter Langman, "Dylan Klebold's Journal and Other Writings," https://schoolshooters.info/dylan-klebolds-journal-and-other-writings-transcribed-and-annotated.

26. Langman, "Dylan Klebold's Journal."

27. Jaime Holguin, "Eerie Letter from University Killer," https://www.cbsnews.com/news/eerie-letter-from-university-killer.

28. Holguin, "Eerie Letter."

29. "Communication from the Dead," https://www.schoolshooters.info/sites/default/files/Flores-final-letter.pdf.

30. "Communication from the Dead."

31. "Letter after Killing Mother," https://www.schoolshooters.info/sites/default/files/Whitman_letter_mother.pdf.

32. "Letter about Killing Wife," http://www.schoolshooters.info/sites/default/files/Whitman_letter_wife.pdf.

33. Tom Jacobs, "What Mass Murderers Have in Common," https://www.salon.com/2013/07/31/are_mass_murderers_all_cold_unfeeling_psychopaths_partner.

34. Laura E. Hamlett, "Common Psycholinguistic Themes in Mass Murderer Manifestos" (PhD diss., Walden University, 2017).

8. POLICE RESPONSE TO
MASS MURDER SCENES

1. "Unprepared and Overwhelmed," https://projects.sun-sentinel.com/2018/sfl-parkland-school-shooting-critical-moments.

2. "Unprepared and Overwhelmed."

3. Ray Sanchez, "My School Is Being Shot Up," https://www.cnn.com/2018/02/18/us/parkland-florida-school-shooting-accounts/index.html.

4. Sanchez, "My School Is Being Shot Up."

5. Audra D. S. Burch, Frances Robles, and Patricia Mazzei, "Florida Agency Investigated Nikolas Cruz after Violent Social Media Posts," https://www.nytimes.com/2018/02/17/us/nikolas-cruz-florida-shooting.html.

6. Christal Hayes and Emily Bohatch, "I'm Sick to My Stomach," https://www.usatoday.com/story/news/2018/02/14/injuries-reported-after-shooting-florida-high-school/338217002.

7. Adam Goldman and Patricia Mazzei, "YouTube Comment Seen as Early Warning in Shooting Left Little for FBI to Investigate," https://www.nytimes.com/2018/02/15/us/politics/nikolas-cruz-youtube-comment-fbi.html.

8. "FBI Statement on the Shooting in Parkland, Florida," https://www.fbi.gov/news/pressrel/press-releases/fbi-statement-on-the-shooting-in-parkland-florida.

9. "New Florida Governor Suspends Sheriff over School Massacre," *USA Today*, January 12, 2019, 1B.

10. "Unprepared and Overwhelmed."

11. Patricia Mazzei, "Slow Police Response and Chaos Contributed to Parkland Massacre, Report Finds," https://www.nytimes.com/2018/12/12/us/parkland-shooting-florida-commission-report.html.

12. Mark Berman and Laura Meckler, "Parkland Shooting Commission Describes School Security Lapses, Police Missteps," https://www.washingtonpost.com/nation/2018/12/12/parkland-shooting-commission-finds-security-failures-improper-law-enforcement-responses-rampage.

13. Megan O'Matz, "Cops in Parkland Shooting under Investigation for Crimes," https://www.sun-sentinel.com/local/broward/parkland/florida-school-shooting/fl-school-shooting-police-response-investigation-20180921-story.html.

14. Tom Jackman, "Police Are Trained to Attack Active Shooters, but Parkland Officer Didn't," https://www.washingtonpost.com/news/true-crime/wp/2018/02/23/police-are-trained-to-attack-active-shooters-but-parkland-officer-didnt-would-armed-teachers-help.

15. Ray Sanchez, "How Columbine Changed the Way Police Respond to Mass Shootings," https://www.cnn.com/2018/02/15/us/florida-school-shooting-columbine-lessons/index.html.

16. Sharon Coolidge, Dan Horn, Cameron Knight, Anne Saker, Max Londberg, and Sarah Brookbank, "Cincinnati Mass Shooting Leaves City Reeling," *Indianapolis Star*, September 7, 2018, 7A.

17. Laura Alix, "Fifth Third Shooting Survivor: 'Every Day Has Been Better Than the Last,'" https://www.americanbanker.com/news/fifth-third-shooting-survivor-every-day-has-been-better-than-the-last.

18. Cameron Knight, "Officials Analyze Fifth Third Shooting Response," https://www.cincinnati.com/story/news/crime/crime-and-courts/2018/09/17/cincinnati-shooting-police-chief-update-fifth-third-center/1333227002.

19. Amber Hunt, "Footage from Bank Shooting Is Revealing," *Indianapolis Star*, September 8, 2018, 6A.

20. Jennifer Edwards Baker, "Fifth Third Shooting Motive May Never Be Known," http://www.fox19.com/2018/09/17/still-no-motive-fifth-third-shooting-ballistic-vests-coming-firefighters.

21. Rick Jervis, Sean Rossman, and Candy Woodall, "'Horrific' Pa. Synagogue Shooting Kills at Least 11," *Indianapolis Star*, October 28, 2018, 1B.

22. "Feds Indict Robert Bowers on New Charges Related to Pittsburgh Synagogue Shooting," https://www.post-gazette.com/news/crime-courts/2019/01/29/robert-bowers-pittsburgh-tree-of-life-synagogue-mass-shooting-superseding-indictment/stories/201901290105.

23. Marina Pitofsky, "Temple Suspect Pleads Not Guilty," *Indianapolis Star*, February 12, 2019, 6A.

24. Kellie B. Gormly, Avi Selk, Joel Achenbach, Mark Berman, and Alex Horton, "Suspect in Pittsburgh Synagogue Shooting Charged with 29 Counts in Deaths of 11 People," https://www.washingtonpost.com/nation/2018/10/27/pittsburgh-police-responding-active-shooting-squirrel-hill-area.

25. Interview by author, April 9, 2019.

26. Police Executive Research Forum, "The Police Response to Active Shooter Incidents," https://www.policeforum.org/assets/docs/Critical_Issues_

Series/the%20police%20response%20to%20active%20shooter%20incidents
%202014.pdf.

27. Jon Schuppe, "California Officer Died While Following a Growing Police Strategy," https://www.nbcnews.com/news/us-news/california-officer-died-
doing-what-he-was-trained-do-stop-n934111.

28. Interview by author, April 23, 2019.

29. Police Executive Research Forum, "Police Response."

30. "Great Mills High Gunman Shot by School Officer, Killed Self: Police,"
https://www.nbcwashington.com/news/local/Great-Mills-High-Shooter-Shot-
by-School-Officer-Killed-Self-Police-477984883.html.

31. Blake McCoy, Alexander Smith, Andrew Rudansky, Erin Calabrese, and
Alex Johnson, "Cedric Larry Ford Kills 3, Injures 14 in Kansas Shooting
Spree," https://www.nbcnews.com/news/us-news/cedric-larry-ford-kills-3-
injures-14-kansas-shooting-spree-n526316.

32. "Year Later, Officer Who Fatally Shot St. Cloud Mall Attacker Speaks
Out," https://www.twincities.com/2017/09/16/year-later-officer-who-fatally-
shot-st-cloud-mall-attacker-speaks-out.

33. "Active Shooter Model Policy," *International Association of Chiefs of
Police*, April 2018, 3.

9. HOW TO SPOT AND SURVIVE A
MASS MURDER

1. Richard C. Paddock and Ralph Frammolina, "Hostages Recall Terror of
Siege in Sacramento," https://www.latimes.com/archives/la-xpm-1991-04-06-
mn-1622-story.html.

2. Steve Geissinger, "Gunmen—Members of an Asian Gang—Were Unhappy in the United States," https://www.apnews.com/
b3e4ccb610b9354220d8de5e2c063cfb.

3. Jane Gross, "6 Are Killed as 8-Hour Siege by Gang Ends in California,"
https://www.nytimes.com/1991/04/06/us/6-are-killed-as-8-hour-siege-by-gang-
ends-in-california.html.

4. Richard C. Paddock and Carl Ingram, "3 Hostages, 3 Gunmen Die in
Sacramento Store Siege," https://www.latimes.com/archives/la-xpm-1991-04-
05-mn-1983-story.html.

5. Paddock and Frammolina, "Hostages Recall Terror."

6. Paddock and Frammolina, "Hostages Recall Terror."

7. *A Study of Active Shooter Incidents in the United States between 2000
and 2013*, US Department of Justice, September 16, 2013.

8. Total Security Solutions, "The Four Ds of Active Shooter Response," https://www.tssbulletproof.com/blog/preparing-active-shooter-response.

9. Becky Lewis, "CRASE Training Helps Schools Fill the Gaps in School Safety Plans," https://www.schoolsafetyinfo.org/stories/Success4CRASE-training.html.

10. "Civilian Response to Active Shooter Events," https://www.alerrt.org/page/CivilianResponse.

11. Elliot C. McLaughlin, "In Active Shooter Situation, Don't Just Stand There," https://www.cnn.com/2016/03/03/us/active-shooter-crase-training/index.html.

12. *A Study of the Pre-Attack Behaviors of Active Shooters in the United States between 2000 and 2013*, US Department of Justice, June 2018.

13. McLaughlin, "Don't Just Stand There."

14. James L. Knoll, "The 'Pseudocommando' Mass Murderer: Part II, The Language of Revenge," *Journal of the American Academy of Psychiatry and the Law* 38, no. 2 (2010): 263.

15. Interview by author, June 6, 1995.

16. Mark Guarino, Kristine Phillips, and Frances Stead Sellers, "Man Accused in Aurora Mass Shooting Had Been Convicted for Beating Girlfriend with Baseball Bat," https://www.washingtonpost.com/nation/2019/02/16/man-kills-five-warehouse-shooting-spree-shortly-after-being-fired-illinois-police-say.

17. Guarino, Phillips, and Sellers, "Man Accused in Aurora."

18. Jonathan Rabinovitz, "Rampage in Connecticut: The Overview," https://www.nytimes.com/1998/03/07/nyregion/rampage-connecticut-overview-connecticut-lottery-worker-kills-4-bosses-then.html.

10. THE FUTURE: WHAT CAN WE DO?

1. Matt McKinney, "Teacher Who Stopped Noblesville Shooter: My Actions 'Were the Only Acceptable Actions,'" https://www.theindychannel.com/news/local-news/hamilton-county/teacher-who-stopped-noblesville-shooter-to-speak-monday.

2. "Police: Ind. School Gunman Asked to Be Excused from Class, Returned with 2 Handguns," https://www.cbsnews.com/news/indiana-school-shooting-today-noblesville-west-middle-school-2018-05-25-live-updates.

3. Stephanie Wade, "I Dropped to My Knees! Students, Parents Talk about Noblesville School Shooting," https://abcnews.go.com/US/active-shooter-reported-indiana-middle-school-police/story?id=55413808.

4. Wade, "I Dropped to My Knees!"

5. Justin Doom, "13-Year-Old Who Allegedly Opened Fire at Indiana School Won't Be Tried as Adult," https://abcnews.go.com/US/13-year-allegedly-opened-fire-indiana-school-adult/story?id=55677685.

6. Carter Barrett, "13-Year-Old Noblesville School Shooter Planned Attack, Apologizes in Court," https://www.wfyi.org/news/articles/noblesville-school-shooting-suspect-admits-to.

7. Vic Ryckaert, Ryan Martin, Chris Sikich, Emma Fittes, Arika Herron, Tony Cook, and Holly V. Hays, "Noblesville Shooting Latest Updates," https://www.indystar.com/story/news/crime/2018/05/25/noblesville-school-shooting-active-shooter-reported-middle-school/644021002.

8. Mike Emery and Jason Truitt, "Police: Juvenile Took His Own Life," *Indianapolis Star*, December 14, 2018, 1A.

9. Audrey J. Kirby, "For Parents, Panic Eases after Being Reunited with Kids," *Indianapolis Star*, December 14, 2018, 5A.

10. Mike Wood, "The Next Generation of Active Shooter Response," https://www.policeone.com/active-shooter/articles/482527006-The-next-generation-of-active-shooter-response.

11. John Bacon, "Arm Teachers, Parkland Shooting Panel Suggests," *Indianapolis Star*, January 4, 2019, 2B.

12. Todd C. Frankel, Brittney Martin, Tim Craig, and Christian Davenport, "Santa Fe High School Had a Shooting Plan, Armed Officers and Practice," https://www.texastribune.org/2018/05/20/santa-fe-high-school-had-shooting-plan-armed-officers-and-practice-ten.

13. Tom Jackman, "Police Are Trained to Attack Active Shooters, But Parkland Officer Didn't," https://www.washingtonpost.com/news/true-crime/wp/2018/02/23/police-are-trained-to-attack-active-shooters-but-parkland-officer-didnt-would-armed-teachers-help.

14. "Judge: Teachers Don't Need Police-Level Gun Training," https://www.apnews.com/c313535fd68c46d0a597dd46343d5918.

15. Mark Berman and Laura Meckler, "Parkland Shooting Commission Describes School Security Lapses, Police Missteps," https://www.washingtonpost.com/nation/2018/12/12/parkland-shooting-commission-finds-security-failures-improper-law-enforcement-responses-rampage.

16. Hailey Branson and Richard Winton, "How Elliot Rodger Went from Misfit Mass Murderer to 'Saint' for Group of Misogynists—and Suspected Toronto Killer," http://www.latimes.com/local/lanow/la-me-ln-elliot-rodger-incel-20180426-story.html.

17. "Omaha Gunman Suicide Notes," http://www.thesmokinggun.com/archive/years/2007/1207072omaha1.html.

18. David Brin, "Names of Infamy: Deny Killers the Notoriety They Seek," http://davidbrin.blogspot.com/2012/07/names-of-infamy-deny-killers-notoreity.html.

19. Malcolm Gladwell, "Thresholds of Violence," https://www.newyorker.com/magazine/2015/10/19/thresholds-of-violence.

20. Owen Amos, "Six Radical Ways to Tackle US School Shootings," https://www.bbc.com/news/world-us-canada-43118865.

21. Amos, "Six Radical Ways."

22. Eli Saslow, Sarah Kaplan, and Joseph Hoyt, "Oregon Shooter Said to Have Singled Out Christians for Killing in 'Horrific Act of Cowardice,'" https://www.washingtonpost.com/news/morning-mix/wp/2015/10/02/oregon-shooter-said-to-have-singled-out-christians-for-killing-in-horrific-act-of-cowardice.

23. Tasbeeh Herwees, "Media's Mass Shooting Coverage Has Got to Change, a Psychologist Says," https://www.good.is/articles/psychologist-connects-media-and-mass-shootings.

24. Jennifer Johnston and Andrew Joy, "Mass Shootings and the Media Contagion Effect," https://www.apa.org/news/press/releases/2016/08/media-contagion-effect.pdf.

25. "'Media Contagion' Is Factor in Mass Shootings, Study Says," https://www.apa.org/news/press/releases/2016/08/media-contagion.aspx.

26. Robyn Merrett, "Woman May Have Prevented School Shooting in Kentucky after Reporting Racist Facebook Message," https://www.people.com/crime/new-jersey-woman-prevents-school-shooting-reports-racist-facebook-message/.

27. Merrett, "Woman May Have Prevented School Shooting."

28. Lindsey Bever, "A Woman Reported a Racist Facebook Message," https://www.washingtonpost.com/education/2018/10/23/woman-reported-racist-facebook-message-she-may-have-helped-stop-school-shooting.

29. Ryan Schmelz, "Woman Credited for Preventing School Shooting Speaks Out," https://www.wtvq.com/2018/10/24/woman-credited-preventing-school-shooting-speaks.

30. "Police in Kentucky Arrest Man with Stockpile of Guns Believed to Be Planning Mass Shooting," https://www.wdrb.com/news/crime-reports/images-police-in-kentucky-arrest-man-with-stockpile-of-guns/article_c9c1cc61-a3b1-5f14-ae7d-547469e5ebc9.html.

31. "Police in Kentucky Arrest Man."

32. Minyvonne Burke, "Police in Kentucky Believe They Stopped Possible Mass Shooting in Arresting Man with Five Loaded Guns in His Car," https://www.nbcnews.com/news/us-news/police-kentucky-believe-they-stopped-possible-mass-shooting-arresting-man-n938676.

33. Burke, "Police in Kentucky Believe."

34. *A Study of the Pre-Attack Behaviors of Active Shooters in the United States between 2000 and 2013*, US Department of Justice, June 2018, 20.

35. *A Study of Active Shooter Incidents in the United States between 2000 and 2013*, US Department of Justice, September 16, 2013, 10.

36. Stephanie Pappas, "The Science of Mass Shooters: What Drives a Person to Kill?" https://www.scientificamerican.com/article/the-science-of-mass-shooters-what-drives-a-person-to-kill.

37. "Deadly Dreams: What Motivates School Shootings?" https://www.scientificamerican.com/article/deadly-dreams.

38. US Secret Service, "Mass Attacks in Public Places—March 2017," March 2018, 6.

39. James L. Knoll, "The 'Pseudocommando' Mass Murderer: Part II, The Language of Revenge," *Journal of the American Academy of Psychiatry and the Law* 38, no. 2 (2010): 270.

40. *Study of the Pre-Attack Behaviors*, 7.

41. Paula McMahon and Brittany Wallman, "Parkland School Shooter: Typical of Today's Mass Killers Studied by FBI," http://www.latimes.com/nation/la-na-parkland-mass-shooters-20180701-story.html.

42. "Texas School Shooting at Santa Fe High School Kills 10, Injures 10," https://www.abc7chicago.com/texas-shooting-at-santa-fe-high-school-kills-10-injures-10/3494817.

43. "Social Sentinel FAQ," https://www.esc20.net/page/open/54649/0/SocialSentinelFAQ2018.pdf.

44. Jerry Davich, "Do Social Media Security Alert Programs Protect or Invade?" http://www.chicagotribune.com/suburbs/post-tribune/opinion/ct-ptb-davich-social-sentinel-alerts-st-0311-20160311-story.html.

45. Alayna Shulman, "Rancho Tehama: Why Do Mass Shooters Target Children, Strangers?" https://www.usatoday.com/story/news/nation-now/2017/11/15/rancho-tehama-why-do-mass-shooters-target-children-strangers/869306001.

46. "Florida Shooting: Updates as They Happened," https://www.bbc.com/news/live/world-us-canada-43066528.

47. Tara Haelle, "Want to Stop Mass Shootings?" https://www.forbes.com/sites/tarahaelle/2018/09/27/want-to-stop-mass-shootings-do-these-two-things-physician-says.

48. Rick Anderson, "Here I Am, 26, with No Friends, No Job, No Girlfriend," http://www.latimes.com/nation/la-na-school-shootings-2017-story.html.

BIBLIOGRAPHY

"Accused Driver Reported Feeling Suicidal at Time of Parade Crash." http://www.cnhinews. com/news/article_419426a8-7cac-11e5-931f-43709fb417d6.html.

"Active Shooter Model Policy." International Association of Chiefs of Police, April 2018, 3.

"Adacia Chambers Sentenced in Deadly Oklahoma State Homecoming Crash." https://www. cbsnews.com/news/adacia-chambers-oklahoma-state-homecoming-crash-sentenced.

Alix, Laura. "Fifth Third Shooting Survivor: 'Every Day Has Been Better Than the Last.'" https://www.americanbanker.com/news/fifth-third-shooting-survivor-every-day-has-been- better-than-the-last.

Allard, Jody, and M. L. Lyke. "Washington Mall Shooting Suspect Confesses to Killings." https://www.washingtonpost.com/news/post-nation/wp/2016/09/25/after-day-long- manhunt-police-arrest-20-year-old-in-washington-state-mall-killings.

Amos, Owen. "Six Radical Ways to Tackle US School Shootings." https://www.bbc.com/news/ world-us-canada-43118865.

Anderson, Rick. "Here I Am, 26, with No Friends, No Job, No Girlfriend." https://www. latimes.com/nation/la-na-school-shootings-2017-story.html.

———. "A Portrait of Violence Emerges of Suspect in the Washington State Mall Killings." http://www.latimes.com/nation/la/na-washington-shooting-20160925-snap-story.html.

Anderson-Maples, Joyce. "UAH Alum Recalls Fateful Night of Las Vegas Strip Shooting." https://www.uah.edu/news/people/uah-alum-recalls-fateful-night-of-las-vegas-strip- shooting.

Associated Press. "Transcript of Letter Purportedly Sent by Binghamton Shooter." https:// www.syracuse.com/news/index.ssf/2009/04/transcript_of_letter_purported.html.

Bacon, John. "Arm Teachers, Parkland Shooting Panel Suggests." *Indianapolis Star*, January 4, 2019, 2B.

———. "Sandy Hook Victim's Dad Dies in Apparent Suicide." *Indianapolis Star*, March 26, 2019, 9A.

Baker, Jennifer Edwards. "Fifth Third Shooting Motive May Never Be Known." http://www. fox19.com/2018/09/17/still-no-motive-fifth-third-shooting-ballistic-vests-coming- firefighters.

Barrett, Carter. "13-Year-Old Noblesville School Shooter Planned Attack, Apologizes in Court." https://www.wfyi.org/news/articles/noblesville-school-shooting-suspect-admits-to.

Berman, Mark, and Laura Meckler. "Parkland Shooting Commission Describes School Se- curity Lapses, Police Missteps." https://www.washingtonpost.com/nation/2018/12/12/ parkland-shooting-commission-finds-security-failures-improper-law-enforcement- responses-rampage.

Bever, Lindsey. "A Woman Reported a Racist Facebook Message." https://www.washingtonpost.com/education/2018/10/23/woman-reported-racist-facebook-message-she-may-have-helped-stop-school-shooting.

Branson, Hailey, and Richard Winton. "How Elliot Rodger Went from Misfit Mass Murderer to 'Saint' for Group of Misogynists—and Suspected Toronto Killer." http://www.latimes.com/local/lanow/la-me-ln-elliot-rodger-incel-20180426-story.html.

Brin, David. "Names of Infamy: Deny Killers the Notoriety They Seek." http://davidbrin.blogspot.com/2012/07/names-of-infamy-deny-killers-notoreity.html.

Brown, Brooks. "Columbine Survivor with Words for Virginia Students." https:www.npr.org/templates/story/story.php?storyid=9658182.

Bui, Lynh, Matt Zapotosky, Devlin Barrett, and Mark Berman. "At Least 59 Killed in Las Vegas Shooting Rampage, More Than 500 Others Injured." https://www.washingtonpost.com/news/morning-mix/wp/2017/10/02/police-shut-down-part-of-las-vegas-strip-due-to-shooting.

Burch, Audra D. S., Frances Robles, and Patricia Mazzei. "Florida Agency Investigated Nikolas Cruz after Violent Social Media Posts." https://www.nytimes.com/2018/02/17/us/nikolas-cruz-florida-shooting.html.

Burke, Minyvonne. "Police in Kentucky Believe They Stopped Possible Mass Shooting in Arresting Man with Five Loaded Guns in His Car." https://www.nbcnews.com/news/us-news/police-kentucky-believe-they-stopped-possible-mass-shooting-arresting-man-n938676.

"Cancer Survivor Sarai Lara Identified as Victim in Cascade Mall Shooting." https://komonews.com/news/local/cancer-survivor-sarai-lara-identified-as-victim-in-cascade-shooting.

Carlsmith, Kevin M., Daniel T. Gilbert, and Timothy D. Wilson. "The Paradoxical Consequences of Revenge." *Journal of Personality and Social Psychology* 95 (2008): 1317.

Carlton, Lindsay. "The Psychology behind Mass Shootings." https://www.foxnews.com/health/the-psychology-behind-mass-shootings.

Cart, Julie. "Sheriff Releases Report on Columbine Shootings." https://www.latimes.com/archives/la-xpm-2000-may-16-mn-30573-story.html.

Chachkevitch, Alexandra, and Liam Ford. "Deaths of All Six Victims in Gage Park Ruled Homicides by Medical Examiner." http://www.chicagotribune.com/news/local/breaking/ct-gage-park-slayings-20160205-story.html.

Chatterjee, Rhitu. "Another Mass Shooting? 'Compassion Fatigue' Is a Natural Reaction." https://www.npr.org/sections/health-shots/2018/11/09/666150361/another-mass-shooting-compassion-fatigue-is-a-natural-reaction.

Chavez, Nicole. "Security Guard Shot by Las Vegas Gunman Breaks Silence." https://www.cnn.com/2017/10/18/us/las-vegas-security-guard-jesus-campos/index.html.

"Cherie Lash Rhoades, Woman Arrested for Tribal Shooting, Known as Bully." https://www.cbsnews.com/news/cherie-lash-rhoades-woman-arrested-for-tribal-shooting-known-as-bully.

"Civilian Response to Active Shooter Events." https://www.alerrt.org/page/CivilianResponse.

Clarkson, Wensley. *Driven to Kill* (London: John Drake Publishing, 2004).

"Communication from the Dead." https://www.schoolshooters.info/sites/default/files/Flores-final-letter.pdf.

Coolidge, Sharon, Dan Horn, Cameron Knight, Anne Saker, Max Londberg, and Sarah Brookbank. "Cincinnati Mass Shooting Leaves City Reeling." *Indianapolis Star*, September 7, 2018, 7A.

Cooper, Alexia, and Erica L. Smith. "Homicide Trends in the United States, 1980–2008." US Department of Justice, 2011.

Cullen, Dave. "At Last We Know Why the Columbine Killers Did It." https://www.slate.com/news-and-politics/2004/04/at-last-we-know-why-the-columbine-killers-did-it.html.

———. "The Reluctant Killer." https://www.theguardian.com/world/2009/apr/25/dave-cullen-columbine.

Cummock, M. Victoria. "The Necessity of Denial in Grieving Murder: Observations of the Victims' Families Following the Bombing in Oklahoma City." *NCP Clinical Quarterly* 5, no. 2–3 (Spring/Summer 1995): 17–18.

Davich, Jerry. "Do Social Media Security Alert Programs Protect or Invade?" http://www.chicagotribune.com/suburbs/post-tribune/opinion/ct-ptb-davich-social-sentinel-alerts-st-0311-20160311-story.html.

"Deadly Dreams: What Motivates School Shootings?" https://www.scientificamerican.com/article/deadly-dreams.

"Deputies on Scene." http://edition.cnn.com/SPECIALS/2000/columbine.cd/Pages/DEPUTIES_TEXT.htm.

DeRuy, Emily. "The Warning Signs of a Mass Shooting." https://www.theatlantic.com/politics/archive/2015/12/the-warning-signs-of-a-mass-shooting/433527.

Dillon, Nancy. "I'll Be Joining You Soon." https://www.nydailynews.com/news/national/christopher-harper-mercer-planned-kill-witness-article-1.2384171.

"DNA, Phone Records Lead to Charges in Gage Park Massacre: Police." http://www.chicago.suntimes.com/news/sneed-gage-park-massacre.

Doom, Justin. "13-Year-Old Who Allegedly Opened Fire at Indiana School Won't Be Tried as Adult." https://abcnews.go.com/US/13-year-allegedly-opened-fire-indiana-school-adult/story?id=55677685.

Downey, Kristin, and Jeanne Huber. "ESL Gunman 'A Nerdie Kid.'" *San Jose Mercury News*, February 20, 1988, A1.

"Dr. Park Dietz: Dangerous Minds." https://www.independent.co.uk/news/people/profiles/dr-park-dietz-dangerous-minds-412116.html.

Duke, Alan. "Timeline to 'Retribution': Isla Vista Attacks Planned over Years." http://www.cnn.com/2014/05/26/justice/california-elliot-rodger-timeline.

"Elliot Rodger Manifesto: My Twisted World." https://www.documentcloud.org/documents/1173808-elliot-rodger-manifesto.html.

"Elliot Rodger's 'Retribution' Video." https://www.schoolshooters.info/sites/default/files/rodger_video_1.0.pdf.

Ellis, Mike. "Call for Legal Protection Highlights Victims' Plight." *Indianapolis Star*, April 26, 2002, A1.

Ellsworth, Monty J. *The Bath School Disaster*. Bath School Museum Committee, 1991.

Emery, Mike, and Jason Truitt. "Police: Juvenile Took His Own Life." *Indianapolis Star*, December 14, 2018, 1A.

Everly, George S. "'Profiling' School Shooters." https://www.psychologytoday.com/us/blog/when-disaster-strikes-inside-disaster-psychology/201803/profiling-school-shooters.

"FBI Statement on the Shooting in Parkland, Florida." https://www.fbi.gov/news/pressrel/press-releases/fbi-statement-on-the-shooting-in-parkland-florida.

"Feds Indict Robert Bowers on New Charges Related to Pittsburgh Synagogue Shooting." https://www.post-gazette.com/news/crime-courts/2019/01/29/robert-bowers-pittsburgh-tree-of-life-synagogue-mass-shooting-superseding-indictment/stories/201901290105.

Fessenden, Ford. "They Threaten, Seethe and Unhinge, Then Kill in Quantity." https://www.nytimes.com/2000/04/09/us/they-threaten-seethe-and-unhinge-then-kill-in-quantity.html.

Feuerherd, Ben. "Yoga Studio Shooter Was a Racist Misogynist Who Found Solidarity with 'Incels.'" https://www.nypost.com/2018/11/04/yoga-studio-shooter-was-a-racist-misogynist-who-found-solidarity-with-incels.

"Fire Kills 87 People at the Happy Land Social Club in the Bronx in 1990." http://www.nydailynews.com/new-york/nyc-crime/dozens-die-fire-illegal-bonx-social-club-1990-article-1.2152091.

Fleeman, Michael. "Bombing Survivors Recall Horror of Blast." *Indianapolis Star*, April 26, 1997, A-3.

———. "Camera Tracked Truck's Movement." *Indianapolis Star*, May 15, 1997, A-3.

———. "FBI Chemist Testifies Explosive Residue Found on McVeigh's Clothing." *Indianapolis Star*, May 20, 1997, A-7.

———. "McVeigh Evidence Lacks Fingerprints." *Indianapolis Star*, May 16, 1997, A-16.

"Florida Shooting: Updates as They Happened." https://www.bbc.com/news/live/world-us-canada-43066528.

Ford, Dana. "Who Commits Mass Shootings?" https://www.cnn.com/2015/06/27/us/mass-shootings/index.html.

Frances, Allen J. "The Mind of the Mass Murderer." https://www.psychologytoday.com/us/blog/saving-normal/201405/the-mind-the-mass-murderer.

Frankel, Todd C., Brittney Martin, Tim Craig, and Christian Davenport. "Santa Fe High School Had a Shooting Plan, Armed Officers and Practice." https://www.texastribune.org/2018/05/20/santa-fe-high-school-had-shooting-plan-armed-officers-and-practice-ten.

Frosch, Dan. "Texas Shooter Spared Students He Liked, Court Document Says." https://www.wsj.com/articles/texas-shooter-spared-students-he-liked-court-document-says-1526735627.

———. "Woman in California Postal Shootings Had History of Bizarre Behavior." https://www.nytimes.com/2006/02/03/us/woman-in-california-postal-shootings-had-history-of-bizarre-behavior.html.

Geissinger, Steve. "Gunmen—Members of an Asian Gang—Were Unhappy in the United States." https://www.apnews.com/b3e4ccb610b9354220d8de5e2c063cfb.

Ghose, Tia. "Mass Shooting Psychology: Spree Killers Have Consistent Profile, Research Shows." https://www.huffpost.com/entry/mass-shooting-psychology-spree-killers_n_2331236.

Gladwell, Malcolm. "Thresholds of Violence." https://www.newyorker.com/magazine/2015/10/19/thresholds-of-violence.

Goldman, Adam, and Patricia Mazzei. "YouTube Comment Seen as Early Warning in Shooting Left Little for FBI to Investigate." https://www.nytimes.com/2018/02/15/us/politics/nikolas-cruz-youtube-comment-fbi.html.

Goodrum, Sarah D., and Mark C. Stafford. "Homicide, Bereavement, and the Criminal Justice System, Final Report." https://www.ncjrs.gov/pdffiles1/nij/grants/189567.pdf.

Gormly, Kellie B., Avi Selk, Joel Achenbach, Mark Berman, and Alex Horton. "Suspect in Pittsburgh Synagogue Shooting Charged with 29 Counts in Deaths of 11 People." https://www.washingtonpost.com/nation/2018/10/27/pittsburgh-police-responding-active-shooting-squirrel-hill-area.

"Great Mills High Gunman Shot by School Officer, Killed Self: Police." https://www.nbcwashington.com/news/local/Great-Mills-High-Shooter-Shot-by-School-Officer-Killed-Self-Police-477984883.html.

Gross, Jane. "6 Are Killed as 8-Hour Siege by Gang Ends in California." https://www.nytimes.com/1991/04/06/us/6-are-killed-as-8-hour-siege-by-gang-ends-in-california.html.

Grossman, Lawrence K. "The Story of a Truly Contaminated Election." *Columbia Journalism Review* 39, no. 4 (January/February 2001).

Guarino, Mark, Kristine Phillips, and Frances Stead Sellers. "Man Accused in Aurora Mass Shooting Had Been Convicted for Beating Girlfriend with Baseball bat." https://www.washingtonpost.com/nation/2019/02/16/man-kills-five-warehouse-shooting-spree-shortly-after-being-fired-illinois-police-say.

Gumbel, Andrew. "The Truth about Columbine." https://www.theguardian.com/world/2009/apr/17/columbine-massacre-gun-crime-us.

Haelle, Tara. "Want to Stop Mass Shootings?" https://www.forbes.com/sites/tarahaelle/2018/09/27/want-to-stop-mass-shootings-do-these-two-things-physician-says.

Hamlett, Laura E. "Common Psycholinguistic Themes in Mass Murderer Manifestos." PhD diss., Walden University, 2017.

Harris, Jake, and Melissa B. Taboada. "Santa Fe Student: Teacher Pulled Fire Alarm to Get Students to Safety during Shooting." https://www.statesman.com/news/20180518/santa-fe-student-teacher-pulled-fire-alarm-to-get-students-to-safety-during-shooting.

Hayes, Christal, and Emily Bohatch. "I'm Sick to My Stomach." https://www.usatoday.com/story/news/2018/02/14/injuries-reported-after-shooting-florida-high-school/338217002.

Herwees, Tasbeeh. "Media's Mass Shooting Coverage Has Got to Change, a Psychologist Says." https://www.good.is/articles/psychologist-connects-media-and-mass-shootings.

Holguin, Jaime. "Eerie Letter from University Killer." https://www.cbsnews.com/news/eerie-letter-from-university-killer.

"How I Tried to Help Elliot Rodger." https://www.bbc.com/news/magazine-28197785.

Hudson, Hayley. "Becky Virgalla, Newtown Shooting Survivor, Says Principal, Others Saved Her in Sandy Hook Rampage." http://www.huffingtonpost.com/2012/12/24/becky-virgalla_n_2357284.html.

Hunt, Amber. "Footage from Bank Shooting Is Revealing." *Indianapolis Star*, September 8, 2018, 6A.

Hussain, Rummana. "Teen Massacre Victim Begged for Mercy: 'I Just Want to Live!'" https://www.chicago.suntimes.com/2016/5/20/18360438/teen-massacre-victim-begged-for-mercy-i-just-want-to-live.

Huynh, Ngoc. "Jiverly Wong's Father: What Prompted Mass Killing in Binghamton Remains a Mystery." https://www.syracuse.com/news/index.ssf/2009/04/jiverly_wongs_father_our_son_w.html.

Jackman, Tom. "Police Are Trained to Attack Active Shooters, but Parkland Officer Didn't." https://www.washingtonpost.com/news/true-crime/wp/2018/02/23/police-are-trained-to-attack-active-shooters-but-parkland-officer-didnt-would-armed-teachers-help.

Jackson, Abby. "Americans Look to Columbine to Better Understand School Shootings—but Myths about the Shooters Have Persisted for Years." https://www.insider.com/columbine-shooters-motives-2018-2.

Jacobs, Tom. "What Mass Murderers Have in Common." https://www.salon.com/2013/07/31/are_mass_murderers_all_cold_unfeeling_psychopaths_partner

Janney, Elizabeth. "Snochia Moseley: 5 Things to Know about Maryland Shooter." https://patch.com/maryland/belair/snochia-moseley-5-things-know-maryland-shooter.

Javanbakht, Arash. "What Mass Shootings Do to Those Not Shot: Social Consequences of Mass Gun Violence." https://www.medicalxpress.com/news/2018-11-mass-shot-social-consequences-gun.html.

Jervis, Rick, Sean Rossman, and Candy Woodall. "'Horrific' Pa. Synagogue Shooting Kills at Least 11." *Indianapolis Star*, October 28, 2018, 1B.

Johnston, Jennifer, and Andrew Joy. "Mass Shootings and the Media Contagion Effect." https://www.apa.org/news/press/releases/2016/08/media-contagion-effect.pdf.

"Judge: Teachers Don't Need Police-Level Gun Training." https://www.apnews.com/c313535fd68c46d0a597dd46343d5918.

Junod, Tom. "Why Mass Shootings Keep Happening." *Esquire*, October 2017.

Kenney, J. Scott. "Survivors of Murder Victims." Paper presented at the X World Symposium on Victimology, Montreal, Quebec, August 6, 2000.

Khazan, Olga. "Why Better Mental-Health Care Won't Stop Mass Shootings." https://www.theatlantic.com/health/archive/2017/10/why-better-mental-health-care-wont-stop-mass-shootings/541965.

Kirby, Audrey J. "For Parents, Panic Eases after Being Reunited with Kids." *Indianapolis Star*, December 14, 2018, 5A.

"Knife Crime: Fatal Stabbings at Highest Level since Records Began in 1946." https://www.bbc.com/news/uk-47156957.

Knight, Cameron. "Officials Analyze Fifth Third Shooting Response." https://www.cincinnati.com/story/news/crime/crime-and-courts/2018/09/17/cincinnati-shooting-police-chief-update-fifth-third-center/1333227002.

Knoll, James L. "The 'Pseudocommando' Mass Murderer: Part I, The Psychology of Revenge and Obliteration." *Journal of the American Academy of Psychiatry and the Law* 38, no. 1 (March 2010): 87–94.

———. "The 'Pseudocommando' Mass Murderer: Part II, The Language of Revenge." *Journal of the American Academy of Psychiatry and the Law* 38, no. 2 (2010): 263–72.

Kristof, Nicholas D. "Japanese Cult Said to Have Planned Nerve-Gas Attacks in U.S." *New York Times*, March 23, 1997, 14.

Kunii, Irene M. "Engineer of Doom." *Time*, June 12, 1995, 45.

Langman, Peter. "Columbine, Bullying, and the Mind of Eric Harris." https://www.psychologytoday.com/us/blog/keeping-kids-safe/200905/columbine-bullying-and-the-mind-eric-harris.

———. "Dylan Klebold's Journal and Other Writings." https://schoolshooters.info/dylan-klebolds-journal-and-other-writings-transcribed-and-annotated.

———. "Elliot Rodger: An Analysis." https://www.schoolshooters.info/sites/default/files/rodger_analysis_2.0.pdf.

Larkin, Ralph W. "The Columbine Legacy." *American Behavioral Scientist* 52 (May 2009): 1309.

Lerner, Melvin. *The Belief in a Just World Hypothesis: A Fundamental Delusion* (New York: Plenum Press, 1980).

"Letter about Killing Wife." http://www.schoolshooters.info/sites/default/files/Whitman_letter_wife.pdf.

"Letter after Killing Mother." https://www.schoolshooters.info/sites/default/files/Whitman_letter_mother.pdf.

Lewis, Becky. "CRASE Training Helps Schools Fill the Gaps in School Safety Plans." https://www.schoolsafetyinfo.org/stories/Success4CRASE-training.html.

Lowery, Don. "Former GA Deputy Convicted of Slaying Boyfriend, Encasing Body in Concrete." *Savannah Morning News*, March 26, 2004.

"Luke Woodham's Writings." https://www.schoolshooters.info/sites/default/files/Luke%20Woodham%20Writings.pdf.

"Man Arrested in Synagogue Plot Inspired by Pittsburgh Attack." *Indianapolis Star*, December 11, 2018, 1B.

Marino, Joe, and Ruth Brown. "Suspected Texas Shooter Was 'Weird' but Didn't Raise Red Flags." https://nypost.com/2018/05/18/suspected-texas-shooter-was-weird-but-didnt-raise-red-flags.

Marino, Melissa. "Middle School 'Satanists' Arrested for Mass Murder Plot in Bartow." https://www.wfla.com/news/polk-county/middle-school-satanists-arrested-for-mass-murder-plot-in-bartow/1546893810.

"Massacre in Michigan—The Bath School Disaster." https://www.legendsofamerica.com/bath-school-massacre/2.

Mazzei, Patricia. "Slow Police Response and Chaos Contributed to Parkland Massacre, Report Finds." https://www.nytimes.com/2018/12/12/us/parkland-shooting-florida-commission-report.html.

McCarthy, Terry. "WARNING: Andy Williams Here." http://content.time.com/time/magazine/article/0,9171,102077,00.html.

McCoy, Blake, Alexander Smith, Andrew Rudansky, Erin Calabrese, and Alex Johnson. "Cedric Larry Ford Kills 3, Injures 14 in Kansas Shooting Spree." https://www.nbcnews.com/news/us-news/cedric-larry-ford-kills-3-injures-14-kansas-shooting-spree-n526316.

McGhee, Paul. "Humor and Mental Health." www.nurseslearning.com/courses/nrp/NRPCX-W0009/html/body.humor.page7.htm.

McKinney, Matt. "Teacher Who Stopped Noblesville Shooter: My Actions 'Were the Only Acceptable Actions.'" https://www.theindychannel.com/news/local-news/hamilton-county/teacher-who-stopped-noblesville-shooter-to-speak-monday.

McLaughlin, Elliot C. "In Active Shooter Situation, Don't Just Stand There." https://www.cnn.com/2016/03/03/us/active-shooter-crase-training/index.html.

McMahon, Paula, and Brittany Wallman. "Parkland School Shooter: Typical of Today's Mass Killers Studied by FBI." http://www.latimes.com/nation/la-na-parkland-mass-shooters-20180701-story.html.

"'Media Contagion' Is Factor in Mass Shootings, Study Says." https://www.apa.org/news/press/releases/2016/08/media-contagion.aspx.

Merrett, Robyn. "Woman May Have Prevented School Shooting in Kentucky after Reporting Racist Facebook Message." https://www.people.com/crime/new-jersey-woman-prevents-school-shooting-reports-racist-facebook-message.

"More Mass Shootings at US Schools in Last 18 Years Than Entire 20th Century: Study."
   https://www.straitstimes.com/world/united-states/more-mass-shootings-at-us-schools-in-
   last-18-years-than-entire-20th-century.
Murderpedia. http://murderpedia.org/male.H/h/harris-eric.htm.
"My Story." https://www.schoolshooters.info/sites/default/files/Christopher-Sean-Harper-
   Mercer-My-Manifesto.pdf.
Navarro, Joe. "Identifying the Next Mass Murderer—Before It's Too Late." https://www.
   psychologytoday.com/us/blog/spycatcher/201506/identifying-the-next-mass-murderer-it-
   s-too-late.
"New Florida Governor Suspends Sheriff over School Massacre." *USA Today*, January 12,
   2019, 1B.
Newman, Katherine. *Rampage: The Social Roots of School Shootings* (New York: Basic
   Books, 2004).
Novotney, Amy. "What Happens to the Survivors?" *Monitor on Psychology* 49, no. 8, http://
   www.apa.org/monitor/2018/09/survivorshttps://www.apa.org/monitor/2018/09/survivors.
Ogas, Ogi, and Sai Gaddam. *A Billion Wicked Thoughts* (New York: Dutton, 2011).
Ohio Crime Victim Services. "Co-Victim Grief." https://www.crimevictimservices.org/
   homicide.html.
"Omaha Gunman Suicide Notes." http://www.thesmokinggun.com/archive/years/2007/
   1207072omaha1.html.
O'Matz, Megan. "Cops in Parkland Shooting under Investigation for Crimes." https://www.
   sun-sentinel.com/local/broward/parkland/florida-school-shooting/fl-school-shooting-
   police-response-investigation-20180921-story.html.
O'Neill, Ann W. "Farley Testifies, Says Obsession Began with Love at First Sight." *San Jose
   Mercury News*, August 21, 1991, A1.
Paddock, Richard C., and Ralph Frammolina. "Hostages Recall Terror of Siege in Sacramen-
   to." https://www.latimes.com/archives/la-xpm-1991-04-06-mn-1622-story.html.
Paddock, Richard C., and Carl Ingram. "3 Hostages, 3 Gunmen Die in Sacramento Store
   Siege." https://www.latimes.com/archives/la-xpm-1991-04-05-mn-1983-story.html.
Pappas, Stephanie. "Female Mass Killers: Why They're So Rare." https://www.livescience.
   com/53047-why-female-mass-shooters-are-rare.html.
———. "The Science of Mass Shooters: What Drives a Person to Kill?" https://www.
   scientificamerican.com/article/the-science-of-mass-shooters-what-drives-a-person-to-kill.
"Pearls before Swine." *Indianapolis Star*, November 27, 2018, 3E.
Pelley, Scott. "What Makes the AR-15 Style Rifle the Weapon of Choice for Mass Shooters?"
   https://www.cbsnews.com/news/ar-15-used-mass-shootings-weapon-of-choice-60-
   minutes.
Perez, Evan, Jason Morris, and Ralph Ellis. "What We Know about Dimitrios Pagourtzis, the
   Alleged Santa Fe High School Shooter." https://www.cnn.com/2018/05/18/us/dimitrios-
   pagourtzis-santa-fe-suspect/index.html.
Pilkington, Ed. "Sandy Hook Report—Shooter Adam Lanza Was Obsessed with Mass Murder." https://www.theguardian.com/world/2013/nov/25/sandy-hook-shooter-adam-lanza-
   report.
Pitofsky, Marina. "Temple Suspect Pleads Not Guilty." *Indianapolis Star*, February 12, 2019,
   6A.
"Police: Ind. School Gunman Asked to Be Excused from Class, Returned with 2 Handguns."
   https://www.cbsnews.com/news/indiana-school-shooting-today-noblesville-west-middle-
   school-2018-05-25-live-updates.
Police Executive Research Forum. "The Police Response to Active Shooter Incidents."
   https://www.policeforum.org/assets/docs/Critical_Issues_Series/
   the%20police%20response%20to%20active%20shooter%20incidents%202014.pdf.
"Police in Kentucky Arrest Man with Stockpile of Guns Believed to Be Planning Mass
   Shooting." https://www.wdrb.com/news/crime-reports/images-police-in-kentucky-arrest-
   man-with-stockpile-of-guns/article_c9c1cc61-a3b1-5f14-ae7d-547469e5ebc9.html.
"The Psychological Ripple Effects of Mass Shootings." https://www.salon.com/2017/10/09/
   the-psychological-ripple-effects-of-mass-shootings_partner.

"Quick Look: 250 Active Shooter Incidents in the United States from 2000 to 2017." https://www.fbi.gov/about/partnerships/office-of-partner-engagement/active-shooter-incidents-graphics.

Rabinovitz, Jonathan. "Rampage in Connecticut: The Overview." https://www.nytimes.com/1998/03/07/nyregion/rampage-connecticut-overview-connecticut-lottery-worker-kills-4-bosses-then.html.

"Rampage in Camden." http://murderpedia.org/male.U/u/unruh-howard.htm.

Roberts, Sam. "Julio Gonzalez, Arsonist Who Killed 87 at New York Club in '90, Dies at 61." https://www.nytimes.com/2016/09/15/nyregion/julio-gonzalez-arsonist-who-killed-87-at-new-york-club-in-90-dies-at-61.html.

Ryckaert, Vic, Ryan Martin, Chris Sikich, Emma Fittes, Arika Herron, Tony Cook, and Holly V. Hays. "Noblesville Shooting Latest Updates." https://www.indystar.com/story/news/crime/2018/05/25/noblesville-school-shooting-active-shooter-reported-middle-school/644021002.

Sanchez, Ray. "How Columbine Changed the Way Police Respond to Mass Shootings." https://www.cnn.com/2018/02/15/us/florida-school-shooting-columbine-lessons/index.html.

———. "My School Is Being Shot Up." https://www.cnn.com/2018/02/18/us/parkland-florida-school-shooting-accounts/index.html.

"Sandy Hook Shootings: Four Things Revealed by FBI Files." https://www.bbc.com/news/world-us-canada-41749336.

Sartorius, Lawrence. "The New Earth." https://www.thenewearth.org.

Saslow, Eli, Sarah Kaplan, and Joseph Hoyt. "Oregon Shooter Said to Have Singled Out Christians for Killing in 'Horrific Act of Cowardice,'" https://www.washingtonpost.com/news/morning-mix/wp/2015/10/02/oregon-shooter-said-to-have-singled-out-christians-for-killing-in-horrific-act-of-cowardice.

Schmelz, Ryan. "Woman Credited for Preventing School Shooting Speaks Out." https://www.wtvq.com/2018/10/24/woman-credited-preventing-school-shooting-speaks.

"School Dynamiter First Slew Wife." https://www.nytimes.com/1927/05/20/archives/school-dynamiter-first-slew-wife-charred-body-of-mrs-kehoe-is-found.html.

Schuppe, Jon. "California Officer Died While Following a Growing Police Strategy." https://www.nbcnews.com/news/us-news/california-officer-died-doing-what-he-was-trained-do-stop-n934111.

Seltzer, Alexandra. "Parkland Victim's Dad: My Daughter Will Be the Last Kid Murdered in School." https://www.palmbeachpost.com/news/local/father-parkland-school-shooting-victim-pledges-meadow-movement/XLfH2mS07kq0uKa0JQfRNM.

"Serious Mental Illness and Mass Homicide." Office of Research & Public Affairs, June 2018.

Shulman, Alayna. "Rancho Tehama: Why Do Mass Shooters Target Children, Strangers?" https://www.usatoday.com/story/news/nation-now/2017/11/15/rancho-tehama-why-do-mass-shooters-target-children-strangers/869306001.

"6-Year-Old Survivor: 'Mommy, I'm OK but All My Friends Are Dead,'" https://washington.cbslocal.com/2012/12/17/6-year-old-survivor-mommy-im-ok-but-all-my-friends-are-dead.

Smith, Matt. "Sandy Hook Killer Took Motive to His Grave." https://www.cnn.com/2013/11/25/justice/sandy-hook-shooting-report/index.html.

Smith, Mitch, and Julie Turkewitz. "Las Vegas Gunman Shot Security Guard Before, Not After, Targeting Concertgoers." https://www.nytimes.com/2017/10/09/us/jesus-campos-las-vegas-shooting.html.

"Social Sentinel FAQ." https://www.esc20.net/page/open/54649/0/SocialSentinelFAQ2018.pdf.

"The Story of the First Mass Murder in U.S. History." https://www.smithsonianmag.com/history/story-first-mass-murder-us-history-180956927.

A Study of Active Shooter Incidents in the United States between 2000 and 2013. US Department of Justice, September 16, 2013.

A Study of the Pre-Attack Behaviors of Active Shooters in the United States between 2000 and 2013. US Department of Justice, June 2018.

"SWAT Team Members: FBI Shooter Rules 'Crazy' at Ruby Ridge." http://www.cnn.com/US/9510/ruby_ridge.

Tavernise, Sabrina, Serge F. Kovaleski, and Julie Turkewitz. "Who Was Stephen Paddock? The Mystery of a Nondescript 'Numbers Guy.'" https://www.nytimes.com/2017/10/07/us/stephen-paddock-vegas.html.

"Texas School Shooting at Santa Fe High School Kills 10, Injures 10." https://www.abc7chicago.com/texas-shooting-at-santa-fe-high-school-kills-10-injures-10/3494817.

"Themes in the Writings of Eric Harris." https://www.schoolshooters.info/sites/default/files/harris_themes_1.7.pdf.

Toppo, Greg. "10 Years Later, the Real Story behind Columbine." https://www.usatoday.com/news/nation/2009-04-13-columbine-myths_N.htm.

Total Security Solutions. "The Four Ds of Active Shooter Response." https://www.tssbulletproof.com/blog/preparing-active-shooter-response.

"Transcript of the May 23–25, 1927 Clinton County, Michigan Coroner's Inquest." https://en.wikipedia.org/wiki/Bath_School_disaster.

Trebilcock, Bob. "I Love You to Death." *Redbook*, March 1992, 103.

"Tribal Shooting Suspect in California Killed 3 Relatives." https://www.seattletimes.com/seattle-news/tribal-shooting-suspect-in-california-killed-3-relatives.

Turkewitz, Julie, and Jess Bidgood. "Who Is Dimitrios Pagourtzis, the Texas Shooting Suspect?" https://www.nytimes.com/2018/05/18/us/dimitrios-pagourtzis-gunman-texas-shooting.html.

"Unprepared and Overwhelmed." http://projects.sun-sentinel.com/2018/sfl-parkland-school-shooting-critical-moments.

US Secret Service. "The Final Report and Findings of the Safe School Initiative." https://www2.ed.gov/admins/lead/safety/preventingattacksreport.pdf.

———. "Mass Attacks in Public Spaces—2017." March 2018, 2.

"Veteran Kills 12 in Mad Rampage on Camden Street." https://longform.org/posts/veteran-kills-12-in-mad-rampage-on-camden-street.

Viegas, Jen. "Mass Shootings in the US: Some Common Characteristics of the Men That Kill." https://www.seeker.com/culture/behavior/mass-shootings-in-the-us-some-common-characteristics-of-the-men-that-kill.

Wade, Stephanie. "I Dropped to My Knees! Students, Parents Talk about Noblesville School Shooting." https://abcnews.go.com/US/active-shooter-reported-indiana-middle-school-police/story?id=55413808.

Wax, Trevin. "7 Myths about the Columbine Shooting." https://www.thegospelcoalition.org/blogs/trevin-wax/7-myths-about-the-columbine-shooting.

"Weapon Types Used in Mass Shootings in the United States between 1982 and November 2018." https://www.statista.com/statistics/476409/mass-shootings-in-the-us-by-weapon-types-used.

Weisbrot, D. M. "Prelude to a School Shooting? Assessing Threatening Behaviors in Childhood and Adolescence. *Journal of the American Academy of Child and Adolescent Psychiatry* 47, no. 8 (2008): 847–52.

Wenger, Daniel. "Pearl Jam's 'Jeremy' and the Intractable Cultural Script of School Shooters." https://www.newyorker.com/culture/cultural-comment/pearl-jams-jeremy-and-the-intractable-cultural-script-of-school-shooters.

"What Characteristics Do School Shooters Share?" https://www.sciencedaily.com/releases/2017/10/171019100756.htm.

Winn, Patrick. "Under Strict Gun Laws, Japan's Mass Killers Must Rely on Knives Instead." https://www.pri.org/stories/2016-07-26/under-strict-gun-laws-japans-mass-killers-must-rely-knives-instead.

Wood, Mike. "The Next Generation of Active Shooter Response." https://www.policeone.com/active-shooter/articles/482527006-The-next-generation-of-active-shooter-response.

Wykes, S. L. "Judge Hears Tape at Farley Trial." *San Jose Mercury News*, July 15, 1988, B1.

"Year Later, Officer Who Fatally Shot St. Cloud Mall Attacker Speaks Out." https://www.twincities.com/2017/09/16/year-later-officer-who-fatally-shot-st-cloud-mall-attacker-speaks-out.

INDEX

ABOUT THE AUTHOR

Robert L. Snow served for thirty-eight years at the Indianapolis Police Department, retiring in 2007 with the rank of captain. While at the police department, he served in such capacities as Captain of Detectives, Police Department Executive Officer, Commander of the Homicide Branch, and Commander of the Organized Crime Branch. He has been a published writer for almost forty years, with more than one hundred articles and short stories in such publications as *Playboy*, *Reader's Digest*, *The Writer*, *Police*, *Law & Order*, and others. He is also the author of twenty books.